BLIND-SIDED

Homicide
Where It Is Least Expected

GREGORY K. MOFFATT

Westport, Connecticut
London

Library of Congress Cataloging-in-Publication Data

Moffatt, Gregory K., 1961–
    Blind-sided : homicide where it is least expected / Gregory K. Moffatt.
      p. cm.
    Includes bibliographical references and index.
    ISBN 0–275–96929–0 (alk. paper)
    1. Homicide. 2. Homicide—Prevention. 3. Violence—Forecasting.
  4. Criminal behavior, Prediction of. I. Title.
    HV6515.M55 2000
    364.15'23—dc21   00–025464

British Library Cataloguing in Publication Data is available.

Copyright © 2000 by Gregory K. Moffatt

Library of Congress Catalog Card Number: 00–025464
ISBN: 0–275–96929–0

First published in 2000

Praeger Publishers, 88 Post Road West, Westport, CT 06881
An imprint of Greenwood Publishing Group, Inc.
www.praeger.com

Printed in the United States of America

∞

The paper used in this book complies with the
Permanent Paper Standard issued by the National
Information Standards Organization (Z39.48–1984).

10 9 8 7 6 5 4 3 2 1

Contents

Preface   vii

Acknowledgments   xi

Introduction   1

1   Homicide—Its Many Forms   7

2   Homicide and Mental Illness   21

3   Homicide in the Workplace   35

4   Homicide at Home: Domestic Violence   55

5   Stalking   79

6   Homicide by Children, Part I   105

7   Homicide by Children, Part II: Columbine   137

8   Assessment of Risk for Homicide   163

9   Intervention and Prevention of Homicide   185

10   Seven Mistakes That Can Cost People Their Lives   209

11   Conclusions   231

Bibliography   241

Index   247

Preface

Over the past several years I have discovered the numerous road-blocks to studying homicides. Police departments, while they can be very helpful, often make it difficult or impossible to get information on homicide cases. Most of the assistance I have received in collecting information has come from my students at the FBI National Academy, an eleven-week training program for law enforcement officers from around the world, based at the FBI Academy in Quantico, Virginia. Aside from these students I have rarely received any cooperation from law enforcement agencies. This happens for several reasons. First, police officers and administrators are very busy. Even when they have good intentions, they simply do not have the time to look up, copy, and send cases to me. Second, if cases have not been fully adjudicated, all agencies are reluctant to release information for fear that outside involvement may compromise them in court. More than once I have been asked by detectives to assist in an active homicide case and then been "uninvited" by superior officers. Finally, and per-haps most frustrating, some agencies do not see any value in this type of research and simply refuse to assist. For example, I spoke with one county sheriff several years ago as I began this line of research. I explained that I was researching the cause of homicide and I wanted to interview an inmate. His response was, "I don't mean to sound rude, but don't we know what causes homicide already?" This officer, based on his years of experience, believed he understood homicide and its causes. The research process does not work that way. We do not rely on personal experience or anecdotal information. The fact is we do not already know all the causes of homicide or I would not have been studying it, but it was pointless to pursue academic logic with the sheriff.

A second obstacle to my research is funding. Homicide research is very expensive. From travel, lodging, and meals to postage and telephone calls, a single thoroughly investigated case can cost thousands of dollars. In order to pass academic scrutiny, this process needs to be repeated many times. Grants of $50,000 or more are the starting point. While grants (both private and public) are available for a variety of areas of research, it is very difficult to get funding for research on the type of homicide I describe in these pages. Homicides involving gangs, drugs, and other youth issues are of interest to granting organizations, but grants for research on homicide among the historically nonviolent are few and far between.

A third obstacle is time. Even when a case has been fully adjudicated and a perpetrator is killed at the scene or sentenced to prison, it takes time to locate the appropriate departments and personnel, request documents, and wait for information. Not surprising, the proper channels rarely result in satisfactory responses. Knowing the right person in the right place and asking for a favor is often what gets the job accomplished.

If an interview with a perpetrator is possible, prisons require various degrees of clearance to gain access. Even my law enforcement associates and I cannot simply walk into a prison and demand to see a prisoner against his or her will. The prisoner must also grant permission. This is all done in writing and can take months. Even when all hurdles have been cleared, any person in the process can change his or her mind at the last minute, setting the process back to the start. For example, I communicated with the prison in South Carolina where Susan Smith was being held during her trial. In surprisingly quick fashion, the prison authorities verbally granted me permission to visit her. However, I had to seek permission from Ms. Smith in writing. My letter was forwarded from her to her attorney. He informed me that I would not be able to see her until the trial ended. Several weeks passed, and when the trial concluded I wrote to Ms. Smith a second time. Again, my letter was forwarded from her to her attorney. His response this time was that I would not be granted an interview. Therefore, it took nearly six months for me to explore a lead that resulted in a dead end.

I know this is not why you are reading this book, but the paragraphs above provide a necessary caveat. Good research is clear and replicable. It is open to scrutiny and it follows certain methodological guidelines. Some of these guidelines were simply impossible for me to follow. For instance, some quotes are unattributed due to their derivation from ongoing investigations and, in some cases, names have been omitted to protect the privacy of the people involved. While I stand firmly by the conclusions presented in this book, this research is an ongoing, lifelong process for me. As new information, funding, and conclusions arrive, modifications in the material presented here are likely.

Acknowledgments

I would like to express my thanks to a number of individuals who either directly or indirectly assisted in this most tedious undertaking. First I wish to thank Mr. Edward F. Davis, instructor at the Behavioral Science Unit, FBI Academy, in Quantico, Virginia, for his friendship, collegial assistance, and mentoring over many years. Thanks to Special Agent George DeShazor, LCSW, also of the Behavioral Science Unit at Quantico, for his encouragement, participation, and shared interest in the area of violence risk assessment.

I am deeply indebted to my good friend Mr. John Otto, former acting director of the Federal Bureau of Investigation, and retired director of corporate security for Delta Airlines. Thank you, John, for all you have done for me.

I also wish to express my appreciation to my wife, Stacey, and children, Megan, Kara, and Benjamin, for enduring my hours at the computer as I prepared this book.

While many police agencies and officers have frustrated me in my work, many others have been extremely helpful and invaluable in providing observations, data, reports, photographs, and other information that have led to the conclusions I present in this volume.

Finally, to all the victims of these murders and their families, I dedicate this work in the hope that from their losses we might learn.

Introduction

"It's him! He is coming for me!" Donna screamed as panic gripped her chest. Coworkers fleeing the office building helped her find someplace to hide. In the parking lot just outside, Scott, with a freshly broken ankle, dragged himself along the ground in the direction of Donna's office. As if in a scene from a horror movie, he had already shot two people and was methodically making his way to Donna. Bullets penetrated the building as he fired his weapon toward her office. She knew it would happen eventually. Scott had threatened her and others. His behavior had told her his intentions and today her fears were realized.

How could she know? Scott had never been violent as far as she knew, but Donna instinctively responded to the cues Scott provided. Unlike many others in her environment, she believed he could be a threat and this may have saved her life. Scott communicated his potential for violence very clearly. Even though seriously wounded, Karla, another woman in the building, survived because she was willing to believe nightmares could come true. As I talked with Donna, Karla, and their colleagues, I learned that they survived because they listened to the warning signals Scott provided.

You will read more about Donna and Karla, both amazing women who saved their own lives, in Chapter 3. What I hope you will learn from reading this book is that you, like Donna, can walk away from violent episodes, if you listen carefully to the signals provided by potential killers.

THE CONCEPT

As you will read in Chapter 1, not all types of homicide are the same. I began my research in this field several years ago when numerous post office shootings were occurring. I was troubled by reports that suggested the perpetrators showed no signs of their intentions. People who knew them said the perpetrators seemed normal and they were shocked to learn of the gunmen's actions. As a clinician, I could not believe that an individual would, with absolutely no warning, commit homicide. My clinical experience with other forms of behavior suggested otherwise.

Around that same time I was working as the vice president for student life at Atlanta Christian College, an undergraduate college in the Southeast. I was working on a case involving a student I believed to be dangerous. I felt this student was a high risk to our community, but I had no training on which to base my assumptions. I began to research the cause-effect relationship between environment/ thoughts/behaviors and homicide, a process that has led to this book. Why was the sheriff wrong when he said, "Don't we know that already?" regarding the cause-effect relationship in homicide? Human behavior is too complicated and multifaceted to suppose that any single factor causes any specific behavior. Any such supposition is reductionist and unrealistic.

My work has focused on perhaps the most difficult form of homicide to predict—homicide among the historically nonviolent. These are people with no apparent violent patterns in their pasts. As with all research in the social sciences, my goals in this line of research are to *describe* what is happening in different types of homicide, *understand* the nature of homicide, *predict* when it is likely or unlikely, and *control* (prevent) it when possible. In the following chapters I address all four elements of the research process as they relate to homicide.

THE HISTORICALLY NONVIOLENT

Even though we may be shocked when we hear of murders involving robberies, drug deals, and other criminal activities, we are most distressed by homicides committed by seemingly normal individuals—people who may have never been arrested or who seem to the casual observer to be productive citizens. This book focuses on homicides committed by people who could be called historically non-violent. Yet, as you will see, the perception of historical nonviolence can be very misleading.

The term "historically nonviolent" is a misnomer. When I began my research many years ago, I used this phrase to describe the type of killer I was interested in studying. However, I found that many of these killers had actually been violent in their pasts, but for one reason or another, this was not reported. This became obvious to me as I prepared my first published journal article.[1] The title of the article included the phrase "historically nonviolent," but as one reviewer pointed out, the very first item on my list of risk factors was a "history of violent behavior." I included "history of violent behavior" for three reasons. First, most of the researchers in violence risk assessment have concluded that a history of violence is strongly correlated with future violence. Second, and perhaps equally important, we tend to overlook behaviors among those we know well and to suppose they are different in some way from those same behaviors exhibited by other people. For example, I was consulting with a business in early 1999 that managed 40,000 employees worldwide. During a meeting with the directors of their employee assistance programs, security staff, and legal staff at their corporate headquarters, one manager told me that a man in his charge had trouble controlling his temper and in a meeting just days before had thrown a chair at another employee. This manager wanted to know if that was a problem.

At first, I thought he was joking. I had just spent an hour telling them to consider all aggression as important. I then realized he was not joking and it was a legitimate question. I said it was indeed a bad sign. I explained that this employee apparently believed that the most effective way to deal with his frustration at a professional meeting was to throw furniture. That seemed clearly dysfunctional to me, but for some reason the manager thought it could be normal behavior. My point is that even when a person acts aggressively, we sometimes do not classify it that way. If the man had pulled a weapon instead of throwing a chair, his friends and supervisors might later have described him as historically nonviolent or a "nice guy." Deeper investigation would have shown quite the opposite to be true.

My third reason for using the item "history of violent behavior" is that I began to see a trend in my own experience that has continued to this day in my research. In nearly every homicide I have studied that was committed by the "historically nonviolent," the perpetrator has, in fact, acted aggressively at some point in the past, but no connection was made with the environment where the homicide occurred. He or she may have a history of spousal abuse, fighting with coworkers, disorderly conduct or reckless driving, child abuse, or simply having a hot temper and striking inanimate objects (or throwing furniture). But if the homicide happened in an environment different from the one where he had displayed violence in the past, reports of his violent history might never have been made. As I suspected at the very beginning of my research, these homicides did not come without warning. However, observers (family, coworkers, and friends) either ignored or were blind to the signs and symptoms that were there all along. Therefore, they were blind-sided by the homicides that followed.

In summary, even though I use the term "historically nonviolent," there really is no such thing as historical nonviolence. As with Scott in the story told at the beginning of this chapter, people who deliberately commit murder have violence in their repertoires. One may appear to be historically nonviolent because of the perceptual errors of observers. These errors may be based on the fact that we often overlook violent behavior by people we know or we mislabel it as something else. Perceptions may also be distorted because a person may never display any violent or aggressive behavior in one environment, yet may have behaved violently elsewhere. To observers in the first environment, he would appear to have been historically nonviolent, but investigation into other areas of his life would show the contrary to be true. Therefore, as you will see even when some observers say the perpetrator has never engaged in any violence, that is almost never the case. The idea that one changes from a "normal" person one day into a mass murderer the next is absurd. Victims who are blind-sided by this type of violence more often than not had available to them the information that they needed to assess the potential risk. For some reason, however, they could not, or would not, see it.

THE PURPOSE

On one occasion as I was lecturing on homicide risk assessment, a student at the FBI National Academy asked me why my research did not include other high-risk people such as armed robbers. My response was this: "If someone is sticking a gun in my face, I'm just going to assume he is a high risk for committing homicide." There is no need for prediction in this case. Prediction is most difficult when the average person cannot see it coming. One does not have to be trained in the psychological sciences to recognize threat during a robbery. Policemen and women on the street are constantly looking for potentially violent situations and making assessments. Psychiatrists, psychologists, nurses, and others who work with the mentally ill also make these assessments routinely. More complicated, however, is recognizing threat in a school, workplace, or other location where people do not expect homicide to occur. In these environments, students, employees, and family members are busy doing other things. They may be aware of risks, but they often do not formally assess the risks until it is too late. Finally, even when they attempt to assess risk, they do not know how.

I have made it my goal to inform laymen on assessment of risk for homicide. When I first began consulting with businesses on assessment of risk for homicide in the workplace, I realized that managers and supervisors did not have the time, training, or resources to fully address risk for violence using traditional psychometrics and interview protocols. I realized, though, that these people could be trained to recognize basic warning signs and did not need formal training in psychology to provide intervention that could save lives. Therefore, even though the rigors of academic process support my research, my presentation is always pragmatic.

My first interaction with business was when my now good friend John Otto, retired director of corporate security at Delta Airlines, called me in response to a research article I had published.[2] He commented that my article was the first one he had ever seen that he could actually use in his work. I was discouraged that a practitioner, a manager of people, could not "use" any of the good research that was in print, but I understood why. Researchers write for other researchers. Their vocabulary is full of jargon and their methodology is so complicated that their work is sometimes unintelligible even to others in the field. Also, researchers are very reluctant to speculate without clear, empirical evidence to back up their statements.

I vowed that my research would not simply end up as a reference in someone else's research. I committed myself to providing information usable by nonacademics and non-psychologists. In this work

I have tried to avoid psychological terminology that may be confusing and I have attempted to portray my research in the simplest form possible. I am not afraid to speculate because the stakes are so high—literally life or death. I do not make haphazard assumptions; I have presented what I believe to be true. My friend at the FBI Academy, Special Agent George DeShazor, a licensed clinical social worker prior to joining the bureau, has shared my interest in this type of writing and is producing similar material for FBI agents with these same thoughts in mind.

CONCLUDING REMARKS

This book is based on police reports, autopsy information, witness statements, discussions with victims, media accounts, and/or other data that I have collected on each case. I have done my best to present these cases as accurately as possible given the information that was available to me. Lest I sound callous in these pages, I must confess that every homicide I have studied has touched me in some way. As much as I try to emotionally distance myself from the personal aspects of these murders, at some point in every case I realized that the dead were not simply "victims" but mothers, fathers, sons, and daughters. They had plans for the future, business to conduct, chores to complete, and the last thing that was on their minds on the day of their deaths was losing their lives. They were thinking about grocery lists, softball games, children's school programs, and other routine matters.

The fragile reality in which we live suggests to us that tragedies like these happen only to other people. Unfortunately, we know deep in our souls that this type of tragedy could, in fact, happen to us. If we pull our heads from the sand we can then seek solutions that could prevent these incidents from happening. I thank you for reading this book and I hope that through it we can gain a better understanding of homicide and save the lives of those we love.

NOTES

1. Gregory K. Moffatt, "A checklist for assessing risk of violent behavior in historically nonviolent persons," *Psychological Reports,* 74 (1994), 683–688.
2. Ibid.

Homicide—Its Many Forms

FORMS AND CAUSES OF HOMICIDE

Homicide is not a monolith. The etiologies of homicide are as diverse as the types of homicide. Homicide has been divided into four categories by the International Association of Chiefs of Police: domestic, confrontational, youth, and robbery related.[1] While these four categories are generally useful in classifying homicide, they can each be subdivided. For example, we can divide domestic homicide into subgroups including partner-to-partner, child-to-adult, adult-to-child, sibling-to-sibling, homosexual partner violence, and so on. Each of these types of violence is different in its etiology, process, and adjudication. In other words, there are significant differences in terms of why perpetrators act on their victims, how they commit their violent acts, and how the law responds.

Serial killers are not the focus of this book, but they show how different homicides can be. While a serial killer may patiently troll for a victim, plan the murder, provide his own weapon, and attempt to cover up the crime, a domestic homicide is often very different. Husbands who kill their wives, for example, usually do not invest much preparation or premeditate their crimes. Their crimes are impulsive and often committed in a fit of rage. They may select any weapon at hand (a blunt instrument, an easily reached firearm, or their bare hands) and they are rarely very good at covering up the crime, even when they try. Likewise, a teenager may take a gun with him as he robs a convenience store. During the intense confrontation of the crime, he may discharge the weapon, surprising himself that he has taken the life of the clerk. These three types of homicides are distinctly different.

One can see how different serial homicide and conjugal homicide are in their process. They are equally different in their cause. Serial killers often have abuse in their pasts and they are deeply disturbed individuals. Unlike this population, a spouse who kills his or her partner may be overcome with rage and impulse at the point of the murder. While their crimes are inexcusable, spouses might never have committed homicide if a number of factors had not converged at the point of the crime, and they may never kill again. Serial killers, on the other hand, evolve into monsters internally driven by their dysfunctions and will continue to kill. The causal factors are more internal than external.

Finally, the law responds differently to different types of homicide. Serial killers, when they are identified as such, attract much media attention. Multi-jurisdictional task forces are organized and many man-hours are committed to the investigation. When a serial killer is arrested and convicted, juries are harsh in their punishments. On the other hand, domestic homicides are often solved within hours or days and may involve few man-hours. Juries can be persuaded that extenuating circumstances were present (such as ongoing spousal abuse) and sentences may be light. Children, on the other hand, often premeditate the murders of their parent(s) and may cover up their crimes for a few days or months. Sentences for children are largely dependent upon how the child is tried—as an adult or as a juvenile.

A look at two actual cases will illustrate these issues. Theodore Bundy is one of America's most notorious serial killers. While there is no evidence of abuse in his background, his upbringing was hardly normal. Born to an unwed mother, Bundy was raised by his mother's parents as if he were their own child, his "sister" actually being his mother. While he was still of preschool age, Ted and his biological mother moved away to Washington state where she later married. Evidence suggests that Ted's stepfather was a well-intentioned man, but Ted never accepted him as a father. It wasn't until Ted was in his early twenties that he discovered his "sister" was actually his mother and his "father" was actually his grandfather. It appears that his killings began sometime after this revelation.[2]

For several years, dozens of officers from several states coast to coast sought the man wanted in connection with killings in their various jurisdictions. Bundy was arrested in Utah and later transferred to face charges in Colorado. While in Colorado, he escaped from a courthouse where he had been taken to use the library. He was eventually recaptured, this time in Florida. Unfortunately, his arrest came too late to prevent further tragedy. Before he could be caught, Bundy killed Margaret Bowman and Lisa Levy at the Chi Omega sorority house at Florida State University and assaulted two other students. On the very same night, Bundy assaulted yet another woman just blocks from the Chi Omega sorority house. His final known victim was 12-year-old Kimberly Leach. Some of Bundy's victims were sexually assaulted post mortem. They were beaten severely and in some cases bitten, stabbed, and strangled.

Bundy became a suspect in the Florida homicides not long after he attempted to abduct the daughter of the chief of detectives for the Jacksonville Police Department. Bundy was charged with the deaths of the two women of Chi Omega and Kimberly Leach. He was convicted in each case and sentenced three times to death. In an interview with Dr. James Dobson, a psychologist from California, Bundy argued that his killings arose from his fascination with pornography.[3] The credibility of this statement is questionable, but pornography plays a role in the lives of many serial killers. Ted Bundy would claim responsibility for the deaths of twenty-eight women and he was executed in January 1989.

On the other hand, John Frye was seemingly a normal husband, father, and successful business man. His family was described as the "perfect American family."[4] Fifteen years into their marriage the Fryes had their daughter, Amanda. John Frye poured himself fully into his daughter's school and church life as well as her other interests, learning about softball and basketball, formerly of no interest to him, in order to please her.

Frye was an employee of Georgia Power and his job allowed him to provide a comfortable living for his family. He and his family divided their time between their $225,000 home in suburban Atlanta and their vacation home on a lake in northern Georgia. Acquaintances said Frye seemed introverted in the months before the killings, but he showed no other signs of unusual behavior. A niece had contacted Frye and invited him to a birthday party that was scheduled for the day Frye took the lives of his family members and himself.

In the early morning hours of Wednesday, December 14, 1995, a neighbor saw Frye's home engulfed in fire and called emergency personnel. When the fire department arrived and extinguished the blaze, they made a gruesome discovery. On the floor in the basement they found 52-year-old Madge Frye dead of a bullet wound to the torso. In the daughter's bedroom, they found 11-year-old Amanda Frye in bed with a bullet wound to the chest. On the floor at the foot of her bed was her father, dead of a self-inflicted gunshot wound to the head.

A neighbor had noticed a strong smell of gasoline around the Frye home the night before. It was later determined that Frye had soaked the house in gasoline to accelerate the flames. Frye most likely shot his wife first. It appears that she was killed in the den on the ground floor, but as fire engulfed the home, the den floor collapsed into the basement where she was found. Frye then proceeded to his daughter's room and he killed her in her sleep.

Frye had collected his bank records, stock certificates, will, family pictures, and other documents and placed them in an envelope. Along with these documents was a note written on the back of an envelope. He left this material in his truck parked in the driveway, addressed to his nephew.

Igniting the gasoline, he went back to his daughter's bedroom where he took his own life, dying beside the daughter he adored. His .38 caliber revolver with three spent cartridges in the cylinder was beside him. The 51-year-old man had no history of violent behavior.

Frye was in good health and loved his family dearly. What could have driven him to take their lives and his own? Frye's suicide note was not released to the public, but police said Frye alluded to "pressures" in his life and potential health issues, although they did not elaborate.[5] Some of his stress was caused by an early retirement option from Georgia Power. An acquaintance suggested that Frye did not want to take the option but felt compelled to do so. According to his friend, other employees who had been offered the voluntary early retirement, but had refused, had later been fired.[6] Frye's decision was due the Monday following the murders. His note also stated that he did not think his family could make it without him. It appears that Frye's primary intention was to take his own life, but he did not want his family to have to exist in the aftermath of his suicide. Therefore, he took them with him.

The investigation of this case was less problematic than Bundy's for several reasons. First of all, John Frye was dead and still on the scene when investigators arrived. Even though he left a note and it might seem obvious that he was the perpetrator, investigators still had to follow procedure to determine if, in fact, he was. Even if he had not taken his own life, however, he would have been an immediate suspect. The clear domestic nature of the homicide could be seen in the fact that nothing significant was apparently missing from the home, no other crimes were suspected (i.e., robbery, drug trafficking, dealing in stolen property), and all members of the family were killed.

Local papers announced the next day that police had named Frye as the murderer. Even though some unanswered questions remain in the Frye homicides, the investigation was completed in hours unlike the investigation into Bundy's crimes, which spanned several years. If Frye had survived, one can only speculate how a jury would have responded to his crimes. It is conceivable that if he had been convicted his sentence could have allowed for the possibility of parole, a sentence highly improbable with serial killers.

The difference between serial killers and domestic killers is clear, but serial killings are quite rare, although the public's voyeuristic fascination with serial killers provides for a lucrative book and movie market. Two more cases provide a look at more common homicides and show how they are different from each other.

Richard Rosenthal of Framingham, Massachusetts, killed his wife as she prepared dinner on a quiet evening in August 1995. The 40-year-old man killed her during an argument over burned ziti. He beat her to death with a rock and then cut her open from her throat to her navel and impaled her heart and lungs on a stake in the backyard. He then took his 4-month-old daughter on a car ride. Around midnight, he followed a couple into their driveway and attempted to engage them in a conversation about gun control. He was arrested after he told the couple he "did something terrible" and the couple called the police. In conversation with a psychiatrist, Rosenthal flatly referred to his deceased wife as the "unknown victim."[7] Rosenthal reportedly believed his wife to be a space alien and claimed he saw "portents in dead rats,"[8] but the jury at his trial rejected his insanity defense. Rosenthal was found guilty of murder and sentenced to life in prison without the possibility of parole. Could something so insignificant as overcooked ziti lead one to savagely murder a loved one? Surely there are other significant factors at work in a case of this nature.

Nineteen-year-old Jillian Robbins, a resident of State College, Pennsylvania, was trained as an army reservist and was also reported to be a hunter. She was known by her acquaintances as "Crazy Jill."[9] Reportedly having a history of mental disturbance, on September 17, 1996, she calmly laid out a tarp on the grass on the campus of Penn State University and proceeded to fire randomly at students with a rifle. Her hair cut in a Mohawk, Robbins's brief volley of gunfire killed a 19-year-old female student and wounded a 27-year-old male. A third student was hit, but by a stroke of luck, the bullet lodged in a book in his backpack, sparing him from injury. As the shooter attempted to reload her high-powered rifle, an engineering student tackled her. Robbins pulled a knife and attempted to stab the student, but instead she unintentionally stabbed herself in the leg.

Robbins was charged with several counts of attempted murder and several counts of aggravated assault. Initially, prosecutors planned to seek the death penalty, but in the trial that followed, Robbins pled guilty to third-degree murder and trying to kill four students. She was sentenced to 30–60 years in prison. It was suggested that she may have told acquaintances what she was planning.[10] After her arrest, when Robbins was asked why she did it, she said she "just wanted to shoot."[11]

In light of these varied forms of homicide, perhaps one can see the near-sighted nature of my sheriff friend's statement and why we don't already know what causes homicide.

COPING

As you have read, Ted Bundy's killings seem to have begun sometime after the discovery that his father was actually his grandfather and that his sister was actually his mother. An obvious response is that many of us have experienced dramatic revelations in our lives and yet we never chose to kill. Spouses discover their partners have lovers or have committed crimes. Adopted children learn that their parents are not their biological parents. Adults and children learn that their conception was the product of rape or incest. This begs the question as to why some choose to kill and others do not. One mitigating difference separates all of us in our behaviors and the likelihood of our committing a violent act.

While many people are sexually and physically abused as children, very few become serial killers. Even though spousal abuse occurs daily in America, only a very small number of these victims will kill their abusive husbands or wives. It is impossible for all factors to be identical between any two people, but when circumstances are similar, some people choose to respond in legal and socially acceptable ways while others choose to respond in illegal or socially inappropriate ways. Some internalize their aggression through depression, alcohol use, and other responses while others externalize it through violence, aggressive behavior, or even overachievement in business or academics.

A major difference between these two types of individuals involves coping skills and strategies. Through hundreds of clinical hours I have come to believe that people make what they believe to be the best choices with the resources they see available to them. These choices are sometimes illegal and often dysfunctional, but the choice was the best the client could make (in his or her mind) at the time. Few of my clients who committed crimes were "evil" people. They are often well-intentioned individuals who have made poor choices. For example, a person is arrested for child abuse. He believed he was disciplining the child and yet he caused bruises or broken bones while "spanking." Why did the perpetrator choose to hit the child rather than use some other form of discipline? Why did the perpetrator not have a healthier outlet for his frustration? These people selected the option they believed to be most effective. In cases like this the choice is subconscious and made very quickly. I am not suggesting that these people are not culpable for their actions and I am not saying they should not be prosecuted. I am suggesting, however, that they reviewed their options and selected the behavior they perceived to be most efficient at the time.

When a person enters a situation, she is required to draw upon her experience and perceived options for a response. The more options a person has stored away in his or her repertoire, the better. I liken this to a toolbox full of tools. When working on a car, a mechanic uses different tools for various jobs. The more tools in the toolbox, the more likely the mechanic will be able to efficiently fix the automobile. Suppose, however, the mechanic has only four tools; a hammer, a pair of pliers, a screwdriver, and a crescent wrench. He may be able to work on the automobile, and he may even be able to repair it. However, it will be more difficult, it will take more time, and he may cause further damage while fixing the original problem. Coping is similar to this. When we have many tools or resources available to us (such as multiple methods for dealing with our anger, frustration, and disappointments, a variety of disciplinary options for dealing with our children, methods for pursuing our goals, and so forth) we are more likely to select healthy, appropriate responses (tools for the job).

Suppose a parent finds himself frustrated with his child. He has three response options in his pool—yelling, spanking, and withdrawal. He selects from these options and reacts by withdrawing to his bedroom, shutting and locking the door. It is possible that none of his options are appropriate, but withdrawing breaks no law. Suppose, however, that the individual chooses instead to spank the child and also suppose that he hits too hard, injuring the child. As in the first circumstance, he has chosen from his narrow pool of options, but this time he breaks a law and a child suffers. His coping skills are few. He has developed ineffective strategies for controlling anger and he has few options for disciplining his child. In both cases, a poor choice was made, but in the latter case, the law was broken.

On the other hand, let's give our subject more coping skills. Suppose he has learned to effectively cope with his anger and he has a multitude of options at his disposal for dealing with a disobedient child (i.e., time out, spanking, withdrawal of privileges, discussion, reinforcement of other behaviors). While it is still possible that this individual could strike the child, it is much less likely.

As we run out of options for dealing with our frustrations and as our coping strategies fail us, we move toward primitive behaviors—from reason to impulsive reaction. This is why our subject is less likely to act aggressively if he has effective coping skills and many strategies available to him for dealing with his child. Human beings are the only creatures that can reason their way through conflict and frustration. All other species, when faced with conflict, will either flee or fight. It is distinctly human to face a conflict and think through it. However, when our reason fails us, we regress to fight or flight. Have you ever watched a perfectly reasonable person strike a vending machine? The reasonable person deposits the money and presses the button for a soft drink. When nothing happens, she begins to select responses from her pool of options. First, she will calmly push the button again. Next, she will try the coin return lever several times. If that fails, she may try the soft drink button again. Eventually, she may kick or hit the machine in exasperation. Reason has failed, so primitive aggression takes over.

At Georgia State University, where I was a graduate student for many years and later an instructor, waiting on the elevators was inherently frustrating because they were very slow. A student would approach the elevator on the ground floor and push the button even if others were waiting and the button was already lit. If the elevator did not arrive fast enough to suit the student, he would push the button again—perhaps several times. When the elevator still did not respond to his satisfaction, he would huff and grimace, clearly displaying his anger. Note that the individual was calm and fairly reasonable until he ran out of options. At the point when he realized his reason was defeated and he had no control over the situation, his behavior regressed to a childlike, or primitive, state.

We all regress to primitive behaviors when we run out of options and coping strategies. However, a mature individual has many coping skills and strategies. He or she rarely, if ever, runs out of options. Therefore, he or she usually responds in socially acceptable ways. However, if a person has poor, ineffective, or few coping skills, his or her behavior is much more likely to be socially unacceptable.

Murder is a choice. The murderer selects this option from a set of coping strategies. It is, therefore, implicit that killing is the murderer's perceived best choice among options. This is most important in assessing risk of violent behavior. As a consultant to businesses, I am often called upon to assess the probability of violence by an employee. I look for a number of variables (as discussed in Chapter 8). However, before I present any conclusions, I look carefully at the individual's coping skills. How has he coped in the past? Does he resort to aggression easily? Does he have a social support network that assists him in coping with stress? The more effective strategies and coping skills in the person's repertoire, the less likely he or she is to act in a violent manner. One might not be surprised to note, however, that those with few effective coping strategies are often on the receiving end of company discipline, which leads to their eventual termination and my involvement.

CONTEXT

Homicide also differs in context. The circumstances surrounding the planning and execution of a homicide are changed by place, time, and presence of others. I am especially troubled at the time of writing by recent school shootings. Homicides are always troubling, but I see a frightening contextual trend in school shootings. While initially they were perpetrated by lone gunmen, several recent shootings have involved conspirators. As place, time, and presence of others changes, the likelihood of violence changes.

School shootings like the ones in Paducah, Kentucky, and Springfield, Oregon, were committed by children who planned and acted alone. When one plans such an act in isolation there is always the option to change the plan or back out while still saving face. If Kip Kinkel in Springfield, Oregon, for example, had changed his mind at the last minute and decided not to kill his parents and the students at his high school, no one would have known any different. He could have continued his daily life without shame or fear of being perceived as a coward. However, when several perpetrators are involved, change in behavior is much more complicated. Suppose one of the two boys in Littleton, Colorado, had a change of heart on the way to Columbine High School and decided to back out. He would have been under pressure to conform (either real or imagined) from his accomplice. Even in a group of three or four, if all members except one decide they do not want to follow through with the plan, the one can exert pressure on the majority to conform.

Gang behavior is incredibly volatile for this reason. Members must maintain their appearance of control, lack of fear, and dominance in order to retain the respect of the others. Therefore, a shop owner can fully comply with robbers and yet be murdered in cold blood because a gang member believed he would lose face if he did not take the owner's life. This is why teenage thugs are often caught. They either commit the homicide deliberately in the presence of others who later inform police or, if they acted alone, they talk about it with pride for days or weeks. These conversations lead to their arrest.

One final part of the context issue involves triggering mechanisms. All of us are potential killers, but few of us will kill. We have the capacity to commit the crime, but even the thought is repulsive to most of us. Even among those at high risk for committing homicide, most will never kill. The triggering mechanism acts as the "straw that broke the camel's back." Pressure within the individual rises and falls with the changing contexts of his world. When the pressure rises to a point where he can take no more, the triggering mechanism is the next pressure-inducing event. Suppose a man is in his mid-forties. He is dealing with the developmental issues of midlife, questioning his purpose and accomplishments. He is dissatisfied in his work and unhappy with himself. He has worked at his current job for twenty years and is unhappy with his career choice, yet he sees no other option for employment and he is afraid of making any changes. His boss is an aggressive, oppressive individual who cannot be pleased. The man is consistently criticized for his work and has been disciplined many times over the years. Perhaps he is also frustrated at home. His teenage children frustrate him and he believes he has done all he can to no avail. His marriage falls apart, leaving him alone.

The pressure has built within this individual to a boiling point. If he were healthy in his coping skills, he would have many options for defusing his increasing rage. However, he is not healthy and can only contain the pressure as best he can. He enters his office, only to find that he is being fired. Feeling hopeless and enraged, he returns home, gets his hunting rifle from the closet, and returns to work, shooting everyone he sees. Before he can be arrested, he takes his own life.

In this fictitious example, the triggering mechanism was the dismissal. If he had been fired at some other time in his life, he might not have chosen murder and suicide as his response. The pressure would have been more manageable and he might have accepted the firing and moved on. What if he had been fired first and then came home to find his wife packing her bags and leaving with the children? In this scenario, his wife's attempted departure could be the triggering mechanism and instead of the victims being coworkers, they could be his family members.

One last issue involves how the killer selects his or her victims. The person who kills often blames his or her problems on the individuals whose lives are taken. The husband in the above scenario will select the workplace as his place for killing if he blames his woes on his company, his boss, or his coworkers. On the other hand, even if the triggering mechanism is his dismissal from work, if he perceives his wife to be at fault for his "life falling apart," she will be the more likely victim. Crimes like the above example have happened in the past and in some cases, the killer has blamed both his family *and* his workplace. In a case like this, he kills them all.

On a hot July day in 1984, James Huberty entered a McDonald's restaurant in San Ysidro, California, carrying weapons and ammunition. Huberty ruthlessly killed twenty-one men, women, and children and injured nineteen others before he was killed by police. Those who lived through this event will never forget the haunting image of a dead child lying on the ground near his bicycle outside the restaurant. Huberty blamed society for his life's ills; therefore, his victims were random members of society—people he had never met.

Identifying triggering mechanisms after the fact is much easier than identifying them beforehand. The list of potential triggers is unlimited. The best I can do as a consultant and clinician is to recognize the rising stress within an individual, consider the person's history of coping, consider perceived response options to situations, and identify contexts where homicide is more likely. As I discuss at length in Chapter 8, assessment of risk involves identifying a *probability* of a behavior, not a *prediction* of whether and when it will occur.

CONCLUDING REMARKS

Homicides differ in their etiologies and processes. From investigation and arrest through adjudication and sentencing, our legal system responds differently to the various forms of homicide. As we try to understand homicide, we must begin by identifying the type that interests us. We must also consider the perpetrator's context and coping strategies, especially when we are trying to assess risk for violent behavior.

The varieties of our human experiences and our differing contexts create for us a world of fascinating diversity but also present an overwhelmingly complex formula for understanding human behavior. Assessing the interactive effects of our internal and external differences rivals the complexity of our genetic makeup. The next several chapters provide an overview of various forms of homicide and their causes, while the concluding chapters address risk assessment and provide suggestions for prevention and treatment.

NOTES

1. "Murder in America: recommendations from the IACP murder summit," International Association of Chiefs of Police, Alexandria, VA, 1995, 7.

2. "Theodore Robert Bundy or Ted Bundy," *www.crimelibrary.com/bundy/attack.htm*.

3. "Fatal Addiction," *Focus on the Family*, Denver, CO, 1987.

4. Bill Torpy, "The Fryes appeared loving, successful, wholesome," *Atlanta Journal/Constitution*, December 14, 1995, D5.

5. Doug Payne, "Full reason for killings may never be known," *Atlanta Journal/Constitution*, December 15, 1995, E11.

6. John C. Johnson, "Letters to the Editor," *Atlanta Journal/Constitution*, December 23, 1995, A23.

7. "Man suspected of butchering wife," *Prodigy News Service* (Internet Edition), August 30, 1995.

8. Brian MacQuarrie, "Once again, the bizarre fails to sway a jury," *Boston Globe*, November 8, 1996, B1.

9. Dave Ivey, "Shooter kills one, wounds one at Penn State," *Atlanta Journal/Constitution*, September 18, 1996, A5.

10. "She may have told friends about her plans," *USA Today*, September 19, 1996, 3A.

11. "Woman is charged in campus slaying," *Washington Post*, September 19, 1996, A15.

Homicide and Mental Illness

It has been my experience that the term "mental illness" is rarely understood by those outside the mental health profession. Twice a year I teach an "Introduction to Psychology" class to college students. I have come to expect from them an understanding of mental illness that is seriously skewed by what they have absorbed from the media, from movies, and from books.

While some of the jargon of mental health clinicians may be familiar to the general public, terms such as "sanity" and "crazy" do not exist in our mental health vocabulary. "Crazy" is a colloquial term that the culture uses to describe individuals whose thoughts or behaviors fall outside the population norm on some measure. While you might hear a clinician use this term (or some similar derogatory term) in non-professional settings, this word has no place in the clinical setting.

The term "sanity" is a legal term, not a clinician's term. Many observers are confused about this word. Jeffery Dahmer committed unspeakable acts of horror. Yet before he was tried, a psychiatrist had to determine whether or not he was sane at the time of the killings and whether or not he was competent to stand trial. Any reasonable person could deduce that the behaviors exhibited by this seriously disturbed individual were abnormal. However, sanity is not defined in terms of normal or abnormal. Neither is it defined by the *Diagnostic and Statistical Manual, 4th Edition (DSM IV)*,[1] the manual by which mental health professionals identify and code mental disorders. In a court of law, a person is sane if he or she could distinguish between right and wrong at the time of the crime. One can also be considered insane if one is determined to have been incapable of preventing one's actions at the time of the crime. This legal issue is only connected to mental health in that it is a court-appointed mental health professional who must make a recommendation to the court of a defendant's sanity at the time of the crime—a very complicated and difficult task. A determination of competency is also made by the court on the recommendation of a mental health professional. One is competent to stand trial if one can understand the charges that have been made.

THE MENTAL HEALTH CONTINUUM

All mental illness exists on a continuum. Every mental disorder falls somewhere on the continuum from absent to full-blown. My students are sometimes shocked to hear me say that all of us are diagnosably "mentally ill" in one way or another.

Consider an example that may be easier for you to relate to. If you were to have a full, head-to-toe physical examination (blood work, heart, x-rays, skin and bone analysis, etc.), a physician could probably find something wrong with you. Perhaps it would only be a wart or a potentially troubling mole. For example, I had my appendix removed in 1998. The surgeon told me I had a small tumor on my kidney, but that it was not uncommon and it was nothing to worry about. Other defects, however, might be more serious. The physician might find a heart problem, a malignant form of cancer, or some other problem that needs immediate attention. While we would certainly be shocked and troubled if our problem was serious, none of us would find a minor defect surprising.

Likewise, most of us could be classified with some form of mental disorder. The *DSM IV* leaves a great deal of room for diagnosing minor disorders as well as major ones. Therefore, if a skilled mental health diagnostician carefully examined us, he or she could probably find some diagnosable disorder. Perhaps you are afraid of spiders. Maybe you find it difficult to quit smoking. You may be having significant difficulty interacting with one of your children. The *DSM IV* provides a diagnostic code for all of these.

While the disorders listed above are common but manageable, it is also possible that you could be diagnosed with a degenerative brain disorder (i.e., senile dementia or Alzheimer's disease). These diagnoses would be troubling, although unlikely outside the geriatric population.

The *DSM IV* provides a set of criteria for each disorder. However, not all criteria must be met in every case. For example, a given diagnosis may include six criteria, but the *DSM IV* may only require three of the six for the diagnosis to be made. One may have only three presenting symptoms, or one may have all six. In both cases the same diagnosis is made.

Just as there are different disorders, each disorder affects each patient differently and patients respond differently to treatment. A person may be diagnosed with schizophrenia, but medical intervention may make it possible for him to function quite well. Acquaintances may be unaware that the person has any mental health problem. On the other hand, one may be diagnosed with schizophrenia and respond poorly to pharmaceutical interventions. This patient may be incapable of caring for himself and require full-time inpatient care. Most people interacting with this patient would know something was not quite right. Therefore, in addressing mental illness, one must consider the type of illness, the place on the continuum where the patient falls, and the individual's response to the illness and to treatment.

LEVEL OF FUNCTIONING

As one can see, there are various forms of diagnoses. My job as a clinician is not merely to identify the presence of a mental disorder and treat it, but also to assess the level at which the disorder interrupts the individual's functioning. Let's return to my psychology class for a moment. In class, as we move through the various classifications of mental disorder, we discuss phobias. Some students are troubled to know that their fear of snakes can be a classifiable mental disorder. My response to them is always the same. How often do you have to be around snakes? Does your fear of snakes make it difficult or impossible for you to do the things you need and want to do each day? If you are rarely around snakes and the phobia creates no difficulty for you in accomplishing your daily tasks, then you do not need to worry about it.

On the other hand, if one is a forest ranger or a navy seal, a fear of snakes would most likely make it difficult or impossible to do one's job. In this case it is a problem that needs attention. While exactly the same diagnosis exists in both patients, the level of functioning is the distinguishing feature. The issue in mental health that I try to communicate to my students is not the presence or absence of a disorder (or disorders) in and of itself, but rather the level at which the disorder affects one's functioning.

I receive a number of unsolicited letters each year from individuals who appear to be mentally ill. Most of these letters are addressed generically to my office and appear to have been mailed to a number of people, although some are addressed to me personally. I suspect that the authors of these letters are desperate for help and look up names and addresses in the phone book, mass mailing their letters in the hope of some positive result. Sometimes they are seeking help, other times they are sending warnings. The common theme is that the writers seem to have difficulty functioning. The best example of this is a letter I received from a woman in the western United States. If we take her letter at face value and assume it was not a prank, this woman is paranoid, delusional, and probably has difficulty functioning on a day-to-day basis. Here is what she wrote (spelling as in the original):

To Whom It May Concern:
This letter is in regards to the invasion of my privacy. I would appreciate any direct information leading to the explanation of this. Periodically, for nine years there have been famous and non-famous strangers watching me in the privacy of my home. I am greatly incompacitated and maimed by this intrusion. As I am typing this letter I am being watched by complete strangers.
People such as Ron Howard, Tom Hanks, Steven Spielberg, Kate Capshaw, Bill Gates, Paul Allan, Harry Anderson, Eddie Money, Ivanna Trump, Tom Petty, George Lucas, Troy Aikman, Rachel Hunter, Jack Nicholson, Goldie Hawn, Kenny Loggins, Jackson Brown, Wesley Snipes, Melinda Gates, Seal, Garrison Keilor, Don Bluth, some members of the Rolling Stones, Pink Floyd, The Who, B.T.O., Led Zepplin, and Fleetwood Mack to name very few of the people who have watched me in the privacy of my own dwelling place for several years have added to this hate crime and harassment.
Despite my pleas to ask them to leave me alone, these people keep finding new people to watch me. Sometimes, some of these people gratify themselves or each other sexually while invading my privacy in all arenas in which I choose to live. There is also drug use at times by some of these people

while invading my privacy. At times these and other people are accompanied by prostitutes and or somebody's children while intruding on my life.

I am greatly incapacitated by all this and the talk that surrounds such treatment. This exploitation of my life has proved to be excruciatingly painful for me. Along with the pain that is ever present due to this unwanted intrusion by these famous and non-famous strangers, I am not employable because of the reputation I have been handed by these strangers.

Before these famous people held charity dinners on behalf of the cause that they fabricated around my life and exploited me in every way imaginable, I had a happy, typical, conservative, affluent, dignified, respectable, middle-class life. I had no reputation as did none of my naturally selected piers [peers]. I have no idea how any famous person even knows that I exist. I have never had the first thing to do with any famous person or anyone who has ever had anything to do with them or anyone they knew.

I have been conservatively waiting for nine years for this hate crime and intrusion to end and there is no end in sight. Someone tied to some famous person obstructs the delivery of this letter at times. So, if you receive this letter and are able to shed any light on this please call or write. I look forward to hearing from you.

Sincerely, Xxxxx

While there is an extremely remote possibility that the allegations in this letter could be true, it is clear to me that this woman does not see reality as it is, she believes she is being persecuted, and she has difficulty functioning. Could she be dangerous? I have no way of knowing from one letter and without interviewing her, but I doubt it. The reason I doubt it is that she has chosen letter writing as a coping strategy. According to research on threatening letters that has been conducted by the Secret Service, "persons who pose threats most often do not make threats, especially explicit threats."[2] There are no threats, either direct or veiled, in this letter. Many patients could be diagnosed with paranoia, delusions, depression, or similar problems and yet function successfully in their daily lives. It does not appear that this woman is one of them. I presume that anyone who knows this woman is aware that she has serious difficulties. What she seeks is relief of her pain.

HOMICIDE BY THE MENTALLY ILL

The purpose of the above discussion is to point out that what most people think of as mental illness is too narrowly defined. While we like to think of ourselves as "normal" it is possible, perhaps even likely, that we are mentally ill at some level. Normalcy is not the absence of mental disorder; it is something that is culturally determined and related to our ability to function. To be normal is to function in a way that is not exceptionally out of step with the ordinary behaviors of people of similar age and gender in a given culture. One can be "normal" and yet suffer from a diagnosed mental illness. Most of us have some abnormalities in our behavioral or cognitive repertoire, but our general level of functioning is the issue on which our peers judge us.

It is for this reason that most people who are mentally ill are not violent. Many of the people you interact with at work, at church, or on the golf course are probably taking psychotropic medications for a mental disorder. These medications may be for depression, for anxiety, or perhaps even for schizophrenia or some other serious disorder. It is more common than you might think. The small number of people with mental disorders that are at high risk for violence are more likely to be violent toward themselves rather than toward others. When one chooses violence, suicide or self-mutilation is more likely than homicide.

In about half of all the homicide cases I have studied, the perpetrator had a diagnosed mental health condition. In light of the discussion at the beginning of this chapter, one can see why I suspect that most of the others had some form of mental disorder that was never diagnosed. Keep in mind, however, that having a mental disorder is a poor predictor of violent behavior, especially homicide. In fact, males are represented in as many as 97% of homicides in the workplace, for example, while only 10–40% of all mentally ill patients commit a physical assault prior to hospitalization.[3] The fact that there may be some correlation between mental illness and homicide does not mean mental illness causes one to commit homicide. If that were so then we could also say that being male causes one to commit homicide. Of course this is not the case.

The varieties of mental illnesses, the various points on the continuum where each patient falls, the individual's response to treatment, and the individual's level of functioning must all be considered when addressing mental illness and homicide. Even though mental illness is common among the general population and is rarely a primary cause of homicide, there are cases where mental illness has contributed significantly to homicides. Here are a few of those cases.

Russell Eugene Weston, Jr.

Friday, July 24, 1998, started like every other Washington, D.C., summer day. It was hot and sunny and tourists filed through the United States Capitol observing its statues, documents, and architecture. Legislators were busy answering phone calls, talking to journalists, and attending meetings. But it would not be an ordinary day. It was on that day that Russell Eugene Weston, Jr., entered the United States's most prominent public facility with a .38 caliber handgun. Within minutes he lay in the hallway critically wounded. A tourist was wounded and two security guards lay dead by his hand.

As a young man, "Rusty" Weston planned to become a draftsman, but with symptoms of schizophrenia emerging he never pursued this goal. Moving from job to job, his mental illness becoming more pronounced and he moved to Montana a few years after his high school graduation in 1974. There he lived in a small cabin near Helena, just forty miles from the place where federal agents would later arrest Theodore Kaczynski, the Unabomber.

In 1983, he complained to police that his 86-year-old landlady had assaulted him with a cane. No charges were filed and Weston became convinced that a conspiracy existed between his landlady and the police. In 1991 he was arrested for selling drugs, but the charges were dropped.

By this time, Weston's dementia was apparent to all who knew him. According to neighbors, Weston believed that the government was using a nearby television satellite disk to spy on him, and he had been seen several times shouting at the satellite dish.[4] He believed that the government was seeking to kill him because he had information on the Kennedy assassination.

Two years prior to the shooting, Weston had made threatening comments about President Clinton. At that time he had been investigated by the U.S. Secret Service, but agents determined that he was not a threat. In October 1996, Weston was involuntarily committed to a mental facility. After a fifty-two-day stay in the facility and having been diagnosed as a paranoid schizophrenic, Weston moved back to his parents' home in Valmeyer, Illinois.

Valmeyer is a small town that was destroyed during the floods of 1993. It moved to higher ground near the original location of the town. Weston's family had lived in this community since 1937. Weston's father, a retired warehouse worker, and his mother, an employee at Wal-Mart, loved him deeply despite his unusual behaviors. They would later state in interviews with police that their son frequently wrote letters to government agencies expressing "irrational ideas and accusations."[5]

According to his father, Weston also exhibited compulsive behaviors, once cutting so much firewood that his father had to demand that he stop for lack of a place to put it all.[6] His compulsive behavior was exhibited in an episode of gardening and another of flower collecting. In both cases, his compulsion drove him to collect so many items that he had be be instructed to stop. Another symptom of his compulsivity was displayed in an incident involving his cats. Weston's grandmother complained about his cats creating a problem and asked him to take care of it. Weston killed them all with a 12-gauge shotgun. He buried all but two, which he left in a bucket. This event upset his father so much that he gave Rusty ten days to move out.

The episode with the cats occurred only days before Weston took a .38 caliber revolver from his parents' home and drove his pickup truck from Illinois to Washington, D.C. Once in Washington, he visited the Capitol building. As Weston approached the metal detectors at the entrance, Officer Jacob J. Chestnut, with his back to the metal detectors, was giving directions to a man and his son. Weston approached him from behind and shot Officer Chestnut in the head. Weston rushed past the dead officer and the blood-splattered visitors.

Groups of Boy Scouts, Girl Scouts, and other tourists ran for cover as Weston proceeded into the building. He encountered a second officer, who fired at him. At this point flying shrapnel wounded a female tourist. Weston followed a woman through the halls and toward the office of Majority Whip Tom DeLay. As the screaming woman approached DeLay's office, Capitol Police Special Agent John M. Gibson, assigned to protect DeLay, met her in the doorway. Weston fired nearly point-blank at Gibson, hitting him in the chest. Gibson returned fire, hitting Weston three times.

Ironically, it was U.S. Senator Bill Frist, a surgeon, who provided the first aid that probably saved Weston's life. In the days that followed, the wounded tourist would be treated and released from the hospital. Gibson and Chestnut both died. Weston, shackled to his bed after surgery, was given only a fifty-fifty chance of survival. He would survive, later to be examined by seven court-appointed psychiatrists and questioned by a host of other officials.

After the shootings, FBI agents confiscated numerous files from

Weston's home, including letters to the CIA and the military as well as several boxes of ammunition. This information and numerous interviews would paint a picture of a seriously disturbed man.

An acquaintance told investigators that Weston's frustrations with the government began in 1988 over a dispute concerning his working an abandoned ore mine in Montana.[7] However, when asked about a motive, Weston would claim that he was attempting to gain access to "the ruby satellite," a device he thought would stop cannibalism and an ailment he called the "Black Heva."[8] He believed that Chestnut and Gibson were cannibals and he told CIA agents that both he and President Clinton were clones. He would also describe many other individuals as cannibals including a judge and a court-appointed psychiatrist. He was not troubled by the killings because he believed that the ruby satellite could reverse time, bringing the two officers back to life.[9]

Weston had a host of delusions of grandeur. Throughout his adult life he believed he was an army colonel under the Kennedy administration, that he was the favorite son of John F. Kennedy, and that he had made a movie with Bill Clinton. He also believed that he had been a Harvard medical and law professor in a previous life. A belief that Clinton had commissioned the navy seals to assassinate him and that the Secret Service was trying to poison him with soap were among his many persecutory thoughts.[10]

Throughout his interviews, Weston saw nothing unusual in his thoughts or behavior. He even instructed his doctors on how to test him for brain problems, telling them that the appropriate test was to "put your tongue out and hold your tongue out for longer than a minute."[11] He informed them that brain problems might exist if the tongue turned purple.

According to the *Washington Post*, his "psychiatric problems were well known long before he allegedly gunned down two U.S. Capitol Police officers: by his frustrated family, his irritated neighbors, the courts, two state mental health departments and at least three federal agencies."[12] Despite his history, Weston had been granted an Illinois gun permit. When authorities were later questioned about Weston and his freedom to move about in public even though he was clearly impaired, one government official responded, "Look, the guy seemed like a garden-variety nut. In the United States of America, you're allowed to be a garden-variety nut."[13]

I attended the solemn memorial ceremony for the two slain officers at the Capitol. Hundreds of flowers covered the steps of the building while police officers from around the world honored the two officers slain in the very halls where Washington, Jefferson, and Lincoln walked. Thousands of citizens filed through the rotunda where the two officers lay in state. The sound of bagpipes echoed across the shady lawn as horses and police in parade formation processed before us.

In a bitter irony, just prior to the ceremony I watched as an apparently homeless, disheveled, and disoriented man wound his way through the crowd. He was tall and thin, taking a moment every few steps to look toward the sky and say a few words. Tourists ignored him and policemen on duty chuckled as they patronized him in his plight. I suppose people responded to Rusty like this. They probably laughed at him as he explained his beliefs. No one took him seriously—he was just another confused man until his actions publicly demonized him.

De-Kieu Duy

The Triad Center is a building in Salt Lake City, Utah, that is home to the offices of KSL television and radio studios. On January 14, 1999, 24-year-old De-Kieu Duy entered the Triad Center and attempted to get into the KSL newsroom, demanding to speak to a reporter that she believed was harassing her. An employee informed her that she could not go into the news reception area. Thwarted in that effort, she drew a 9mm handgun and again demanded to be allowed in the newsroom area.

Employees attempted to steer her toward an engineering area, but Duy did not leave. After "spinning around in circles and talking in the air," she allegedly began firing with the handgun.[14] Her first shot was toward the floor, but it is alleged that she then pointed her gun at KSL manager Brent Wightman and fired twice. Her shots grazed him on his right side. Duy walked over to Wightman, who had fallen to the floor and was pretending to be dead. She cursed him and kicked him in the chest.

After allegedly shooting Wightman, Duy fired a number of shots through the glass window near the reception area. Reaching through the broken glass, she opened the door, but two other secured doors prevented her from reaching other employees. While she was in the reception area, Wightman and others fled the area.

Duy then used the elevator and moved to other floors firing at people as she went. Eventually, she made her way to the fourth floor of the building where AT&T's Wireless Services offices were located. As she stood in the doorway, AT&T employee Ben Porter saw her point the gun at his coworker, Anne Sleater, a human resources director who had just returned from maternity leave. Sleater was interviewing a new employee on his first day of work. Duy allegedly shot Sleater in the head and then turned the gun toward Porter, but Porter tackled Duy, taking her gun. He and other employees held her down until police arrested her. Sleater, whose daughter was only six months old, died eight days later.

According to a family friend, everything in Duy's Vietnamese refugee family had been normal until approximately four years earlier when the onset of Duy's mental problems coincided with her initial brushes with the law.[15] In 1996, Duy believed a disc jockey at a local radio station was putting voices in her head.[16] As in the KSL incident, Duy entered the lobby and demanded to see the employee. However, instead of a gun, Duy had concealed a steak knife in her pocket. Police arrested her and charged her with disorderly conduct and stalking as well as assault against the officer who arrested her. These charges were later dropped. Her police record included other misdemeanor charges.

Duy's mother said that she heard voices, consistent with her diagnosis as paranoid schizophrenic, but she apparently had not been taking her medication. In spite of her mental health history and her criminal record, the day before the KSL incident Duy had legally purchased the gun and ammunition she allegedly used in the shootings.

She was found incompetent to proceed with the trial in April 1999 by a district court judge and was remanded to the Utah State Hospital in Provo. A hearing on the charges of aggravated homicide and capital murder (among other charges) was set for July 26. At that hearing, the judge determined that she was still incompetent to participate in a trial and ordered her to undergo a year of treatment. She remains in a mental health facility and won't be tried for some months to come (if ever).

Sergei Barbarin

Just three months after Duy opened fire on the Salt Lake City television station, another tragedy occurred in the same town. On Thursday, April 15, 1999, Sergei Barbarin left the Salt Lake City apartment he shared with his aging wife and went for a walk. Nothing seemed unusual as he left for his daily routine of walking around town. On this day, however, dressed in military-style clothing, he entered the Mormon Church's Family History Library with a .22 caliber handgun.

As he entered the library he immediately started shooting into the crowd of visitors and employees. People began screaming "get down" as numerous shots rang out. A security guard had no time to respond to Barbarin's barrage. Before he could draw his weapon, he was struck in the chest and he died at a nearby hospital. A tourist from California was also shot and killed.

Barbarin reloaded and continued to fire indiscriminately. He remained in the building for the next ninety minutes. During that time, police had taken up positions in and around the library. As Barbarin moved through the building, he encountered police. He exchanged fire with them and was shot. He died minutes later in an ambulance outside the library.

The body count following his actions that day numbered two dead and four wounded. A bullet also grazed a SWAT team member. However, this incident could have been worse. Officials of the library said that on any given day as many as 250 people are in the building. Of the many visitors to the library that day, 180 fourth-grade students avoided any physical injuries. A number of other patrons were trapped on the second floor but were later freed unharmed.

Barbarin, a 71-year-old Russian immigrant, was a husband and father with a history of psychological problems. According to his wife, Barbarin was supposed to be on medication to control his schizophrenia, but he had not been taking his medication prior to the shooting.[17] His son described a history of paranoid behavior, saying Barbarin had also accused him, his mother, and acquaintances of being spies.[18] His son had tried unsuccessfully for nearly a year to get his father committed, but hospital officials stated that they had refused to commit him involuntarily because he showed no signs of an imminent threat to himself or others.[19] Barbarin had refused his medication because he feared the doctors were trying to poison him.

This shooting was not Barbarin's first act of aggression. He was arrested in 1995 after an altercation in a department store. At that time police found a .22 caliber handgun in his possession and confiscated the weapon. He was charged with carrying a concealed weapon and assault. In May 1998 he knocked a neighborhood boy from a bicycle by sticking an umbrella in the spokes as the boy rode past. Barbarin's explanation was that he believed the boy to be a spy.

CONCLUDING REMARKS

There are many cases of individuals with mental illness who have committed homicide. Psychiatrists and psychologists are among the victims of homicide by the mentally ill. In June 1999, a 27-year-old patient diagnosed with paranoid schizophrenia shot and killed his psychiatrist and a woman in the office area before taking his own life. However, many thousands of patients come through our doors and never present any threat to our welfare or the welfare of others.

In all the examples I have presented, the patients were diagnosed as paranoid schizophrenics, but some research suggests that schizophrenics are no more likely to be dangerous than any other members of the population.[20] Other diagnoses are present in those who commit homicide, including substance abuse disorders, depression, and mania.

When I was an undergraduate student, I toured a state mental health facility in the Midwest. The supervising psychiatrist made a point that I have used often in my own classes. He noted that the fence around the facility was not just to keep the patients in; it was to keep others out. He informed us that most of the patients were there voluntarily and could walk away any time they wanted. This changed my perspective on mental illness. Prior to that conversation I, like my introductory psychology students, believed that mentally ill people were either maniacal individuals looking for people to kill or catatonic patients in dimly lit psychiatric hospital wards like the one I was visiting. Fortunately, while both of these populations do exist, they represent only a small number of the mentally ill. Mental illness is represented across our population in business, in recreation, and among those who commit homicide. The mental illness factor by itself, though, rarely causes people to kill.

NOTES

1. American Psychiatric Association, *Diagnostic and statistical manual for mental disorders, 4th edition* (Washington, DC: American Psychiatric Press, 1994).

2. R. A. Fein and B. Vossekuil, "Preventing attacks on public officials

and public figures: a Secret Service perspective," in J. Reid Meloy, ed., *The psychology of stalking: clinical and forensic perspectives* (San Diego, CA: Academic Press, 1998), 183.

3. Charles E. Labig, *Preventing violence in the workplace* (New York: RHR International Co., 1995), 29.

4. "United States v. Russell Weston Jr.," *Court TV Online, www.courttv.com/trials/weston/index.html.*

5. Michael Grunwald and Bill Miller, "Officials seek clues to Weston's 'state of mind,' " *Washington Post* (Internet Edition), July 29, 1998, A01.

6. Gabriel Escobar, "Before the shootings, a string of excesses," *Washington Post* (Internet Edition), August 10, 1998, A1.

7. Grunwald and Miller, "Officials Seek Clues," A01.

8. Bill Miller, "Capitol shooter's mind-set detailed," *Washington Post* (Internet Edition), April 23, 1999, A1.

9. Ibid.

10. Ibid.

11. Ibid.

12. Michael Grunwald and Susan G. Boodman, "Weston case 'fell through the cracks,' " *Washington Post* (Internet Edition), July 28, 1998, A01.

13. Ibid.

14. "Eyewitness interview KSL shooting," *KSL News* (Internet Edition), *www.ksl.com/dump/news/cc/whiteman.htm.*

15. "Background on Triad shooting suspect," *KSL News* (Internet Edition), *www.ksl.com/dump/news/cc/shxsusp2.htm.*

16. E. Fuller Torrey and Mary Zdanowicscg, "Utah must change its law governing involuntary commitment of mentally ill," *Salt Lake Tribune* (Internet Edition), April 25, 1999, AA6.

17. Greg Beacham, "Motive unknown in rampage at Mormon site," *Atlanta Journal/Constitution*, April 16, 1999, A3.

18. "Officials debate whether Salt Lake shooting could have been averted," *CNN On-line, www.cnn.com/US/9904/17/PM–MormonLibraryShooting.ap/,* April 17, 1999.

19. Ibid.

20. G. T. Harris and M. E. Rice, "Risk appraisal and management of violent behavior," *Psychiatric Services, 48*, 9 (1997), 1168–1176.

Homicide in the Workplace

My original interest in homicide risk assessment and prevention was not in the area of workplace homicide, but an interesting trend has evolved over the past few years, a trend I should have seen coming. Most of the interest in the field of homicide prevention has come from businesses interested in workplace violence. My work at the FBI Academy and with Delta Airlines, US Airways, Westinghouse Corporation, and other businesses has directly involved workplace homicide.

It is only when a school shooting occurs that I get many phone calls regarding school homicide. Interestingly, though, schools certainly qualify as workplaces. Rarely does any organization ask me to speak on youth or domestic homicide. Never have I been asked to address random shootings like road rage, gang shootings, etc. The sad reason why businesses seek my input and few other organizations do is that businesses can directly attach a dollar value to the issue. Other forms of homicide are much less conducive to quantification. I do not doubt for a minute that people care about the deaths of the innocent. When we hear of tragedies involving random shootings, domestic violence, and youth homicide, it moves us. I believe that. However, it is only when it happens to someone we know that the issue becomes real and prominent for us. Otherwise, we go about our daily lives assuming it will always happen someplace else.

When the director of corporate security at US Airways first contacted me, he said something that drove this point home. In my experience, I had noticed that some businesses balked at my suggestions for improving the safety of their work sites and preventing workplace homicide. Others were open to my suggestions and willing to spend money on them. In the very first phone conversation when the US Airways security director was considering hiring me as a consultant, he said, "You don't have to convince us of its importance."

Why not? You may recall the December 7, 1987, crash of a Pacific Southwest shuttle flight. A disgruntled former employee gained access to the aircraft with a .44 caliber handgun. While the plane was in flight, he shot and killed his manager, who was a passenger. Then, he entered the cockpit and shot the flight crew before taking his own life. Before putting the gun to his own head, the perpetrator put the plane in a nosedive causing it to crash to the ground at 800 miles per hour. Forty-four passengers and crew perished, making it one of the largest mass murders in U.S. history. US Airways was in the process of buying Pacific Southwest. Workplace violence is very real to them. They know the cost in public relations, damages, legal fees, lost air time, and so forth. They are also caring individuals who are starkly aware of the emotional cost of such a tragedy to family members, coworkers, and others.

When I address a business for the first time, if managers are resistant to making changes, I ask them how much just one incident would cost them in manpower, public relations, legal fees and restitution, training, and so on. With this perspective, spending a few thousand dollars on safety improvements becomes more reasonable to them.

Workplace homicide has touched businesses all across the spectrum. Educational institutions, hospitals, libraries, day care centers, government offices, law offices, financial institutions, and restaurants are all places where an employee or former employee has killed a person or persons. Also represented are small businesses as well as large, private as well as public, big city as well as rural. Presented in this chapter are several cases of workplace homicide. In all these cases, with one exception, the perpetrator was an employee or former employee. However, perpetration of homicide at work is not limited to employees. As you will see in the one exception, people in the workplace can be at risk from a shooter who has no connection at all to the work site.

THE POST OFFICE

The term "going postal" has been used to describe an unhappy employee who opts to kill at work as a means of dealing with his or her frustrations. Even though I do not like the term because it unfairly associates a dysfunction with one environment, the post office is clearly prominent in the workplace homicide field. Broad public interest in homicide at work largely stems from post office shootings during the 1980s. Since 1983, there have been at least sixteen shootings by post office employees around the country. This does not include shootings and other violent acts that occur on these sites during the commission of other crimes (i.e., robbery, rape). Table 3.1 lists a number of incidents at post offices.

The nation's deadliest post office shooting happened in Edmond, Oklahoma, on August 20, 1986. Patrick Henry Sherrill killed fourteen coworkers that day and injured seven others. After a standoff with police, Sherrill killed himself.

On May 6, 1993, Mark Richard Hilburn killed one person and injured two others at the Dana Point post office in California. That same day a second shooting occurred two time zones away in Dearborn, Michigan. There, Larry Jasion killed one coworker. Like Sherrill, Hilburn and Jasion died of self-inflicted gunshot wounds at the scene.

Bruce William Clark was a 58-year-old employee at the City of Industry mail processing and distribution center. He had worked for the post office for twenty years. In the early morning hours of July 9, 1995, police were summoned to the post office to investigate a shooting. They found Clark pinned to the floor by fellow employees. Nearby, Clark's supervisor, James Whooper III, lay dead with two gunshot wounds to his body.

Clark had a master's degree in mathematics and had taught at two colleges in California during a short leave of absence from the post office in the 1970s. A former marine, he had few problems in his personnel file and his only legal trouble was a drunk driving arrest in the early 1970s. Just days before the shooting, Clark had contacted a private investigator saying he was afraid of Whooper and he wanted the private investigator to see if Whooper had a criminal history. Clark believed that Whooper was stealing from his employer and, according to the investigator's statement, Clark sought information to take to superiors in order to get Whooper fired. No evidence of any wrong-

Table 3.1
Post Office Incidents

Perpetrator	Location	Date	Deaths	Injuries	Status
James Brooks	Anniston, AL	12/2/83	1	1	unknown
Stephen Brownlee	Atlanta, GA	3/6/85	2	1	incarcerated
Bruce William Clark	City of Industry, CA	7/9/95	1	0	incarcerated
Anthony Deculit	Milwaukee, WI	12/19/97	1	2	suicide
Christopher Green	Montclair, NJ	3/21/93	4	1	incarcerated
Joseph Harris	Ridgewood, NJ	10/10/95	4	0	incarcerated
Mark Richard Hilburn	Dana Point, CA	5/6/93	1	2	suicide
David Lee Jackson	Denver, CO	12/24/97	hostages unharmed		incarcerated
Larry Jasion	Dearborn, MI	5/6/93	1	0	suicide
Charles Jennings	Las Vegas, NV	4/16/98	1	0	incarcerated
Thomas McIlvane	Royal Oak, MI	11/14/91	4	5	suicide
Warren Murphy	New Orleans, LA	12/14/88	4	1	incarcerated
Patrick Henry Sherrill	Edmond, OK	8/20/86	14	7	suicide
Perry Smith	Johnston, SC	8/19/83	1	2	unknown
Jesus Tamayo	Miami Beach, FL	9/2/97	2	0	suicide
John Merlin Taylor	Escondido, CA	8/10/89	3	1	suicide
Dorsey Thomas	East Palatine, IL	8/30/95	0	2	incarcerated

doing by Whooper existed. Clark told a coworker the month before the shooting that he believed his supervisor was picking on him and driving him crazy. He did not elaborate on his allegations.

The shift Clark was working operated from 10:00 P.M. until 7:00 A.M. Around 2:00 A.M., coworkers witnessed Clark in a verbal confrontation with Whooper. Thirty minutes later, Clark came up behind Whooper, who was seated at a machine, and, with both hands clenched together, struck him on the back of the neck. At this point another employee grabbed one of Clark's arms and Whooper grabbed the other. The employee asked Clark if he was on medication, if he was having family troubles, and if he had a gun. To each of these questions Clark replied, "No." Whooper sent Clark back to his work station and then called his supervisor, who came to the area. As the supervisor was talking with Whooper, he witnessed Clark approaching them with his hand in a paper bag. Twice he asked Clark what was in the bag, but he got no answer. Then Clark pulled a revolver from the bag and pointed it at Whooper. Whooper backed into a machine as Clark fired two shots. An employee grabbed the gun as Clark tried to fire a third round. The gun's hammer struck his thumb, preventing the round from being discharged. He then wrestled the gun away from Clark as other employees assisted in detaining Clark.

After the incident, Clark told police that some employees believed he was a postal inspector, but provided no evidence as to why he believed this. He also believed that during the previous year an employee had followed him on at least two occasions. Upon examination of the house where Clark lived alone, police found six cats and a hand-drawn map of the street where Whooper lived.

Clark made it clear at the scene and later to police that Whooper was his only intended victim. Witnesses stated that they had seen Clark carrying a paper bag around for several weeks and on the night of the shooting had seen him pull his revolver from what appeared to be the same paper bag. This incident is representative of many workplace shootings. Clark believed a coworker was wronging him, yet there was no evidence of truth in his allegations against Whooper. Clark never made any attempt to deny his involvement in the shooting.

My intuitive response when I first started research in the area of workplace homicide was that the post office was no more common as a site of homicide at work than any other location. I assumed the media were feeding on public interest in their coverage of these incidents to the exclusion of others. However, the post office is a dangerous place to work. While the Centers for Disease Control has found the post office to have a lower homicide rate than other industries,[1] others question this statistic. Statistics for homicide are often calculated per thousand workers.[2] If you consider the number of postal locations rather than the number of employees, the homicide rate at post offices is higher.

A number of suggestions have been made about why the post office is so often a target. Some argue that poor management is to blame. Poor management would include poor hiring practices, poor promotional policies, dysfunctional or nonexistent grievance procedures, and unhealthy management skills. Others have suggested that the quasi-military structure of the post office, stress to deliver on time, and questionable job security because of increased automation are all to blame.[3] Stress by itself seems an unlikely cause since air traffic controllers deal with significant job stress on a daily basis, but I am not aware of any shootings at air traffic control towers. Some also have suggested that the post office is targeted because the public has very high expectations and yet a very low opinion of the postal service. Most likely, the cause is a combination of all of these factors.

The U.S. Postal Service has not ignored the problem of violence in the post office. In 1998, U.S. Postmaster General William J. Henderson formed the United States Postal Service Commission on a Safe and Secure Workplace. According to a post office memo, "The five-member commission is an independent body that will investigate, analyze and report to the Postmaster General on workplace violence in the Postal Service, giving special attention to factors such as work-related stress, substance abuse and the workplace environment. The commission's report will detail concrete steps the Postal Service can take to make its 38,000 post offices and related facilities the safest possible environment for its employees."[4]

Setting up the commission is not the only measure the postal service is taking to address workplace violence. Henderson calls safety at work a priority.[5] In addressing safety in the workplace, Henderson has identified the grievance system as part of the problem, calling it inefficient and ineffective. He said, "On grievance handling, we can't have this huge bureaucracy that constantly reinforces management's decisions with no accountability."[6] The post office is not to blame for the choices of individuals, but I am encouraged that it has taken a lead in addressing problems that may perpetuate violence in the workplace.

CLIFTON McCREE

More often than not, in fact nearly 70% of the time, perpetrators of workplace homicide are Caucasian. An exception is Clifton Mc-Cree. Clifton McCree was born to Emily McCree in Thomasville, Georgia, in November 1954. Little is known of his activities through high school, but in January 1975 he joined the United States Marine Corps and was assigned to Camp Pendleton, California. His recorded troubles began that same year when he was disciplined twice for disrespect and disobeying a lawful order by a superior. Yet again, in 1976, he was punished for disrespect toward an officer. He was transferred to the inactive reserve in January 1977. He attempted to re-enlist in 1979 but was denied.

It was in 1977 that he began his work with the City of Fort Lauderdale, Florida, as a maintenance worker. He would eventually take his own life and the lives of five coworkers. During the next seventeen years, McCree's employment records are full of reprimands and warnings for unacceptable behaviors. He argued and fought with coworkers, on numerous occasions arrived at work late, used a city vehicle for personal use, left work early, was disciplined for being abusive to the public and harassing his coworkers, and was finally dismissed in 1994 for failing a drug test. In the meantime, McCree made several attempts to join the police force, but he failed the written exam and later the oral exam.

While still employed with the city, McCree took on a second job at a security firm. Following his dismissal from the city, he worked for other security firms, but his aggression and other problems continued. He was dismissed from at least one of these jobs as a result of such problems.

Married in 1979, McCree had three children. In winter 1996, he fell into financial trouble. He was unemployed and three months behind on his house payments. With electrical service to his home about to be disconnected, his wife and children moved out, leaving him alone. Four days later and fourteen months to the day after his dismissal from the city, McCree attempted to reacquire his city job. At city hall, he talked with a city employee about his old job and began the application process. However, when he asked about the possibilities of getting his old job back, he was informed that city policy prohibited him from being rehired because his termination involved a failed drug test. McCree calmly thanked the employee for her help and left the building. Just hours later he would carry out threats he had made over a year earlier.

According to employees who worked with him during his service with the city, McCree had a volatile temper. He accused others of discriminating against him because of his race, when there was no evidence of such bias. For example, on one occasion while eating lunch with coworkers in a fast food restaurant, McCree verbally attacked two elderly patrons because they looked at him. He believed they were staring at him because he was black. His outburst stunned and frightened both the customers and his coworkers. Eventually, his aggressive and threatening behavior was directed at his fellow employees. Upon his dismissal, McCree swore revenge on them.

At approximately 4:45 on the morning of February 9, 1996, McCree arrived at the trailer where beach maintenance workers gathered at the beginning of the workday. McCree entered the trailer and began shooting. One employee, Nancy Ann Ellers, escaped through a rear door as McCree fired in her direction. Six other employees were not as fortunate.

Several men sitting around a break-room table were shot in one room. One of these men, Joe Brookins, was wounded, but he fell to the floor and pretended to be dead. McCree stood over him and shot him again. McCree moved down the hall to an office where another employee was working. He shot and killed him on the spot.

Minutes later, Brookins, who was still feigning death, realized that the gunfire had stopped. He opened his eyes and saw McCree lying on the floor with blood around his body and thought McCree had shot himself. He crawled to a phone and contacted police. McCree was dead when the police arrived, but Brookins recovered from his wounds.

One employee survived that day because he remembered McCree's threats. Ivan Herman McDonald had worked with McCree prior to McCree's dismissal in 1994. He remembered the volatile temper and told fellow employees that he believed McCree would live up to his threats. McDonald made it a habit to greet fellow employees at the beginning of the day, clock in, and then leave the trailer. He would wait in his vehicle and then join the crews as they prepared to leave for their maintenance tasks. On the day of the shooting he was sitting in his vehicle when he heard the shots and saw Nancy Ellers running from the trailer. Fearing the shooter might follow Ellers, McDonald hid in his vehicle for a few minutes. He then left in his vehicle in an attempt to find Ellers, eventually locating her at a convenience store near the scene.

The tragic circumstances of the Fort Lauderdale shooting are unfortunately characteristic of workplace homicide. As in many of the other homicides I have studied, McCree provided numerous warnings of his intentions. His overt threats to kill his coworkers were completely dismissed by many and minimized by others. As for McDonald, believing McCree's threats probably saved his life.

McCree was an angry man who indiscriminately vented his rage on others. He repeatedly threatened his coworkers and failed to operate according to the rules of his superiors. When he found himself alone, unemployed, and broke, and when it became obvious to him that he would not be able to return to his former workplace, McCree decided others would pay for his misfortunes. To the very end he blamed others for his problems.

THOMAS HAMILTON

Several years before the shooting at Columbine High School in Littleton, Colorado, a 43-year-old former scout leader and boys' club operator assassinated sixteen children and one teacher in cold blood and wounded seventeen others in a primary school in Dunblane, Scotland. On March 13, 1996, Thomas Hamilton entered Dunblane Primary School. In his possession were four handguns and 743 rounds of ammunition. In a matter of minutes, Hamilton fired over one hundred rounds, saving the final round for himself.

Hamilton was born to Thomas Watt and Agnes Graham Hamilton Watt in 1952. The marriage was troubled and it dissolved before young Thomas was four. Thomas and his mother moved in with her parents, and the Hamilton family later adopted him. Like Ted Bundy, Thomas was raised believing that his mother was his sister. It is not clear whether he ever knew the true identities of his birth mother and his adoptive parents. Hamilton never married and was described as a lonely, isolated individual. He continued to live with his grandparents until his adopted mother's death in 1987. A few years later his "father" moved into "sheltered housing," leaving Thomas alone.[7]

In 1973, Hamilton became a scout leader. He seemed exceptionally interested in young boys and the scouting program. However, Hamilton's unusual behavior led to questions concerning his activities and motives. For example, on more than one occasion, Hamilton forced boys to sleep with him in a vehicle. He provided excuses for these events to his superiors, but they finally asked him to resign his leadership position in 1974.

For a number of years, Hamilton attempted to regain his position in the scouting organization, but was repeatedly denied the warrant needed to operate a sanctioned troop. It was Hamilton's belief that the scouting organization had tarnished his name, seemingly because of accusations of misconduct. Therefore, in the late 1970s he ended his struggle to be reinstated into the scouting organization.

In 1981, Hamilton opened a private boys' club, the Dunblane Rovers Group, which he operated until 1983. During the next fifteen years, Hamilton opened and operated fifteen separate clubs for boys from 7 to 11 years of age. These clubs provided games and gymnastics training (for which Hamilton held a Grade 5 certificate from the British Amateur Gymnastics Association).[8] Some of these clubs operated on school property. While some of his clubs started out successfully, many of them later declined in attendance and closed. As late as 1995, he accused the scouting organization of conspiring against him to destroy his clubs.

Using titles like "Boys' Clubs Sports Group Committee," Hamilton attempted to give his clubs credibility by presenting the impression that they were run by committees. However, according to the head of the inquiry into the Dunblane shootings, Lord Cullen, there was never any clear committee functioning in any of Hamilton's organizations.[9]

While he operated these clubs, Hamilton was accused of being verbally abusive to boys and their parents. He also appeared to some to be paranoid, believing the scouting organization and the police were linked in an effort to promote scouting to the detriment of his own organizations. He was also believed to exaggerate his own importance, using names of important individuals as "contacts."[10]

During this time, Hamilton became an avid gun enthusiast. Despite Scotland's strict firearms laws, Hamilton was able to legally acquire numerous pistols and rifles as well as thousands of rounds of ammunition. Between 1977 and 1996, Hamilton legally held several .22 caliber pistols, a 9mm semiautomatic pistol, a .357 caliber pistol, and several .22 caliber rifles. Records indicate that during this period he acquired over 20,000 rounds of various types of ammunition. Because of his participation in shooting clubs, his requests for firearms and ammunition purchase permits did not attract attention and were readily approved by police.

At the beginning of the school day on March 13, 1996, Hamilton drove to Dunblane Primary School. He cut telephone lines near the building, apparently thinking he was disabling the school's phone system. However, the lines he cut served residences adjacent to the school. Hamilton entered the school through a side door by the gymnasium. His first two shots were fired outside the gymnasium, but he quickly entered the gym where Mrs. Gwen Mayor's primary class of twenty-eight pupils had assembled for a physical education class. As he entered the gymnasium, Hamilton fired at random into the crowd of students. Mrs. Mayor was killed instantly. In the minutes that followed, teachers, some of whom were wounded, tried to shelter the children in a storage area as Hamilton continued to fire in the adjacent room. As they cowered in confusion and fear, Hamilton strolled through the gym, shooting injured and fallen children at point-blank range.

Hamilton fired several shots out of a doorway toward an external classroom structure. The teacher in that classroom instructed her children to get down to the floor. A round penetrated a seat that only moments before had been occupied by a child.

During the few minutes of his rampage, Hamilton fired both indiscriminately and with deliberation. His final shot was from a revolver he placed in his mouth. Pulling the trigger, he died among the dead and wounded children in the gymnasium.

The state's formal inquiry into Hamilton's actions failed to provide a clear motive for his behavior. While there was evidence of financial trouble in his life, and while he had exhibited symptoms of mental illness (paranoia), it is unclear why he chose Dunblane Primary School for his unconscionable act. According to acquaintances, nothing seemed unusual about Hamilton prior to the incident and he had plans to meet with an associate the following Monday.

Dunblane is a most troubling homicide for many reasons. Homicides where there are multiple victims and when the victims are children are especially difficult to accept. However, most disconcerting to me is the fact that Hamilton seems to have chosen the Dunblane school at random. There is little we can do to protect ourselves when a perpetrator blind-sides us by choosing a location out of the blue. With few exceptions, in all the homicide cases I've studied, even when authorities have been reluctant to speculate on motive, I have always been able to see a potential motive. Dunblane is one of the exceptions. Perhaps one day there will be an explanation for this tragedy that will help to make sense out of it. For now, however, we are left with the truth that our lives are not always under our control. They can be taken from us at any time.

ROBERT SCOTT HELFER

Greely, Colorado, is a quiet town about sixty miles northeast of Denver. On a cold December morning in 1998, state Department of Transportation (DOT) employee, Robert Scott Helfer, was to have a disciplinary hearing with a regional director and an equal employment representative. At the day's end one of them would be dead, another hospitalized with gunshot wounds, and a state trooper would have taken the life of an acquaintance.

Like Clifton McCree, 50-year-old Robert Scott Helfer, an accounting technician, had a long history of difficulty getting along with his coworkers. He was described by some unstable and many were concerned that he might some day "go postal." Helfer had a variety of problems with coworkers and received several warnings from superiors concerning his behavior. He had filed grievances against his workmates and been involved in several situations that required intervention by superiors.

The incident that finally led to the shooting at the Colorado DOT involved fellow employee Donna Archuleta. In July 1998, Helfer had requested a new desk, extra file cabinets, and other office furniture. Archuleta had altered the order upon instructions from supervisors. It was determined that Helfer had not only requested expenditures that equaled the entire office's budget for the year, but that the desk and other equipment Helfer requested would not even fit in his office. Therefore, a smaller desk as well as other scaled-back items were ordered. Furious with the change, Helfer blamed Archuleta and threatened her. He was disciplined for his aggressive response. In the weeks that followed, superiors responded to statements from Archuleta that she feared for her safety by moving Helfer's office to an adjacent building.

On the morning of December 8, 1998, Helfer was scheduled to

have a disciplinary hearing (called an 8-3-3 meeting) with regional director Karla Harding. The purpose of the meeting was to seek facts concerning allegations of sexual harassment against Helfer. Sharlene Nail, an employee representative, was to sit in on the interview to ensure that Helfer's employee rights were not violated.

Helfer arrived at work as usual that morning, but he left the DOT offices, saying he had to pick up his daughter who had missed the school bus. There was no evidence that his daughter had missed the bus and it appears that Helfer may have left in order to collect his firearm. When he returned to the office he was ten minutes late for his hearing. He went directly to the meeting room on the second floor of the DOT building where the hearing was to take place. Harding asked Helfer if he wanted to hang up his coat, but he chose to keep it with him. Harding noticed that Helfer had something under his coat and he kept his hand under the coat for the entire meeting. Her first thought was that he was concealing a tape recorder, but then she wondered if he might have a gun. As the hearing proceeded, Harding became more concerned about Helfer's behavior and her fear that he had a weapon increased. She decided that if he pulled a weapon she would charge him. Ms. Harding explained to me that she did not know what she would do once she charged him, but she knew that rushing him was her only hope. Her plan saved her life.

Toward the end of the meeting, Helfer became agitated. He complained that he was being treated unfairly and that fellow employees were preventing him from being promoted. He then drew a 9mm Ruger pistol from beneath his coat. He aimed the weapon at Nail, who was sitting closest to him, and fired, striking her in the hip and chest. As Helfer was shooting Nail, Harding put her escape plan into action by lunging toward him. Helfer turned the gun in her direction, shooting her three times. Harding fell to the floor pretending to be dead. As she lay there bleeding, she opened her eyes and saw Nail motionless across the room. Harding heard a window open and then the room fell silent. She saw that Helfer had left the room through a window, escaping onto the roof of the structure below.

Even though Harding was seriously wounded when she implemented her escape plan, the fact that she was a moving target probably saved her life. Help for Harding and Nail arrived in minutes. Attempts by coworkers to revive Nail were unsuccessful and she later died. In an unusual twist of fate, one rescuer responding to the scene was Harding's brother.

Helfer, however, was not finished with his shooting spree. After leaving the second story office, he ran across an adjacent roof and jumped to the parking lot below. As he landed on the pavement, he severely fractured his ankle. He sat on a curb in the parking lot for several minutes, firing shots into the building where Archuleta worked. Two rounds narrowly missed an employee in the building.

Helfer then crawled into the building searching for Archuleta. Sliding across the floor from office to office he met other coworkers, telling them, "Don't worry. I'm not here for you."[11] As Helfer headed in the direction of Archulata's office she screamed, "It's Scott. He's after me."[12] She ran to another office and hid behind a large printer. When Helfer reached Archuleta's office it was empty. He then returned to the parking lot.

The state DOT offices were next door to a Colorado State Patrol post. One employee ran to the State Patrol office and found Captain Gary Myers on duty at the desk. Myers ran to the parking lot, where he saw Helfer approximately seventy-five feet away, sitting on the curbing and waving a gun in the air.

Myers drew his service weapon and ordered Helfer to drop his gun. Helfer fired in Myers' direction, yelling, "Shoot me! Do your duty."[13] Again, Myers instructed Helfer to drop his weapon and again, Helfer fired toward the officer. Returning fire, Myers walked toward the gunman. As the two exchanged fire, Myers saw his rounds missing their target. He paused and took careful aim. His next five rounds hit the gunman, who died at the scene.

As is often true in workplace homicide, some employees were afraid of Helfer. Archuleta was afraid for her safety and she repeatedly expressed her fear to coworkers, supervisors, and her husband. Fearing any interaction with Helfer, she went out of her way to avoid the building where he worked. The day of the shooting, she was nearly paralyzed with fear as she hid from the gunman. In statements following the shooting, numerous employees recounted previous conversations involving their own concerns that Helfer would someday kill some or all of them.

In an odd twist of circumstances, the day before the shooting Helfer had talked with Captain Myers in the parking lot between the DOT and State Patrol buildings. Helfer had purchased a new Ford Taurus and discussed it with Myers, who congratulated him on his purchase.

Tragically, Sharlene Nail, present in the room as Helfer's advocate, was the only employee who died as a result of Helfer's actions. Harding recovered from her gunshot wounds. Captain Myers, a veteran officer, was left to recover from the emotional scars involved in taking the life of another human being. In 1999 he was commended for his bravery.

Helfer provided many clues to his instability. Among these were his reputation as temperamental, his threatening behavior, his grievances against other employees, his history of inability to get along with his coworkers, as well as others' fear of him. Helfer was an active member of his church and a member of its choir. His neighbors described him as helpful "almost to the point of being annoying."[14] One neighbor recalled "shouting matches" at the Helfer home and another stated that he feared for the safety of Helfer's children.[15] Helfer was suffering from depression and had undergone counseling. No shooting can be predicted with total accuracy, but this situation would have ranked as a high risk if an assessment had been done.

MATTHEW BECK

Like Robert Helfer, 35-year-old Matthew Beck was an accountant. Beck had worked for eight years for the Connecticut Lottery Corporation. For months Beck had accused his superiors of misconduct. He had twice approached newspapers with his allegations. After returning from several months on stress-related disability leave, Beck entered his office, worked about thirty minutes, and then proceeded to kill four of his bosses.

Newington, Connecticut, is a town eight miles south of Hartford and home to the offices of the Connecticut Lottery Corporation. Prior to his employment at the Lottery Corporation, Beck had jobs with the Internal Revenue Service, a security company, and the state Department of Special Revenue. He had undergone treatment for anxiety and depression, and his dysfunctional behavior dated back to his days as a student at Florida Institute of Technology when he made his first attempt at suicide.[16] Never married, Beck lived alone for years, but just months before the shootings, his parents had successfully convinced him to move in with them. They were concerned about his welfare because of his struggle with depression.

Beck had been unhappy at work almost since the beginning of his employment with the Lottery Corporation. Initially he complained of his working conditions and pay. He believed that his coworkers did not care about him, despite the fact that several of them called to ask about him during his stay at Elmcrest Psychiatric Hospital the year before the shooting.

His discontent at work escalated as he accused lottery officials of misconduct. As it turned out, lottery officials admitted they had, indeed, inflated Lotto jackpots for years by rounding sales up to the nearest $500,000.[17] Beck alleged that these inflated amounts were used to increase ticket sales. He also alleged other forms of misconduct by employees that were never confirmed. Beck also said he was not being paid appropriately for the job he was doing. He believed he was doing work that was outside his assigned area, for which he should have been paid an additional $2 per hour.

He took a disability leave from the Lottery Corporation in October 1997. During his leave he wrote letters to the governor, state officials, lawmakers, and later reporters expressing his concerns about the Lottery Corporation.[18] Beck also wrote letters to his superiors complaining about his job, requesting a special orthopedic chair, and asking for a copy of his personnel file. Beck had originally planned a six-month leave of absence, but he returned after only four months. His accrued sick time ended on the day of the shooting.

The day before the shootings, Beck had contacted a reporter for the *Hartford Courant*. He left a message saying he wanted to talk about "lottery-related issues," exposing "flaws in the system that compromised the integrity of the state lottery," but the reporter was out of town and did not get the message until after the killings.[19]

On the morning of March 6, 1998, Beck arrived at work and worked for about a half hour. He had a discussion with his boss, the lottery's director of information systems, Michael Logan. Nothing seemed unusual. Linda Mlynarczyk, the chief financial officer, asked Beck if he wanted to take his coat off, but he replied he did not. At some point, Beck went to a supply closet. The reason for this is unknown, but he was seen emerging from the closet prior to entering Michael Logan's office.

Security officers heard screams or yells. Investigating these, a female security officer knocked on Logan's door. Beck answered, telling her everything was "OK." She left the area to report what had happened to a colleague. While she was speaking with her associate, gunshots rang out. Beck shot Logan twice with a 9mm Glock semiautomatic handgun and stabbed him several times in the chest and abdomen. Beck reportedly was stabbed in the leg during this encounter.

After killing Logan, he left the knife in that room and then moved to a room where his supervisor and four others were engaged in a meeting. Looking at Linda Mlynarczyk, the corporation's chief financial officer, Beck held up his hand and said, "Bye, bye." He shot her numerous times. A trail of blood from his leg wound marked his movements. Leaving the office where Mlynarczyk was killed, he came upon Rick Rubelmann, the lottery's vice president of operations, in a hallway. Beck shot Rubelmann four times on the spot.

During the shooting spree, a security guard ushered employees out of the building. As they ran across the parking lot, lottery president Otho ("Otto") Brown yelled for everyone to take cover. Witnesses say that Brown, apparently realizing he was a target, slowed down to draw attention from the fleeing workers.[20] As Beck exited the building he shot Brown in the buttocks causing him to fall to the ground. As frightened employees watched from nearby woods, Beck stood over the corporation's president and pointed the gun at him. The terrified employees yelled for Beck not to shoot him, but their cries fell on deaf ears. Pleading for his life, Brown raised his arm in self-defense. Beck fired two more times into Brown's head, killing him. An unmarked police car entered the parking lot and two officers emerged with weapons drawn. Immediately, Beck put the gun to his head and shot himself. Bystanders thought the police might have shot him, but they had fired no rounds.

As with most workplace killers, Beck's coworkers recognized him as a potential threat. Several employees told police they had had various levels of concern about Beck. One stated he had carried his gun to work specifically because of Beck.[21] Mlynarczyk's husband released a "farewell" letter he had written to his slain wife, stating she had discussed her concerns about Beck twice in the week prior to the killing.[22] Another employee of the Lottery Corporation told police that Rubelmann had feared Beck might damage computer equipment in the offices.[23]

Despite his mental health history, Beck had a license to carry a handgun and had access to weapons. He was involved in paint-ball games and, according to an acquaintance, was fascinated by "soldier of fortune–type stuff."[24] Police say he owned at least six different firearms including two assault rifles. Beck had been treated for psychiatric conditions, having twice been admitted to mental institutions, and he is reported to have attempted suicide at least twice.

The role Beck's mental health played in this tragedy is unknown;

however, I believe that his mental health history is not solely responsible. Beck's coping skills were weak and he had a very difficult time functioning in his social environment. I believe that a combination of variables lead to the tragic events of March 6, 1998. Beck's inability to get along with coworkers, his mental health struggles, his weak social skills, and his weak coping strategies all played a role.

Beck's parents were deeply grieved at the actions of their son. These well-intentioned individuals did not foresee his fatal plans. Mr. and Mrs. Beck apologized to the victims and their families for their son's behavior. There is little doubt that they would have intervened if they had known what the future held. A year after the killings, Beck's parents petitioned state police to return his gun and knife so that they might sell these items and other things that once belonged to their son. Their intent was to donate the proceeds to the victims' families. The Lottery Corporation has since moved its offices and it has introduced significant security measures in its new facility. Unfortunately, these precautions come too late to save the four who died that day.

CONCLUDING REMARKS

My files are full of homicides that occurred at work. Even though workplace homicide is on the decline, in 1996 there were nearly one thousand murders in the workplace in the United States. In California, one in five deaths at work are homicides, and workplace violence costs this country millions of dollars every year. The typical workplace murderer is Caucasian, male, and between the ages of 23 and 45. However, as with several of the cases described in the preceding paragraphs, not all workplace killers fit this profile.

The first step toward prevention of workplace homicide is to believe that it can happen. One of the ways we cope with tragedies around us is to believe they will not happen to us. We see house fires and car accidents on the evening news and we suppose it happens to other people and we are somehow immune. I am quite sure that as you read this chapter, you scarcely even considered the fact that this same sort of event could take place in your own working environment. Any insurance salesperson will tell you that the first hurdle in selling insurance is convincing customers that tragedies can strike at home. As we have seen in the cases described in this chapter, there are warning signs. Some potential victims are alive because they heeded these warning signs and believed that the unimaginable was indeed possible. Others, for reasons we may never know, did not heed these signs and their disbelief may have cost them their lives.

The victims of these homicides are not to blame for their own deaths. My purpose is to learn from these cases and teach others how to avoid the same fate. Hindsight is much easier than foresight, I admit, but we would be foolish not to take advantage of information that might save our lives.

NOTES

1. Robert I. Simon, *Bad men do what good men dream* (Washington, DC: American Psychiatric Press, 1996), 247.

2. Charles E. Labig, *Preventing violence in the workplace* (New York: RHR International Co., 1995), 132.

3. Simon, *Bad men do what good men dream*, 246.

4. "Postmaster general established commission on a safe and secure workplace," *Memo to Mailers*, *www.usps.gov/business/mtm/mtm1198 workplace.htm*, November 1998.

5. Irene Middleman Thomas, "Are you afraid to come to work?" *Postal Life* (Internet Edition), *www.usps.gov/history/plife/p1090198/afraid.htm*, September/October 1998.

6. Ibid.

7. *Public enquiry into the shootings at Dunblane Primary School on March 18 1996*, The Stationery Office, *www.official-documents.co.uk/document/*
scottish/dunblane/dunblane.htm, 1996.

8. Ibid.

9. Ibid.

10. Ibid.

11. Donovan Henderson, "Gunman: 'Shoot me! Do your duty!' " *Greeley Tribune*, March 14, 1999, A10.

12. Ibid.

13. Ibid., A1.

14. Carla Crowder, "Brother could see frustration but not violence," *Denver Rocky Mountain News*, December 9, 1998, D5.

15. David Olinger, "Gunman's neighbors in 'shock,' " *Denver Post*, December 9, 1998, 4A.

16. Lynne Tuohy, "Killer's parents apologize," *Hartford Courant* (Internet Edition), March 8, 1998.

17. Lyn Bixby, "Matt Beck took his grudge to the newspaper," *Hartford Courant* (Internet Edition), March 7, 1998.

18. Andrew Julien, Lyn Bixby, and Colin Poitras, "Friends saw anger growing in Beck," *Hartford Courant* (Internet Edition), March 7, 1998.

19. Bixby, "Matt Beck took his grudge to the newspaper."

20. Mike McIntire, Al Lara, and Matthew Hay Brown, "Horrified workers witness killing in parking lot," *Hartford Courant* (Internet Edition), March 7, 1998.

21. Bixby, "Was it avoidable?" *Hartford Courant* (Internet Edition), February 28, 1999.

22. Andrew Julien, "Lottery gunman deeply troubled, records show," *Hartford Courant* (Internet Edition), March 12, 1998.

23. Bixby, "Was it avoidable?"

24. Julien, Bixby, and Poitras, "Friends saw anger growing in Beck."

Homicide at Home: Domestic Violence

In 1998, an 80-year-old Kansas man stalked a 77-year-old woman with whom he was infatuated. She dated and then married another man, enraging her stalker. He then broke into the home of the newlyweds, bludgeoned the woman's husband to death with a baseball bat, and beat the woman. Police called by the woman found the elderly stalker hiding behind a chair in the couple's home, holding the blood-covered bat. He claimed he found the man dead and the woman beaten and was only trying to help them, but a jury later convicted him of murdering the 77-year-old man. He was sentenced to life in prison plus four years.

A 41-year-old woman in Florida was arrested and accused of deliberately making her child sick in order to gain attention and to defraud her insurance company as well as charitable organizations. She had allegedly poisoned her daughter's food and medicine with, among other things, fecal matter. The child had been hospitalized more than 200 times, had her gall bladder, appendix, and part of her intestines removed, spent 640 days in the hospital, and endured 40 surgeries. The child's illness even attracted the attention of Hillary Clinton, as the mother claimed the child suffered from a genetic disorder. Police, however, charged the mother with aggravated child abuse. She was convicted and sentenced to five years in prison for child abuse. Fortunately the child lived and has not been sick since she was removed from her mother's care.

In 1998, a 37-year-old Pittsburgh man said he was angry because his 5-year-old twins were slow getting ready for day care. When he could not find a toy that the children wanted to take with them, he said he "just lost it." He went to the cellar, retrieved a sledgehammer, returned upstairs, and beat the children in the head. Afterward, he called police and confessed the crime. Police arrived to find the father in the front yard and the children inside the residence, one on the couch and the other on the floor in front of the television. One of the children was dead, but the other was still alive, although he died later. The mother, a bank clerk, was at work at the time. Neighbors said the financially stable family seemed happy and the father often played with the twins outside.

There is perhaps no form of violence more passionate and uncontrolled than domestic violence. Even terrorists, for example, while extremely passionate about their causes, are quite controlled in their behavior. They can and will postpone their aggression, waiting for the right place and time. Aggression fueled by the emotion involved in personal relationships, however, is uncontrolled and explosive. Some domestic partners stalk and deliberately plan the murders of their spouses, but many kill in the heat of passion. For this reason, as I stated in Chapter 1, domestic homicide is distinctive.

Research on domestic violence indicates that 33% of all women killed in America are murdered by their husbands or boyfriends.[1] If we include all domestic perpetrators, as many as 50% of all murders occur within the family.[2] On several occasions I have addressed medical students on the topic of domestic violence. They are always shocked to hear the statistic that regardless of their specialty or place of practice they will see a battered woman in their offices every two weeks.[3] Because these numbers are so high, when a homicide occurs, family members are always suspects. As you read this chapter you will see why.

DESPERATELY CLINGING TO CONTROL

A domestic situation that turns violent is like a swimmer who begins to drown. All is well as long as the swimmer believes he is in control of the situation, but as he tires and finds it difficult to stay on the surface, he thrashes around and begins to panic. Once this happens, he may even fight those who are there to help him, to the point of drowning his rescuers. Relationships operate in the same way. While a partner in the relationship believes he is in control, he may be rational and calm, but once the other person begins to slip away, the partner becomes more desperate. He may threaten, fight, scream, or even kill the very one that he loves. This kind of behavior precedes some forms of stalking that I address in Chapter 5. During the O. J. Simpson trial, I heard many people say that he would not have committed the murders of his ex-wife and her friend because he was rich, influential, and famous. None of these things matter to a drowning victim. Simpson was found not guilty, but his wealth and status would in no way have prohibited him from committing those murders. It is completely plausible that a person could be so obsessed with a former love interest that he could stalk and kill her regardless of his financial status, power, or prestige.

A rule called the *principle of least interest* operates in every relationship. This principle says that the person who has the least interest in maintaining the relationship has the most power. This is because he or she has the least to lose if the relationship dissolves. You may have wondered why women stay in relationships with men who treat them poorly or cheat on them. One reason is that the husband has the most power; therefore, he can do what he wants and get away with it because he knows his partner will not leave. Sometimes, however, these roles reverse. A woman may decide she has had enough and choose to leave. When she leaves, the husband discovers that he has lost power or control and, even though she may not realize it, the wife has gained immense power in the relationship. In an attempt to regain power and control, the husband will make promises, beg for forgiveness, or threaten. The more he sees that he cannot regain the power in the relationship, the more desperate he becomes—just like a drowning person.

In his book *Rose Madder*, Stephen King presents the story of a woman dominated and abused by her husband. She has no friends, no money, and no place to go, but she decides to leave her abusive mate anyway. Even though this is a fictional story, King's description of the woman, her life, her thoughts, and her husband's behaviors are very realistic. The husband in the story controls her friendships, free time, money, and telephone conversations, leaving her with nothing except him and their relationship. He strengthens his position every time she loses a friend or a freedom. Yet when she decides to leave, he sees that he has lost his power in the relationship and he loses control of his normally controlled behavior. He abandons all of his responsibilities including his job, personal business, and relationships in a desperate attempt to regain control of the woman.

The security director of a business asked me to review the case of an employee who was making threats, wanting to know how likely the employee would be to actually carry them out. The general impression of the security staff was that the man was a low risk and simply a "blowhard." They were probably right, but I asked about his domestic situation. He was in the midst of a divorce, they told me, and I asked who initiated it. They were not sure, but they said they assumed he did because he had moved to another state the previous year and had been living apart from his family during that time. I know it makes sense to suppose he did not care very much about his family, but that is not necessarily the case. The *principle of least interest* tells me that a person may do outrageous things because he believes he can always go home. I have worked with many clients whose spouses have had multiple affairs, beaten them, threatened them with knives and guns, or engaged in drug use or illegal activities, yet as long as my clients put up with it, their partners would continue to do whatever they want. In one case, the husband of my client had even convinced her to let his mistress move into their home, saying he was trying to "help" her. My client said she "didn't know" if anything was going on between the two of them. Obviously, this woman was in deep denial, but she stayed with her husband because, in her mind, she had more to lose by leaving than by staying. For this reason he could get away with his selfish behaviors. Therefore, if the employee I was evaluating had initiated divorce proceedings himself, I would be less worried than if his spouse had done so. If she had been the one to file, even though he might have seemed unconcerned about their relationship, his apparent apathy could have been symptomatic of his belief that she would not leave. Her filing for divorce would have been a signal to him that he had lost his power and, therefore, he would be a higher risk to her and perhaps to others.

The following case studies provide a glimpse of relationships that tragically turned to murder because of poor coping skills, dysfunctional thinking, mental illness, and clear attempts to capture, maintain, or regain power.

SAMUEL JACKSON QUICK, JR.

Peachtree City, Georgia, is a very quiet, upscale, suburban Atlanta community just a few miles from my home. The city is interwoven with walking paths and golf cart trails that residents use to travel to the store, the theater, and the library. It was in this quiet suburb that Samuel Jackson Quick, Jr., committed only the second murder in the city in the thirty-six years of its incorporation.

Hoshizaki America, Inc., a Japanese-owned business that produces ice machines, is located in Peachtree City. Among the employees at Hoshizaki America were Samuel Quick and Tracy Lavallie. Quick was a 25-year-old resident of a neighboring town and Lavallie was a 31-year-old mother of two, wife of a police sergeant, and resident of an adjacent county. During the course of their employment, Lavallie and Quick began some kind of relationship, but the nature of that relationship remains in dispute. According to Lavallie's family, there was never any "domestic" relationship between Quick and Lavallie. Tracy's husband, Richard Lavallie, said that his wife was a kind woman who had attempted to befriend a lonely coworker, but that Quick had misinterpreted her intentions. Quick, on the other hand, perceived their relationship to be much deeper than a simple friendship. At his trial, the judge called the situation a "classic example of domestic violence."[4] Whichever version was closer to the truth of their relationship, it is undisputed that in October 1995, Lavallie wanted it to end. Quick found it difficult to suppress his feelings for her since they had to interact with each other daily at work. Therefore, both Quick and Lavallie pleaded with Hoshizaki managers to move them to separate areas of the facility because they found it difficult to work together. Their requests were denied and they were threatened with disciplinary action if they asked again or if there was trouble between them.[5] During this time, Quick tried in vain to renew their relationship.

In spring 1996, the city of Atlanta and its suburbs were preparing to host the centennial Olympic Games. The papers were full of news of construction, pre-Olympic events, and other information. That same spring, the situation between Quick and Lavallie was reaching a climax. On April 3, 1996, the two of them talked while at lunch. Then, claiming to be sick, Quick left the factory, but he returned that afternoon. Quick brought flex-cuffs, the plastic ties often used in mass arrests by police, and a firearm, planning to abduct Lavallie. He confronted her in the parking lot in front of Hoshizaki America. Employees inside the building saw the two struggling and they called the police.

By chance, four high-ranking Peachtree City police officers were traveling together nearby when they heard the call. They responded and were on the scene within two minutes. As they pulled into the parking lot, they saw that Quick was holding Lavallie in a headlock and she was desperately struggling against him. As the four officers approached in their vehicle, Quick put a .38 caliber pistol to Lavallie's head and pulled the trigger. As the officers left their vehicle, Quick dropped his weapon and said, "Please don't shoot me."[6] Lavallie was airlifted to a local hospital, but she died that evening.

What exactly occurred was a point of contention between the defense and the prosecution in the subsequent trial. While still at the scene, Quick told police chief Jim Murray that he shot Lavallie because he heard sirens, but that he did not know officers were there until he shot her.[7] However, in court he would claim that he shot Lavallie by accident and that he merely intended to take her to his home to force her to tell him why she would not consider renewing their relationship.

In court, Quick said that his infatuation with Lavallie was in part due to her striking resemblance to his deceased mother and that he thought that she was estranged from her husband.[8] This excuse may seem reasonable on the surface, but the obvious dysfunction in his thinking is reflected in his decision to abduct her by force. Responsible, mature men do not kidnap people when they want to ask them questions. He eventually pled guilty to charges of felony murder, kidnapping with bodily injury, and possession of a firearm during the commission of a crime. He was sentenced to two life terms plus five years and will be eligible for parole in twenty years. He had no prior criminal record.

A year after the killing, Lavallie's family filed a wrongful death lawsuit against Quick and they also sued Hoshizaki America, saying the corporation should have known Quick was a danger to Lavallie but failed to act. Ironically, Quick also filed suit against Hoshizaki America, arguing that Hoshizaki should "pay him damages equal to the amount of any damages he may be required to pay Richard Lavallie or his two children," because the corporation did not separate the two as they had requested.[9]

SUSAN SMITH

Few homicides rival the powerful but mixed emotions that our country experienced in response to the murders committed by Susan Smith. Smith claimed that her children were abducted by a black carjacker, but later she confessed to murdering the two innocent boys herself. October 25, 1994, was a day that changed our nation.

I first heard the name "Susan Smith" as I watched the news broadcast her desperate plea for a carjacker to return her two sons. With her estranged husband at her side, Smith stood before television cameras in her hometown of Union, South Carolina, and pleaded for the return of her sons. She told police that she and her children, 3-year-old Michael and 14-month-old Alex, were at a stoplight on a deserted highway when a man forced his way into her vehicle at gunpoint. A few miles down the road he forced her from the car but did not allow her to take the boys with her. The day after this story became public, one of my students asked me what I thought of the case. I said it was unlikely that the boys were still alive. Carjackers want cars, not children. When carjackers take a vehicle with a child on board, they usually let the child out in a public place or abandon the vehicle as soon as they discover the child inside—usually within hours of the carjacking. Because I did not know much about the case, however, I suggested that the police would certainly look into the possibility that a relative had taken the children. This is common in divorce and custody disputes. I concluded that if there was no custody battle going on, the children had probably been killed. Unfortunately, I was right, but not in the way I had thought. Nine days after the alleged carjacking, the concern of people across the country turned to outrage when it was revealed that Smith had rolled her car into a lake with her helpless children strapped into their car seats, and she had stood by as they drowned.

People who knew Susan Smith described her as a God-fearing woman and loving mother. She had been voted the friendliest girl in her 1989 senior class, and her teachers, principal, friends, relatives, and acquaintances all found her a likable, cheery woman who was never in any significant trouble. This cheery veneer, however, concealed a deeply troubled woman. In 1978 when Susan was only 6 years old, her unemployed father, who had separated from her mother, shot and killed himself. When she was 13, she attempted suicide, but her mother and stepfather refused to follow the psychiatric recommendation that she be hospitalized.[10] She would attempt suicide again at age 18. At 23 years of age, she would yet again consider ending her life but would, instead, take the lives of her sons.

When she was 15, her stepfather, Beverly Russell, began molesting her; he continued to engage in sexual relations with her until three months before she killed her sons. Russell, a leader in the local Christian Coalition and the local Republican Party leader, was reported for abuse, but Susan and her mother, Linda Russell, decided not to pursue charges against him.[11] Mrs. Russell's reasoning was that she wanted to keep the family together. In the meantime, Susan met David Smith while working at a grocery store. In March 1991 she married David after learning that she was two months pregnant. A year before the murders, she left the grocery store and became secretary to Cary Findlay, the owner of Conso Products, a company with 600 employees manufacturing decorative tassels and trim. While married, both David and Susan engaged in extramarital affairs.[12] During their three-year marriage, Susan had sexual relations with her husband, her stepfather, her boss, and her boss's son, Tom Findlay.

She eventually separated from her husband and filed for divorce in September 1994 stating "adultery" as the cause. She hoped to pursue a relationship with Tom Findlay. By mid-October, however, he had decided to end this relationship. He told Susan that, among other reasons, he was not ready to be the father of two boys. At age 23, she had been dumped by her wealthy boyfriend, she was separated from her husband, and she felt hopeless, desperate, and alone. On the night of October 25, seven days after her breakup with Findlay, Smith put her children in the back seat of her 1990 maroon Mazda. Her mother, knowing she was upset, had invited her over for the evening, but Smith would not take her mother up on the offer. She fastened the boys into their safety seats and began driving. At one point, she stopped on the Broad River Bridge and contemplated jumping to her death. As she stood there looking into the dark water and contemplating suicide, her crying son caused her to reconsider. She got back into her car and continued to drive. After three hours, she found herself on the boat ramp near the dam at John D. Long Lake, an eighty-acre, man-made lake. She had planned to kill herself and also kill her children so that they would not have to live without a mother. She released the parking brake and let the car roll toward the water, but then she stopped. A second time she did the same thing and stopped.

What happened next has been disputed. The prosecution said that Smith left the vehicle, stood on the bank, and watched her son struggle to free himself as the car turned over on its back, slowly filled with water, and sank—a process that took six minutes. Smith's attorney adamantly denied reports that Smith watched the boys struggle and drown. The defense said that Smith left the vehicle and ran, covering her ears and screaming, "Oh, God! Oh, God, no!" never looking back as her children drowned. Smith said she ran as if propelled by "some survival instinct."[13] Unfortunately, that instinct did not include saving her boys. Regardless of which version is most accurate, after the car sank, she made her way to a nearby house where she told the carjacking story.

Smith told police that the carjacker forced his way into her car at a deserted intersection and warned her to "drive or die."[14] She said that when he forced her from the vehicle near the lake, she begged him to let her have the boys, but he was in "a too much of a hurry."[15] Hundreds of people searched on foot and on horseback, divers combed the lake for clues, and a nationwide manhunt was undertaken to find the black male who allegedly took the boys. Companies pledged $10,000 as a reward for information leading to the return of the boys, and over 100 law enforcement officers from federal, state, and local jurisdictions participated in the case.

In Union, a town of only 10,000 people, it is not surprising that Sheriff Howard Wells, aged 43, knew the Smith family. He was also the godfather to Susan Smith's nephews.[16] Wells recognized problems in Susan's story early in the investigation but was hesitant to accuse her. There were numerous inconsistencies in her story, she failed two lie detector tests, there was no clear motive for the "kidnapping," and there were absolutely no clues that substantiated her story. The press began questioning her story and suspected her involvement even before she confessed. Yet Smith maintained her innocence, acting the part of the grieving mother. I suspect she had little trouble producing tears and playing the role of the grieving mother. She was severely depressed and deeply remorseful for her actions, and deep down she knew her story would eventually unravel.

There were reports that Sheriff Wells bluffed Smith into confessing. Some said that he threatened to tell the media of the inconsistencies in her story if she did not tell him where the boys were.[17] However, other sources said that investigators did not bluff her, but that they did consult with behavioral science experts.[18] While some people suspected Susan's participation in the boys' disappearance, others were convinced she had nothing to do with it. "I saw the love that they [Susan and David] had for these children . . . and there would be no way you would convince me that they had anything to do with what happened to these children," a neighbor said.[19] David Smith stood by his estranged wife, calling her "a very dedicated, devoted mother."[20] Susan's hysterics and grief convinced the woman who first spoke with her after the incident that she was innocent of any involvement.[21] Susan even appeared to take some personal responsibility for the boys' disappearance when she said, "I just feel hopeless. I can't do enough. My children wanted me. They needed me. And now I can't help them. I just feel like such a failure."[22]

Susan's tearful pleas gripped the hearts of people around the country. "I know right here," she said, touching her heart, "what the truth is. . . . [T]he Lord and myself both know the truth. I did not have anything to do with the abduction of my children."[23] She begged the kidnapper to return her children and she told him through television reporters that she prayed daily that he was taking good care of them. "I want to say to my babies that your Mama loves you so much and your Daddy and your family loves you so much . . . and that you've got to be strong. You've got to take care of each other. Your Mama and Daddy are waiting right here for you at home. I just love you so much."[24]

On November 3, however, nine days after the boys' disappearance, Smith confessed to Sheriff Wells. Within a few days the Mazda, found eighteen feet below the surface, was dragged from the murky water of the lake with the boys still fastened in their car seats. The compassion of thousands of supporters turned to rage. Citizens of the small town, as well as people across the country, were outraged that a mother would kill her own helpless children, but they were also angry that they had been duped. The black community was furious that the country had so readily accepted the stereotypical image of the alleged abductor as a black male. Some of the same people who had stood by and encouraged the Smith family for nine days screamed "murderer!" as Susan was led to her bond hearing under police escort.

A grand jury quickly indicted Smith on murder charges and the prosecution announced that the state would seek the death penalty. However, a sentence of death was unlikely. South Carolina had not executed a woman in decades. Only 1% of the women convicted of murder are sentenced to death and more than 98% of these sentences are overturned.[25] The trial was expected to last ten weeks, but it was over in seventeen days. Each day as Smith was driven to trial, her vehicle passed a sign for John D. Long Lake, a painful reminder of her sins. During the trial, jurors watched a videotaped reenactment of the event. A camera was mounted in the back seat of a car giving jurors the same perspective the boys would have had. The jury of nine men and three women found Smith guilty of murder. Ironically, the verdict came about the same time of night as the killings.[26] At one point as she was being led from the courtroom, she whispered, "I'm sorry," to her ex-husband who sat crying on the witness stand.[27]

During presentencing comments, Beverly Russell read a letter taking responsibility for failing his stepdaughter. "I must tell you how sorry I am for letting you down as a father. . . . All you needed from me was the right kind of love. You don't have all the guilt in this tragedy."[28] David Smith asked for the death penalty for his ex-wife, saying, "All my hopes, all my dreams came to an end."[29] "Everything I'd planned," David said, "teaching them to play ball, taking them fishing, teaching them to ride a bike, watching them go to school that first day, watching them grow up—all that has been ripped from me, and I don't know what I'm supposed to do about it."[30] He published a book that was released the same day he testified, but he claimed he was not trying to profit from the tragedy, saying most of the profits would go to charity. Susan's brother, Scotty, argued that Susan's life should be spared, saying there was enough tragedy in their family already.[31]

The jury spent only two and a half hours deliberating her sentence. Initially, the jury voted eleven to one for life in prison, but after further discussion, the vote for a life sentence was unanimous. One juror later said that he wanted Susan to suffer the consequences of her actions and he believed she would be tortured by other inmates. He said he wanted her to live "every day wondering if she would make it to the next day."[32] Another juror said that there were others who should have been punished, including Beverly Russell, for molesting his stepdaughter.[33] Others have laid partial blame on Susan's mother. Referring to her mother's refusing Susan hospitalization when she first attempted suicide, they said that even though it is unthinkable "that a mother could kill her own children, it is not a whole lot less unthinkable that a mother could reject a chance to help a child bent on killing herself."[34] When the judge read the sentence, "You, Susan Smith, shall remain in the custody of the Department of Corrections for the balance of your natural life," Susan replied, "Thank you."[35]

I believe that Susan Smith was deeply remorseful. She said that she wanted to save her boys, but it was too late. This deeply troubled young woman made a tragic mistake that cost her sons their lives. I do not agree with reports that Smith was a scheming monster who cold-bloodedly drowned her children for selfish reasons. She was confused, mentally ill, and had very few coping skills at her disposal to deal with life's stressors. I also believe the sentence she received was just.

Smith is now an inmate at the South Carolina Women's Correctional Institution in Columbia. The chances are poor that she will ever be released, but she will be eligible for parole after thirty years. On behalf of the Smith family, Scotty Vaughn, Susan's brother, issued a formal apology to the black community. In 1996, the mansion that once belonged to Tom Findlay's father was turned into the Inn of Fairforest, a bed and breakfast inn. The children were buried in the cemetery of the Bogansville United Methodist Church, the church where Susan and David were married. Susan's mother, Linda, divorced Beverly Russell in 1995 and still lives in Union. In one final twist in the Smith saga, the 39-year-old step-grandmother of Michael and Alex died in 1999 of a suspected drug overdose—an apparent suicide.[36] Evidence of the two boys still remains at the home of Linda Russell. A black-and-red plastic toy lawn mower is tucked away, dusty, on the screened back porch.[37] During her trial, a sociologist summarized the paradox that is Susan Smith. "Susan Smith was a splendid mother with a strong moral code who regularly slept with married men and killed her children. There was one area of her life she was good at—being a mother."[38]

MARK ORRIN BARTON

Many of the homicides that I describe in these pages could be classified in a variety of ways. For example, the case discussed at the beginning of this chapter could have been classified as a stalking case.

The homicides committed by Mark Barton could be classified as either domestic or workplace homicides. Statistics for various forms of homicide are somewhat dependent upon how the reporter chooses to classify them. Even the government's uniform reporting procedures do not guarantee that interpretation of crimes will not vary from one agency to another. Mark Barton was responsible for the deadliest workplace shooting in Atlanta history, but I have included him in this chapter on domestic homicide because that is how he started his career as a murderer. You will see as you read through this case that even though many people thought the Boy Scout leader and seemingly loving father was "normal," he was a distinctly disturbed individual.

Barton, born in 1955, was the only son in an air force family. His father moved the family to Germany where they spent many years, but at age 11, Barton returned with his family to the States. There is little reliable information about Barton during his high school years, but one thing seems constant—he perceived himself as an outsider and he resented it. Signs of his hedonism and dysfunctional thinking were evident during these years. He was arrested for breaking into a drug store at age 14 and then again at age 20 but he did not receive a jail sentence in either instance. An acquaintance said he "fancied himself as a criminal mastermind."[39] Like many young people, he claimed to have experimented with drugs during his early years.

Barton married Debra Spivey in 1979, but his life was unsettled. In spite of the fact that some people saw them as a "normal family," Barton was a mean and controlling husband who did not allow his wife to do anything without his permission and was said to have routinely referred to her as "stupid." His personal problems were apparent at work as well. His educational background as a chemist helped him land a job at TLC Manufacturing Inc. in 1984. Within two years he was named president, but his internal disturbances were evident to coworkers. They described the 6'4", 220-pound man as paranoid and said he would lock himself in his office and tape the telephone conversations of other employees; he even sabotaged one employee's work because he disliked him.[40] A former secretary recalled Barton heartlessly belittling his wife to coworkers when she had a miscarriage. In 1990, the TLC board of directors fired Barton, but he broke into the offices a few days later, and stole files and formulas, and erased computer hard drives. He was questioned and then arrested by police who charged him with felony burglary, but TLC chose not to prosecute, having apparently reached some agreement with him.

Barton began dating Leigh Ann Lang, aged 21, while he was still married to Debra. In 1993, he told Leigh Ann that he would be "free by October."[41] The day before Labor Day that year, Leigh Ann, who was also married, left her husband. The next day, Debra, 36, and her 59-year-old mother were found brutally murdered in a camper at Weiss Lake in Alabama, hacked to death with a hatchet-like weapon, which was never found. Because several hundred dollars were left at the scene, investigators presumed the murderer had unsuccessfully attempted to make the scene look like a robbery. Barton was immediately suspected in the crime, but he claimed he was home in Atlanta with his children the night of the murders. A mass of circumstantial evidence, however, linked him directly to the murders. He had recently taken out a $600,000 insurance policy on his wife, and a witness in Alabama had seen a man matching Barton's description asking for directions to the lake. In fact, police determined that Barton would have had time to drive to Alabama, commit the crime, and return home before his children awoke. Additionally, blood was found in his car, garage, and kitchen, and investigators knew of his affair with Leigh Ann, even though Barton twice lied to them about it.[42] In spite of all of this evidence, however, investigators said they did not have enough evidence to charge him with the murders. For the next few years, he would remain the only suspect in the eyes of the police, Spivey's relatives, and the relatives of his new wife, Leigh Ann. Investigators even told Leigh Ann and her parents that Barton was dangerous, warning her that he would kill her when he got tired of her.

Barton had settled with the insurance company about Debra's life insurance, accepting $450,000 with $150,000 to be placed in a trust fund for the children. He also received approximately $70,000 from other policies. The money was soon gone, however, as he attempted to make a living as a day-trader selling stocks over the Internet. In the meantime, Barton had come under the scrutiny of Georgia law enforcement and social services when his daughter told a day care worker that he had sexually abused her. In the course of the investigation, a psychologist was hired to evaluate Barton. The psychologist's report found no evidence of sexual abuse of the child, but he reported that Barton was capable of homicidal thoughts and he appeared "controlling, power oriented, and very suspicious."[43]

By October 1998, Barton was unemployed, struggling financially, and depressed. He called his wife at work and said he was suicidal, but when she arrived home he said, "Never mind. I've already killed the cat."[44] Indeed, Barton had shot and killed his daughter's cat. For two days he pretended to be concerned as he helped his 7-year-old daughter, Mychelle, search for the "missing" cat even though he had already buried the animal. Leigh Ann was the last to acknowledge that Barton was a disturbed man, but after this incident, she moved out, renting an apartment for herself. Barton and his two children from his first marriage, 11-year-old Michael and Mychelle, were on their own, but by July 1999, he was begging Leigh Ann to take them in. He had lost thousands of dollars day-trading and he told Leigh Ann the three of them had nowhere else to go. Even though divorce proceedings were under way, she reluctantly allowed them to move into her apartment.

By July, Barton had lost approximately $450,000 in Internet stock trading, his marriage had collapsed, he felt alone, and he blamed others for his circumstances. In a note found after the murders, he said of his wife, "I killed Leigh Ann because she was one of the main reasons for my demise."[45] In regard to others he said, "I don't plan to live much longer. Just long enough to kill as many of the people that greedily sought my destruction."[46]

The 44-year-old Barton carefully planned a week of destruction. On Monday, July 26, he called his attorney and changed his will, leaving everything to his children. He would change the will again on Thursday, leaving everything to his aging mother and stipulating that his children be buried next to their mother, Debra Spivey.[47] On Tuesday, Barton lost about $20,000 on the stock market. At home that night he beat his 27-year-old wife to death with a hammer as she slept, and then he placed her body in the closet of their bedroom. The next day, Barton took the children to get their hair cut. It appears he was already planning to kill them that night. Sometime that day he spoke with his mother, who said she felt something was amiss but did not know what it was.[48] That night, as the two children slept, he crept into the bedroom they shared and beat them about the head with the hammer he had used the night before on Leigh Ann. After beating the children, he submerged them facedown in a bathtub filled with water. He appears to have washed their limp bodies and then tucked them neatly in bed, covers around their necks. One officer at the scene in the Barton home said the children's hair smelled of shampoo and they appeared to be snuggled in "like it was real cold."[49] Beside his daughter, Barton left a favorite doll, and with his son's body he left a Swiss Army knife, Pokemon trading cards, and Boy Scout patches. He also left handwritten notes with each body asking God to care for the children, as well as a longer typewritten letter in the living room. Sometime that night he tried to clean blood from the bathroom and bedroom carpets.

On Thursday, the Dow-Jones industrial average was down by 180.79 points when Barton returned to Momentum Securities where he had worked as a day-trader. Just outside the building, he met a man who had gone outside to smoke and asked him, "Are you going to stick around for the blood bath?"[50] Inside, he asked to see a supervisor in an apparent attempt to get back his position as a day-trader. He had previously attempted to reopen an account with the firm by writing a check for $50,000, but the check bounced. The supervisor was out of the building. Around 2:50 P.M. Barton talked with another coworker for a few minutes and then said, "It's a bad trading day and it's about to get worse."[51] At that point he drew a 9mm Glock and a .45 caliber Colt from under his shirt and shot the employee. With guns in both hands, he proceeded to shoot employees in the trading room, missing his mark only three times in the thirty-nine shots he fired. One of the people he missed was Nell Jones, who said he "looked at me and pointed the gun and fired."[52] The bullet struck the computer terminal on her desk, narrowly missing Jones.

"I hope I'm not upsetting your trading day," Barton mocked as he shot workers while they sat stunned in their chairs or cowering beneath their desks.[53] He fired one round into the computer terminal at the trading spot he had once occupied. Two employees, Glenn Miller and Joe Skipper, barricaded themselves in an office. Miller tried to call 911, but he was put on hold and had to call back. Skipper had talked with Barton just minutes before he began shooting; Barton had smiled and asked Skipper how he was doing.[54] Barton tried unsuccessfully to force his way into the room where the two men were hiding and then fired two rounds through the door, narrowly missing Skipper. The men then broke a window using a computer terminal so that they would have an escape route if Barton managed to get past their barricade, but they were spared the need to use that option.

Calls flooded the 911 service identifying the shooter as a male wearing a pink shirt, but Barton was already leaving the building on his way to All-Tech, a trading organization across the street. In fact, in the pandemonium Barton walked right past a security guard. As police arrived at Momentum, Barton was across the road at All-Tech preparing to continue his violence. He said to a secretary, "I hope this doesn't ruin your day" and then walked into a conference room where several employees had gathered for a meeting.[55] After getting a soft drink for a terrified employee, he said, "I've got something you're going to want to see," showed them the guns, and began shooting.[56]

When 911 operators began receiving calls from All-Tech, they were unaware that this was a second crime location. Barton was identified as the shooter by 3:30, but it was not until approximately 3:45 that officers realized there had been shootings in two different buildings. By that time, Barton had already left All-Tech. Ironically, several miles south of downtown Atlanta, a maintenance man at the Bartons' apartment complex had been asked to check on Mrs. Barton because she had not shown up at work for two days. Around 3:20, he entered her apartment and found the bodies of Barton's family.

By 4:00 P.M., police were searching cars and they detained a man driving a red Jeep Cherokee who met the description of the shooter. After determining that he was not the suspect, the police released him, but other officers mistakenly continued searching for Barton in a red Jeep. By 4:30, they finally checked his driver's registration and realized they had been looking for the wrong vehicle. Meanwhile, Barton had fled the scene and traveled north of Atlanta. In his vehicle he had packed clothes for several days, a thirty-day supply of disposable contact lenses, two other pistols, 200 rounds of ammunition, and $4,500 in cash (as well as two pairs of handcuffs). Several miles north of Atlanta he stopped at a shopping mall and attempted to abduct a shopper from the parking lot. Most likely he wanted the woman's vehicle. He threatened to shoot her if she ran or screamed, but the woman fled anyway and sought refuge inside a store. Another person who had seen the description of Barton and his vehicle on the news recognized him and called police. Initially, 911 operators did not believe the caller, but after she provided a description of the vehicle and the license number, police were notified.[57] A county officer then spotted Barton's vehicle on the interstate and positively identified the driver, but he remained behind Barton until other officers could assist. Mark then exited the interstate and pulled into a gas station about a quarter of a mile from the highway as other officers closed in. As they exited their vehicles with weapons drawn, Barton took the .45 caliber Colt and fired one round into the side of his head. Five hours after he started shooting at Momentum Securities, he sat alone in the front seat of his van, still wearing his glasses, dead from the self-inflicted gunshot wound.

When the smoke had cleared, five people were dead at All-Tech and four at Momentum Securities. Five of the twelve injured people were hurt as they tried to escape. Employees hid or played dead while others were shot and killed at their workstations. Some of the dead and wounded were shot in the back, and many of them were shot at point-blank range as they hid under their desks. One man played dead momentarily and then realized Barton, unflinching in his rampage, might shoot him again, so he fled. "He was just shooting anyone just sitting there," a witness said.[58]

Barton's delusional thinking was most evident to me in the letter he left in his living room. Referring to killing his children, he said he "forced himself to do it" in order to spare them future pain and said, "It was over in five minutes." He said he used a hammer because he thought it would be a quiet and "relatively painless" way to die, but his supposition that "only five minutes of pain" was minimal is absurd. Five minutes is a very long time and even though the children may have died instantly, people survive severe head injuries all the time, sometimes not even losing consciousness. I know he was aware of this possibility because he said he held them under the water in the bathtub to make sure they did not regain consciousness. Therefore, he was willing to force his innocent children to endure brutal batterings to the head as well as drowning, believing their suffering was minimal. It is possible that they did not suffer, but a normal loving parent would balk at even the slightest possibility of causing his child pain. His thoughtlessness was also evident in the murder of his wife. Barton left Leigh Ann's battered body in a closet where his children could have found her. Even though it was unlikely that they would snoop in his bedroom closet, it was certainly possible.

Another symptom of Barton's dysfunction can be seen in his comments regarding these murders and the murders of his first wife and her mother. His note denied that he had anything to do with the murders of his first wife and his mother-in-law in Alabama, but I do not believe him. His note said, "There's no reason for me to lie now."[59] I believe he had plenty of reason to lie. In his note he said that he loved his family with all his heart, but he wanted to justify killing them as well as justify what he was about to do (killing his coworkers). He blamed his wife for his problems and he blamed his employers for his work-related difficulties. He said it would be better for his children to suffer for a few minutes than to suffer for a lifetime without mother, father, or relatives. For him to admit murdering his first wife and mother-in-law, he would have needed to develop a justification for these murders. If no such justification existed, he could not admit his involvement; otherwise, in his mind he would be just a run-of-the-mill murderer. The circumstantial evidence in that crime and the choice of weapon in both the Alabama slayings and his family's slayings lend credibility to his guilt in both cases.

In yet another sign of his delusional state of mind, at the end of his note he appeared to seek forgiveness, saying, "if Jehovah is willing, I would like to see all of them [his children and wife] again in the resurrection, to have a second chance." But in the very next sentence he again displays his rage and lack of remorse by saying he wanted to live only long enough to kill the people he blamed for his demise.

Few people who knew Barton expressed surprise when they learned of his involvement in the shootings. Law enforcement officers in two states, a social worker who had investigated the abuse allegations, and relatives of Debra and Leigh Ann said they had known it would happen sooner or later. A cousin of Barton's first wife said Barton was "colder than a cucumber" at Debra's funeral.[60] Leigh Ann's father was constantly afraid for his daughter's safety, having once panicked when he could not contact her for several days and did not know she had been traveling on business. After Leigh Ann's murder, her sister said, "I'm sorry it happened to my sister, but I'm not surprised. I've felt that this has been coming for a couple of years."[61] Perhaps even Leigh Ann had begun to believe the stories from the Alabama killings, expressing concern for her safety to her sister as early as October 1998.[62]

Barton's father had died in 1997, but his mother released a statement saying, "There is no explanation for a tragedy such as this. I have been praying for the victims and their families. Even though I am very hurt by the actions of my son, Mark, I wish there was some way to explain why this tragedy occurred or some way that it could have been prevented."[63]

Among the grieving survivors was Bill Spivey, Barton's former father-in-law, who lost his wife and his daughter in the 1993 murders in Alabama, and then had his grief compounded when he lost his two grandchildren to Barton in 1999. At the funeral for the two children, their caskets were draped with wreathes that said, "Gone to be with Mama." The evidence shows that Barton was a paranoid burglar, a saboteur who referred to his first wife as "stupid" and who allegedly killed her and her mother with a hatchet. He had affairs, dominated both his first and second wives, even dictating what they wore, killed his daughter's kitten, and squandered thousands of dollars on business ventures before cold-bloodedly and savagely wounding twenty-one people and murdering twelve others including his own children. Was this former scoutmaster a loving father? I hardly think so.

CONCLUDING REMARKS

How can we kill the ones we love? Barton and Smith killed their children while others killed their spouses or other loved ones. Regardless of the specifics, the desperation and loss of control these murderers experienced is evident. The murders described in this chapter were committed by a boyfriend, a mother, and a father and husband. The passion of these murderers attests, in part, to their deluded thinking, but it also lends credibility to the argument that they cared, as distorted as their emotions were, about the family members and loved ones that they killed. Even as I write, the news is occupied by accounts of stalking and murders of passion. In New Jersey in September 1999, just hours before her wedding, a bride-to-be was in her home with some members of her wedding party. They were having their pictures taken while her fiancé waited at the church. The woman's ex-boyfriend arrived and allegedly shot and killed the bride-to-be. She died just hours before her wedding. We are more at risk of murder at the hands of those who know us than we are at the hands of strangers. As you have discovered by reading these cases, this should be no surprise. Recognizing that potential threats may exist in our own living rooms is of little help, however, unless we know what to do about it. In Chapters 8, 9, and 10, I will discuss some ways for us to protect ourselves.

NOTES

1. Melinda Beck, Debra Rosenberg, Farai Chideya, Susan Miller, Donna Foote, Howard Manly, and Peter Katel, "Murderous obsession: can new laws deter spurned lovers and fans from 'stalking'—or worse?" *Newsweek*, July 13, 1992, 61.

2. Robert I. Simon, *Bad men do what good men dream* (Washington, DC: American Psychiatric Press, 1996) 49.

3. Ibid.

4. Ralph Ellis, "Man gets 2 life sentences for murder of co-worker," *Atlanta Journal/Constitution*, July 27, 1996, C06.

5. Ralph Ellis, "Admitted killer says his former company is liable for slaying," *Atlanta Journal/Constitution*, July 3, 1997, M02.

6. Diane Wagner-Price, "Quick justice sought," *Fayette Neighbor*, April 11, 1996, 3A.

7. Ralph Ellis, "Co-worker held in woman's death: shooting suspect blames failed affair," *Atlanta Journal/Constitution*, April 4, 1996, B3.

8. Ellis, "Admitted killer says his former company is liable for slaying," M02.

9. Ibid.

10. Barbara Ehrenreich, "Susan Smith: corrupted by love?" *Time* (Internet Edition), August 7, 1995.

11. Ibid.

12. Gail Cameron Wescott, "The reckoning," *People Weekly* (Internet Edition), August 7, 1995.

13. Steve Wulf, "Elegy for lost boys," *Time* (Internet Edition), July 31, 1995.

14. Chris Burritt, "Mother charged with murder," *Atlanta Journal/Constitution*, November 6, 1994, A01.

15. "Desperate S.C. search presses on; sheriff won't say if mom failed lie detector test; officials unable to find any clues to missing boys," *Atlanta Journal/Constitution*, October 31, 1994, A01.

16. Chris Burritt, "Sheriff says movie could help town," *Atlanta Journal/Constitution*, July 31, 1995, A04.

17. "Up to speed: postscript," *Atlanta Journal/Constitution*, November 13, 1994, A18.

18. "S.C. mom reportedly remorseful: Smith in isolation since confession," *Atlanta Journal/Constitution*, November 10, 1994, A04.

19. Jerry Adler, Ginny Carroll, Vern Smith, and Patrick Rogers, "Innocent lost," *Newsweek*, November 14, 1994, 29.

20. " 'I believed Susan,' father of drowned S.C. boys says: story of kidnapping called convincing," *Atlanta Journal/Constitution*, November 15, 1994, A01.

21. "Desperate S.C. search presses on," A01.

22. "Two tots, suspect in S.C. carjacking still missing; no new leads reported in case," *Atlanta Journal/Constitution*, October 27, 1994, B01.

23. Adler, Carroll, Smith, and Rogers, "Innocent lost," 29.

24. Chris Burritt, "Hopes soar, then crash in carjack: 'exciting' lead fizzles; parents issue new plea for boys," *Atlanta Journal/Constitution*, November 2, 1994, A01.

25. Gerrie Ferris, Bill Hendrick, and Chris Burritt, "Women who kill usually escape ultimate penalty," *Atlanta Journal/Constitution*, July 29, 1995, A10.

26. Wulf, "Elegy for lost boy."

27. Elizabeth Gleick, "No casting of stones," *Time* (Internet Edition), August 7, 1995.

28. Ibid.

29. "David Smith: 'All my hopes, all my dreams came to an end,' " *Atlanta Journal/Constitution*, July 26, 1995, A01.

30. Gleick, "No casting of stones."

31. William F. Buckley, Jr., "The Susan Smith case," *National Review* (Internet Edition), August 28, 1995.

32. "Jurors in Susan Smith trial say they don't have any regrets," *Atlanta Journal/Constitution*, August 28, 1995, C06.

33. Chris Burritt and Jack Warner, " 'Giving Susan death wouldn't serve justice': S.C. jury weighs tortured past, votes for mercy," *Atlanta Journal/Constitution*, July 29, 1995, A01.

34. Ehrenreich, "Susan Smith: corrupted by love?"

35. Chris Burritt and Jack Warner, "An end to ordeal of trial, not conscience: life in prison, lifelong torment?" *Atlanta Journal/Constitution*, July 29, 1995, A01.

36. "Continuing tragedy," *Atlanta Journal/Constitution*, June 8, 1996, E09.

37. Chris Burritt, " 'She is not a bad person, she loved her children': Linda Russell, mother of Susan Smith," *Atlanta Journal/Constitution*, November 11, 1998, A14.

38. Chris Burritt and Jack Warner, "Susan Smith was a good mother, defense witnesses testify: death sentence wouldn't be 'fair,' brother tells jury," *Atlanta Journal/Constitution*, July 27, 1995, A18.

39. Craig Schneider, Alan Judd, and Lyda Longa, "Details shed little light on riddle that was Mark Barton," *Atlanta Journal/Constitution*, August 7, 1999, F4.

40. Ibid.

41. Ibid.

42. "Georgia investigator: enough evidence to arrest Barton for 1993

killings," *CNN On-Line, www.cnn.com/US/9908/01/atlanta.shootings. alabama./index.html,* August 1, 1999.

43. Jane O. Hansen, "Psychologist saw Barton as capable of violence," *Atlanta Journal/Constitution,* July 31, 1999 A7.

44. Schneider, Judd, and Longa, "Details shed little light on riddle that was Mark Barton," F5.

45. Ibid.

46. Ibid.

47. "Police find Prozac in Atlanta shooter's car," *CNN On-Line, www.cnn.com/US/9909/01/atlanta.shooter.reut/index.html,* September 1, 1999.

48. "Atlanta chief: office shooter had firepower for more carnage," *CNN On-Line, www.cnn.com/US/9907/31/atlanta.shooting.03/,* July 31, 1999.

49. Bill Montgomery and Bill Torpy, "Barton children buried; hundreds pack service in Lithia Springs, where 'it's hurt everybody,' " *Atlanta Journal/Constitution,* August 3, 1999, A5.

50. Jay Croft and Alan Judd, "The day Atlanta can't forget," *Atlanta Journal/Constitution,* September 26, 1999, Q1.

51. Ibid., Q6.

52. "Investigators search for answers after 12 die in Georgia killings," *CNN On-Line, www.cnn.com/US/9907/30/atlanta.shooting.01/index.html,* July 30, 1999.

53. Bill Montgomery, " 'I have come to hate this life': mass killer of 12 describes in detail how he murdered family," *Atlanta Journal/Constitution,* July 30, 1999, A8.

54. "Shooter lost $150,000 in month, but motive still a mystery," *CNN On-Line,www.cnn.com/US/9907/30/atlanta.shooting.08/index.html,* July 30, 1999.

55. Croft and Judd, "The day Atlanta can't forget," Q6.

56. Ibid.

57. Kathy Pruitt and D. L. Bennett, "Cobb mall sighting put cops on killer's trail to suicide," *Atlanta Journal/Constitution,* July 30, 1999, A1.

58. "Investigators search for answers after 12 die in Georgia killings."

59. Arthur Brice, "Killer's letter a cry of pain," *Atlanta Journal/Constitution,* July 31, 1999, A6.

60. "Suspected Atlanta killer was focus of earlier murder probe," *CNN On-Line, www.cnn.com/US/9907/30/alabama.deaths.01/index.html,* July 30, 1999.

61. "Atlanta chief: office shooter had firepower for more carnage."

62. Ibid.

63. Brice, "Killer's letter a cry of pain," A6.

Stalking

Kristin Lardner was a 21-year-old student at the School of Fine Arts in Boston and the daughter of a Pulitzer Prize–winning reporter for the *Washington Post*. In 1992, she began dating Michael Cartier. Just a few weeks into the relationship, Lardner wanted to discontinue contact with Cartier, but he would not let go. The night she tried to sever their ties, Cartier followed her home and beat her into unconsciousness, kicking her with steel-toed shoes. During the beating he screamed, "get up or I'll kill you."[1] She survived the beating, but during the next several weeks, Cartier contacted her repeatedly, calling her home and showing up at her workplace. His discussions with her fluctuated between two extremes, alternately begging her to accept him and threatening her life. Lardner sought and was granted a temporary restraining order, which Cartier repeatedly violated, but he was never arrested.

Investigations by police determined that Cartier had told a friend that he was going to kill Lardner. On May 30, 1992, he tried one last time to convince Kristin to see him again. When she refused, Cartier pulled a gun and shot her three times in the head, killing her. He then returned to his apartment and killed himself. This was not the first time that Cartier had demonstrated that he had problems with relationships. He had been named as the offender in two other restraining orders in Massachusetts.[2] He also had an extensive rap sheet and had once attacked a girlfriend with a pair of scissors.[3] Cartier had violated the restraining order taken out by the woman he had stabbed and he was on probation at the time he murdered Lardner. These incidents violated his probation and, therefore, he was to be arrested, but on the day that he killed Kristin, the paperwork authorizing his arrest lay on a desk where it had been for three weeks waiting to be typed.[4]

Sarah Auerbach was 35 years old and an executive investment banker at Salomon Brothers in New York. For a year she had dated Rick Varela, but she decided to end their relationship. Varela was a 46-year-old divorced man who was not about to accept this rejection. After their breakup, Varela stalked his former girlfriend, but she never sought a restraining order. At one point, he forced his way into her apartment and raped her at knife-point.[5] Eventually, Varela decided if he could not have her, then he would not allow her to live. He went to Illinois where he acquired a 9mm handgun. Returning to New York, he rented a car and donned a disguise, including a wig, sunglasses, and a trench coat. He found Auerbach at the Best Cleaners where she was picking up her dry cleaning. In front of several witnesses, Varela came up behind Auerbach and shot her six times, hitting her in the head, neck, chin, chest, hip, and back. Auerbach died soon afterward.

After shooting Auerbach, Varela fled the scene, went to a movie, and then called his ex-wife. He did not confess the crime to his family, but they were concerned about his "farewell tone" so they contacted police.[6] At 3:35 A.M., Varela was found on a bench on the promenade at Brooklyn Heights with a self-inflicted fatal bullet wound to the head. A suicide note left by Varela acknowledged the murder of Auerbach but expressed no remorse for it.[7]

In most of the homicide cases I have addressed in these chapters, the victims have been attacked and killed very quickly. Their ordeals progressed from beginning to conclusion in a matter of minutes or hours. Victims of stalking, however, may endure their tormentor's cruelty for days, months, or years. In fact, according to the Centers for Disease Control and Prevention, the average stalking lasts nearly two years.[8] The terrifying loss of control that one feels when a gunman enters an office building and begins shooting is experienced by the stalking victim each time the perpetrator sends a letter, makes a phone call, or appears at the doorstep. Some victims try in vain to elude their stalkers. They may verbally confront their stalkers, change their phone numbers, even change their addresses. The relentless and obsessive stalker is not deterred by victims' futile attempts at regaining control of their lives. The stalking will continue until the perpetrator selects another victim, is jailed, or is dead. Often, it is only at the stalker's death that the victim's nightmare ends.

Stalkers fluctuate between the extremes of love and hate. One minute they shower their victims with gifts and praise and the next minute they threaten to injure or kill them. In the same week, a victim of stalking may receive a bouquet of roses and a package containing a dead animal or human feces. Even when perpetrators are jailed, they find ways to continue their harassment. They make phone calls, they send e-mail messages, letters, and faxes, and like a banner, they flaunt their looming dates of release in their victims' faces, rejoicing that their victims cannot escape them.

I have listened to dozens of messages left on answering machines and read dozens of letters sent to victims by stalkers. Even in the short span of a telephone message, stalkers fluctuate from love to hate—in one sentence they say how much in love they are and in the next they threaten to kill the victim. My heart aches for these victims because the law does not work quickly in these cases. Even though stalking is against the law in every state, the anti-stalking laws in some states make it much more difficult to prosecute a stalker than in others. Even in states with very powerful anti-stalking legislation, the stalker can continue his or her atrocities for weeks before being arrested. In states with weak legislation, the stalker can harass a victim for years. Unfortunately, that sometimes seals the victim's death warrant.

STALKING—DEFINITION, VICTIMS, AND PERPETRATORS

Stalking is a relatively new phenomenon. Even though all fifty states now have laws addressing it, this has not always been the case. The first anti-stalking legislation was passed in California in 1990 in response to a series of murders committed by stalkers, including the murder of actress Rebecca Schaeffer. I discovered something interesting as I conducted my literature review on this topic. Dozens of articles and studies have been published on stalking in the past few years, but prior to 1990, nearly all of the articles I found on stalking were in hunting periodicals. Before 1990, the term "stalking" was not routinely applied to people. Today, however, the term has become a part of our everyday vocabulary.

There are many definitions of stalking. Each state has identified behaviors that fall under their stalking laws. The Centers for Disease Control and Prevention have also defined stalking in their research on violence against women. However, psychiatrist Robert Simon has provided the most useful definition of stalking as he summarizes stalking legislation. According to Simon, stalking is "a crime in which a person 'on more than one occasion' engages in 'conduct with the intent to cause emotional distress . . . by placing [another] person in reasonable fear of death or bodily injury,' or the 'willful, malicious and repeated following and harassing of another person.' "[9] In summary, a person is being stalked when he or she receives continued, unwanted contact in any form by another person and when those contacts make the person fearful.

Stalking is a significant problem in our culture. It touches approximately one in every ten women. A woman is three times more likely to be stalked than she is to be raped.[10] According to the Centers for Disease Control and Prevention, "an estimated one million women and 370,000 [370,990] men are stalked annually," with 78% of the victims being women and 87% of the perpetrators being men.[11] This study also reported that most women who are stalked by domestic partners have also been physically and sexually assaulted by those partners.[12]

Research has repeatedly shown that stalkers usually know their victims before the stalking begins. One study on stalking demonstrated that nearly all stalkers knew their victims: 57% of the victims had prior relationships with their stalkers and another 34% of the victims were at least acquaintances before the stalking began.[13] Only 6% did not know their stalkers.[14]

Like most of the murderers and victims that I have discussed in this book, these are ordinary people. Stalkers are usually ordinary people who choose ordinary people as their victims. While stalking of celebrities and other high-profile individuals attracts a great deal of media attention, these make up only a small percentage of stalking cases. Victims are typically women between the ages of 18 and 29, but they can also be male, older, younger, famous, or ordinary. Robert Simon says 38% of victims are ordinary people, while other victims are celebrities, corporate executives, employers, and psychotherapists.[15] Most victims of stalking (62%) are either divorced or have never married.[16] They may meet their stalkers at work, at church, at the grocery store, or even in a chance encounter in a parking lot or a shopping mall. Victims live as ordinary citizens until their worlds are consumed with caution and fear because of the obsessions of a stalker.

Stalkers themselves are a diverse group. They are male and female, old and young, from varied races, and from varied socioeconomic classes. Despite their diversity, stalkers share some characteristics. One study has shown that stalkers are most often white (67%), have stalked other people in the past (62%), and range in age from 18 to 50, and that more than half have a mental illness (54%).[17] Robert Simon suggests that the incidence of mental illness among stalkers is much higher than usually reported, according to Simon about 90%.[18] However, these people are often capable of functioning, aside from their stalking behaviors, in a seemingly ordinary way. Robert Snow, in his book *Stopping a Stalker*, relates accounts of stalking by a gynecologist, a bank president, a former school superintendent, a school board member, a police officer, and a professor of architecture. Some very famous people have also been accused or convicted of stalking. Actor John Heard was charged with stalking an actress by whom he had a child.[19] James Farentino was charged with stalking the daughter of Frank Sinatra and was sentenced to three years probation.[20] Actor Mykelti Williamson, well known as "Bubba" from *Forrest Gump*, was arrested and accused of stalking his ex-girlfriend and stabbing her male friend. In spite of their stalking behaviors, these individuals may have seemed rather ordinary to the casual observer, contradicting the media image of the weathered and disheveled stalker working in shadows and alleyways with a maniacal expression on his face.

According to research in this area, the most common method of contact by stalkers is by telephone, but stalkers also watch the homes of their victims, follow them, visit their places of work, send letters, spread gossip, damage their property, threaten them, and break into their homes.[21] They send them gifts, assault them, harm their pets, and send them packages containing urine, dead animals, blood, and other items.[22] Stalkers may even kidnap their victims.

Robert Simon divides stalkers into six types: celebrity stalkers, immature romantic stalkers, dependent, rejection-sensitive stalkers, borderline personality stalkers (these make up the majority of celebrity stalkers), erotomanic stalkers, and schizophrenic stalkers. Despite

these six divisions, the *Diagnostic and Statistical Manual, 4th Edition*
identifies only one type of stalking, erotomania, as a mental illness.
Erotomania is classified as a subtype of delusional disorders, those
disorders in which a person does not accurately perceive reality. Delusional clients may experience, among other things, hallucinations
(delusions) in the form of voices or visions. In the erotomanic subtype, these patients believe that another person is in love with them.[23]
As a therapist working in a field that includes stalkers, I believe stalking as a mental illness is much broader than the *DSM IV* allows.

Because of stalkers' diverse backgrounds, it is difficult to predict
who will be a stalker. However, police officer and author Robert
Snow describes eight symptoms of the stalker personality. Potential
stalkers won't take no for an answer, have obsessive personalities, and
are above average in intelligence.[24] They also have few, if any, personal relationships, lack embarrassment or discomfort at their actions,
have low self-esteem, exhibit sociopathic thinking, and finally, according to Snow, have a "mean streak."[25] Even though these personality traits are present in stalkers, most of them are not evident to
a victim until she or he is already involved in a relationship with the
potential stalker. Therefore, predicting stalking based on these traits
is unlikely.

THE PSYCHOLOGY OF STALKING

I am most troubled by victims of stalking who seek my help, because I know there is little I can do. I cannot stop a stalker. The best
I can do for my client, aside from helping her to cope with her circumstances, is to inform her of her legal options, provide suggestions
for protecting herself, and help her to develop a case against the
stalker. Unfortunately, building a case takes time. I have been fortunate that many of my clients who have been stalked have successfully rebuffed their stalkers. Nothing that I have done has made this
happen. I attribute the good fortune of my clients in part to their
diligence and also in part to the luck of the draw. Their stalkers were
simply among those who could be deterred by direct confrontation
or legal intervention. As you will see in the examples presented in
this chapter, many victims of stalking are not so lucky.

Some behaviors that were regarded as romantic a few years ago are
now considered stalking in most states. Repeated telephone calls,
showing up unannounced at the victim's home or place of employ-

ment, sending gifts, and so forth have, in the past, been portrayed in the movies as endearing. This form of diligence was perceived as a romantic representation of a person's passion for the object of affection. Times have changed. Today, if an individual has implied or stated that he/she is not interested in a relationship with another, the potential stalker is obligated to cease contact.

In a healthy relationship, when one person decides he/she is interested in another, there is some form of courting. In our culture, a date or social meeting is a common beginning to the relationship. If one or both people in the duo decide that they are uninterested in continuing the relationship, they have various ways of ending it. One might clearly state that he/she has no interest in further contact. More subtle indicators, however, are also possible. Not making a second date, avoiding the former partner, not returning phone calls, and so forth, imply to the pursuer that his or her interest in continuing the relationship is not shared. Mentally healthy and socially competent people will usually perceive these social cues as they were intended and will disengage from their pursuit of the relationship.

Socially incompetent or mentally disturbed individuals may misread these social cues. In the movie *Dumb and Dumber*, after a very brief encounter, star Jim Carrey chased a love interest who had no idea he was even interested in her. Toward the end of the film she confronted him and told him she was married and had no interest in him. Responding to a question from Carrey regarding the chances of "a guy like him and a girl like her" getting together, she told him "a million to one." She obviously was gently trying to tell him there was no way a relationship between the two of them would ever develop. Carrey's response was to say excitedly, "So you're saying there is a CHANCE!" His statement amused viewers because they recognized the social cues for what they were. However, the stalker does not always recognize these cues and, like Carrey's character, they misread as interest cues actually intended to discourage further contact. They continue pursuing the relationship.

Not all stalkers misread social cues, though. Perpetrators may, in fact, recognize these cues but refuse to accept them. In one study, 58% of the people surveyed said they were stalked by a person who simply would not accept that the relationship was over.[26] In other words, they know that the victim wishes to end the relationship, but they are simply unwilling to let it end.

Consider this example. Suppose a man works in an office with a woman he finds appealing. He approaches her and engages in conversation that eventually leads him to ask her to accompany him on a date. If the man were socially competent he would interpret her words, her body language, and other cues as he tried to understand her response. If she was reserved or hesitant and if she seemed uncomfortable as she said, "I don't know if I will be available to go out with you," the man would probably get the idea that her words really meant, "No, I'm not interested in going out with you." However, if the man were mentally unhealthy and socially unskilled, he might read her words at face value and think she meant "I need to check my calendar" or something to that effect. Therefore, he would continue to seek her company. Alternatively, he might recognize that she is turning him down, but he might also have personalized his previous interactions with her. He might have assumed that she had been dressing to please him or even to tease him and, feeling she had led him on, he would then be offended. This delusion is not uncommon among stalkers, even when the victim has not even been acquainted with the stalker. His dysfunctional thinking causes him to misread the social context and give it personal meaning. Finally, the man may repeatedly ask the woman out because he has missed her cues altogether.

The mentally unhealthy office worker in my example keeps asking the woman out until she eventually becomes irritated or afraid of him. She is forced to bluntly tell him that she has no intention of going out with him and she wants him to leave her alone. If he is merely socially inept, he may accept this direct statement and sever his contact with her. However, he may continue to misread her words, assuming she is playing hard to get. Therefore, he will continue asking her out. If he is delusional, he may become angry because he believes she has led him on and is now dumping him. He will relentlessly pursue her even if he is jailed. People who become victims of acquaintance stalking sometimes inadvertently set themselves up as victims. Stalkers are often socially isolated and, therefore, have few friends. In an attempt to be polite or perhaps even to befriend someone they see as lonely, they inadvertently give the stalker the impression that there is some romantic interest. The stalker misreads kindness as affection.

RICHARD WADE FARLEY

One of the most widely publicized stalking cases I have been able to review is the case of Richard Wade Farley. Farley captured the attention of the nation when his obsession with a coworker eventually led to the deaths of seven former coworkers and injuries to four others, including the object of his obsession. These murders were the culmination of stalking that lasted for nearly five years. This case involved two people who were not otherwise well-known. These were not actors, politicians, diplomats, or athletes. They were ordinary people, employees of a computer firm, living ordinary lives. As I have already pointed out, cases like this make up the majority of stalking cases.

Richard Farley, the first of six children, was born in Texas on July 25, 1948. There was nothing in his childhood to indicate the future he would choose. Childhood friends and classmates were interviewed after the murders. Some recalled that Farley was introverted and lonely, but that could probably be said about many of us at one time or another. It is my impression that Farley was an average student and an average child. His father was in the military and was required to move with some regularity, but the Farleys eventually settled in California. The Farleys were not a close family. Farley's mother testified at his trial that they loved each other, but "we didn't show it."[27] At the time of the shooting, his siblings were living in various parts of the world and one brother said he had not talked to Richard in ten years.[28]

After finishing high school in 1966, Richard attended Santa Rosa Community College. In 1967 he joined the navy where he would spend the next ten years of his life. His jobs in the navy prepared him for his civilian career with computers. Farley began his work as a software technician at Electromagnetic Systems Lab (ESL) Incorporated, a defense contractor, in 1977. He would not meet the object of his obsession for several more years, even though they both worked for ESL. To many of the people who knew him at ESL, Richard Farley was unusual. He did not endear himself to many people at his place of employment. Some described him as a loner, egotistical and arrogant.[29] Farley and a coworker once discussed a shooting at a McDonald's restaurant where an individual killed numerous patrons. Farley told the coworker that he could see why someone would do something like that. He described himself as one who did not tend to "fly off the handle," but his self-analysis did not prevent his violent outburst in 1988.

In 1984, while visiting an employee in another department, he crossed paths with Laura Black, an athletic 22-year-old woman who had been a high school tennis star and gymnast. Farley immediately became infatuated with Black. He would later say in court, "I think I fell instantly in love with her. It was just one of those things, I guess."[30] He began following Black, writing letters to her, leaving baked goods on her desk, and asking her out on dates. Black consistently turned down his invitations to concerts, dinners, and outings, yet his obsession grew. Their interactions at work fueled his belief that she could be interested in him romantically. As time progressed, his advances became a noticeable problem, both to Ms. Black and to other employees at ESL. It became apparent that he was pursuing her and that she was not interested in him. Coworkers began to warn Black that Farley might be dangerous. His activity was so overt that on the day of the shooting several employees told law enforcement officers they knew exactly who was doing the shooting, even before they saw him.

Prior to his interaction with Black, Farley had no criminal record, but some people who knew him said that Black was not the first woman he had harassed at ESL. One employee told investigators that he was aware of two other employees that Farley had harassed, but he had not obsessed over these women as he would with Black. Farley stalked Black for years. He left letters and notes on her car, he sat in his vehicle outside her home, he called her repeatedly, and he left gifts in her office. He would send messages asking her out and assume her lack of response to be agreement. He would then show up at her house ready to take her out. He was known to go through her desk and personal items at work, even tampering with her computer. Black stated that she became "more annoyed and angered by the unwanted attention."[31] Farley's response was that he had the right to ask her out, she had the right to refuse, and if she wasn't "cordial" in her refusal, he had the right to bother her.[32] On one occasion, Farley found the keys to Black's home on her desk. He had copies made and, in an incredible display of arrogance, mailed copies to her to prove to her that she was vulnerable. On another occasion, Farley discovered the address of Black's parents and he wrote to her while she was visiting them.[33] More than once he tried to move into the apartment building where she lived.[34]

Farley joined Black's aerobics class in an attempt to be near her. He told a coworker that he and Black went to aerobics together, but then corrected himself, saying, "Well, actually, I'm not going with her, I follow her there." He sent Black nearly two hundred letters and as time progressed his words became more aggressive. He eventually threatened her life directly and alluded to other damage that he could do in revenge for his unrequited love. In Farley's letters he specifically said he did not want to kill her because he wanted her to live to regret her unresponsiveness to his romantic advances. Black probably thought her problems would go away when Farley took a company assignment in Australia. Yet even distance did not diminish his passion and he resumed stalking her as soon as his overseas assignment ended. Even his acquaintances in Australia were aware of his obsession with Black.

In an attempt to avoid him, Black tried ignoring his contacts, sought help from her superiors, and even moved three times in order to elude him. None of these actions deterred Farley. As time went on, he became more obsessed than ever. Farley wrote in a letter that it was his choice to make her life miserable.[35] At work, superiors intervened on numerous occasions. In the fall prior to the shooting, the human resources department required Farley to seek counseling.[36] Even though he attended therapy, it had no effect on his behavior. One day while he was conversing with other ESL employees, he said, "Some day a crazy person is going to come in there and shoot up their computers," and he reportedly indicated that he might do it. These comments disturbed his coworkers, but they did not report the incident. Farley's threats went from veiled to overt. His direct threats to Black as well as to other ESL employees continued. At one point he said in a letter to Black that he "could take people with him" if he was provoked.[37] ESL's management could endure these threats no longer. In May 1986 he was fired, but his dismissal would not be the end of his harassment. Farley told Black, "once I'm fired, you won't be able to control me ever again. Pretty soon, I'll crack under the pressure and run amok and destroy everything in my path."[38] Black would endure another twenty months of harassment and stalking before her nightmare came to a terrifying climax.

In her frustration, Black eventually told Farley that she would not date him if he were the last man on earth.[39] Even though he was no longer interacting with her at work, his delusions concerning his relationship with Black never weakened. Evidence of his obsession and delusions was regularly observable. He once suggested that he and Black go to marital counseling since they seemed to "fight like" married people.[40] Just two weeks before the shooting, Farley told a friend that he was going to buy a new house and have Laura cosign for it. Of course, Ms. Black had no intention of doing so. Eventually, Black's government security clearance was threatened because of Farley's behavior.[41] Seeing no other alternative, she filed for a temporary restraining order against Farley. The order was served on February 8, 1988.

Farley's life was disintegrating. He had lost his job, he had lost his house because of financial trouble, the IRS was investigating him, and he was served with the restraining order. He resolved to take action. The day after the restraining order was served, Farley spent nearly $2,000 purchasing weapons and ammunition.[42] He reportedly dropped Black from his will and also sent a package to Black's attorney claiming to have a variety of evidence that showed she was a willing participant in a secret relationship with him. Eight days later and one day before a scheduled court hearing on the restraining order, Farley finalized his plans for revenge. On February 16, in a motor home he had rented the previous week, Farley drove to ESL. Dressed like Rambo with a bandana around his head and bandoliers of ammunition across his chest, he loaded himself down with nearly 100 pounds of weapons and ammunition, left the vehicle, and headed toward the entrance to ESL.

Farley's defense attorney would claim that his intentions were only to destroy equipment in the building and then to kill himself in front of Black. Farley said, "I just felt she had to see the end result of what I felt she had done to me."[43] If those were his original intentions, his plans changed almost immediately. It was just after 3:00 P.M. when Farley parked his vehicle and prepared for his attack. About this same time, two ESL employees, Larry Kane and a female colleague, were enjoying a break together in the cafeteria. After the two left the cafeteria, they walked down the hall together. Kane normally left work around 3:00 P.M. From her office, Kane's colleague heard noises in the parking lot and looked out her window; she saw a man with a gun, and she saw Kane fall to the ground. Just after that, another employee came into her office saying someone was in the building with a gun. By a chance encounter in the parking lot, Kane, an acquaintance of Farley's, became his first victim.

Farley used his shotgun to blast his way through the glass security doors. He proceeded through the halls of ESL searching for Black, shooting computers, doors, office equipment, and anything that moved. Even though word of the gunman spread quickly through the building, some employees were unaware of what was occurring. They poked their heads into the hallway in an attempt to identify the source of the commotion, only to see a heavily armed man shooting their colleagues. One employee heard the shooting and looked into the hall. She saw the body of a coworker "bouncing on the floor" and quivering. Initially, she was not sure what was happening, but then she saw the barrel of a gun extending from the stairwell and saw fire and smoke coming out of the barrel. She hid in her office for several minutes as the sound of the shooting seemed to move away from her. Deciding to attempt an escape from the building, she ran into the hall and came to an intersection; she cautiously looked around the corner and saw Farley. As she ran across the hall he fired at her but missed. She continued to run, trying futilely to work a combination lock on a door. She ran to another room where she saw an employee who told her that he knew exactly who the gunman was and what it was about. She then fled down the stairs and out the main entrance. Another employee blocked her door with a bookcase after she looked into the hall and saw two coworkers being shot in the back and catapulted into the hall. As pandemonium erupted in the ESL facility, some employees escaped as shots flew past their heads, while others hid in closets, under desks, and above the ceiling tiles.

In the meantime, a police officer who arrived on the scene entered the motor home and found, among other things, a rifle with a scope and four gallons of a flammable liquid. As more police officers arrived, they saw both wounded and uninjured employees leaving the building. When the law enforcement officers had identified the perpetrator as Richard Farley, they went to his home and entered it. While they were there, the officers met Farley's girlfriend, Mei Chang, who told police that she knew of Laura Black. She seemed unaware of Farley's obsession with Black, although she said that she knew that Farley liked her and that Laura did not reciprocate.

Back in the building, Farley was far from finished. He approached Laura Black's office. As he entered her doorway, she turned and recognized him. Farley fired the weapon and hit her in the shoulder, seriously wounding her. Despite her wounds, however, she managed to push her office door closed. With the help of other employees, she made her way to another office where they tended to her wounds. Eventually, she was able to escape the building and arrived at the hospital with a broken arm, significant damage to her shoulder, and a collapsed lung.

One employee was shot in the hall and, seeking cover, he crawled back into his office and called security, who advised him that they knew of the shootings. In fact, Farley had called security himself. This employee hid in a closet, but he later returned to his office and heard his phone ringing. He answered and discovered the caller was his wife. A friend who had heard about the incident on a police scanner had notified her and she was calling to check on her husband. While hiding in his office he saw another employee crawl past an opening in the ceiling. He later helped this employee climb down into his office, to which he had barricaded the door.

In another office a female employee had chosen to hide under a desk. Farley came in and fired twice, but then he left. To her horror, she heard Farley coming toward the room a second time. As she desperately tried to remain quiet under the desk, she heard Farley close the drapes and then walk to her very hiding place to use the phone. Some manuals were stacked on the chair and Farley knocked them off and sat down. As he sat down, he saw the woman hiding and said, "Oh, you can come out," and then told her she could leave. Initially, she was afraid to leave, fearing that he would shoot her in the back. After she offered to stay with him, he encouraged her to leave and she did. Police met her as she exited the building.

A hostage negotiator, Ruben Grijalva, arrived on the scene and communicated by telephone with Farley for nearly five hours. Farley told the negotiator at one point that he shot people because he felt threatened. He said they just "popped out from around corners." He said he wanted to destroy computer equipment and that he had specific people in mind, contrary to his later defense argument that he did not intend to harm people. He also said he was not ready to give up yet because he "wanted to gloat" for a while. He indicated that he was sorry that Laura Black and a friend were not there. In fact, when the shooting started, the friend Farley referred to told a coworker that he knew his name was on the list of Farley's potential victims. Farley showed no remorse for his actions as he talked with the negotiator. In an interesting paradox revealing his state of mind, he told the negotiator at one point that he had to use the bathroom and he didn't want to "pee all over the floor" because that would be "rude." After destroying so much of the building and killing so many people, in his delusion he remained selectively concerned about social impressions.

As the evening wore on, Farley told the negotiator that he was hungry. A lengthy discussion about food, what kind to get, where to get it, and how long it would take, ensued. An arrangement was made to bring him a sandwich and drink from a nearby restaurant. In the process of arranging delivery of the food, Farley agreed to surrender. He was taken into custody without a struggle. After Farley's arrest, police investigators began the mountainous task of locating survivors and victims and collecting evidence. A gas mask, smoke bombs, ammunition, exhausted rounds, weapons, and other materials were found in the wake of Farley's carnage. Victims were found in stairwells, offices, and along blood-splattered hallways. The day after the rampage, the restraining order was made permanent, but at that point it was not clear if Black would survive. Farley was charged with seven counts of capital murder and four additional felonies including vandalism, second-degree burglary, and assault with a deadly weapon.

At his trial, his defense attorney, Gregory Paraskou, said Farley was not an evil person.[44] Despite all his obvious preparations for destruction, Paraskou said that Farley did not plan to kill anyone.[45] Assistant District Attorney Charles Constantinides, however, argued that Farley targeted victims, cruelly continued to shoot them to make sure they were dead, and he showed no regard at all for human life. The jury was also informed that Farley said he would "smile for the cameras" if he should be sentenced to the gas chamber.[46] After a three-month trial, jury deliberations lasted six days. On October 1, 1991, the jury found Farley guilty of seven counts of capital murder and four additional felonies. On November 1, 1991, the same jury, after a single day of deliberation, recommended the death penalty. On January 17, 1992, Superior Court Judge Joseph Biafore, Jr., sentenced Farley to death in the gas chamber. He currently resides at San Quentin awaiting appeals or eventual death.[47] Despite his conviction, Farley continued to write to Black from prison.

The deadly violence of February 16 did nothing to abate Farley's delusions. "Sometimes she's happy . . . sometimes she's angry. All this is having a very confusing effect on me. I don't know whether I'm coming or going with her," he would say in court.[48] Farley seems to be the only one who was confused about where he stood in his relationship with Black. The depth of his obsession was clear as he said,

"The more she tries to push me away, the more I try to not have her push me away."[49] Even after his trial, he referred to his relationship with Black in the present tense.[50] Black continued to work at ESL, but she required numerous operations and is permanently disabled. At one point, Farley said he was sorry but he knew he would not be believed.[51]

CELEBRITY STALKERS

Even though celebrity stalkers make up only a small percentage of people who stalk, celebrity stalking is a problem and sometimes leads to assault and murder. Several widely publicized stalking cases involving celebrities have led to some of the stalking laws that exist today. Robert John Bardo stalked and murdered actress Rebecca Schaeffer, a murder that led to the nation's first stalking law. John Hinckley, Jr., shot President Ronald Reagan in an attempt to win the affections of actress Jodie Foster. Even though President Reagan survived, the attack nearly cost him his life as well as the lives of a Secret Service agent and Reagan's press secretary, James Brady. Just one year after the attempt on Ronald Reagan's life, in one of the first widely publicized celebrity stalking cases in recent history, Arthur Jackson stalked and viciously stabbed actress Theresa Saldana. Fortunately, Saldana survived the attack.

Robert John Bardo

Rebecca Schaeffer was a 21-year-old actress who seemed to be riding on top of the world. She was enjoying a successful career in the regular television series *My Sister Sam*. Like many actors and actresses, when she received fan mail she sent back a signed note and a photograph. Her response fed one fan's obsessive desire for a personal relationship with her.

Like many stalkers, Robert Bardo had stalked other women. He repeatedly wrote letters to a teacher when he was in junior high school and threatened to kill her.[52] In fact, he even briefly discontinued his obsession with Schaeffer in 1988 and turned his attentions toward singers Debbie Gibson and Tiffany.[53] On several occasions in his childhood he reportedly threatened to kill himself, a threat he would never carry out. Even though his parents continually denied there was anything wrong with him, he was hospitalized more than once and diagnosed with severe emotional problems.[54] Bardo said he never had a girlfriend, got his "ass kicked" a lot at home, and felt alienated.

Bardo videotaped every episode of *My Sister Sam* and he composed songs about a fantasy relationship with the actress.[55] He went to Los Angeles and tried to contact Schaeffer on the studio set, but he was turned away by security. On a second trip, he took a knife with him, but he was again turned away. In his obsession, he paid a private investigator to find Schaeffer's address. Since he was not yet 21, he sought his brother's help in acquiring a handgun, the weapon that he would use in the murder.[56]

At 19 years of age, Bardo spent hours watching TV, he had no money or friends, and his life was meaningless. After seeing Schaeffer in bed with another actor in a TV program, he became angry. He told a court-appointed psychiatrist, "If she was a whore, God was going to appoint me to punish her."[57] Carrying a bag containing a pistol, a U2 tape, and a copy of *The Catcher in the Rye*, Bardo headed toward Schaeffer's home. On July 18, 1989, he visited Schaeffer's apartment. After a brief conversation with her, he left, but he returned an hour later, armed with his handgun. When Ms. Schaeffer opened the door, Bardo pointed the gun at her chest and fired one round, killing her. Bardo was arrested as he wandered along a freeway exit ramp in Tucson, Arizona.[58] His defense tried to argue that he was too mentally ill to stand trial, but the judge did not accept that argument. Bardo was convicted of first-degree murder and the special circumstance of lying in wait, and he was sentenced to life in prison without parole. Bardo did not deny the murders. Even in his apology, though, his disrupted thinking is evidenced. He said, "I feel kind of guilty about all that's happened."[59] Apparently for Bardo, feeling "kind of guilty" is a form of remorse.

John Hinckley, Jr.

John Hinckley, Jr., was a lonely boy infatuated with actress Jodie Foster. He longed for a relationship, hoping that he could be important to her. Only days before he attempted to assassinate President Ronald Reagan, Hinckley wrote to Foster asking, "Don't you maybe like me just a little bit?"[60] He concocted a plan that would attract her attention. On March 30, 1981, Hinckley stood outside the Washington hotel where President Reagan had given a speech. As President

Reagan and his staff exited the building, Hinckley stepped forward, pulled a handgun from his pocket, and fired six times. As the nation watched on TV, Secret Service agents rushed Reagan into the presidential limousine and sped away. Other agents with automatic weapons swarmed Hinckley while Secret Service agent Timothy McCarthy and press secretary James Brady lay seriously wounded and bleeding on the sidewalk nearby. Initially, Reagan did not know he had been shot, but as agents checked him for injuries, they found a bullet wound later determined to have damaged his left lung. Even though his injury was serious, he survived the attack and was released from the hospital after a two-week stay. Brady and McCarthy were both seriously wounded. McCarthy was able to return to duty, but Brady was permanently disabled by the attack.

After the attempt on Reagan's life, Hinckley asked Secret Service agents, "Is it on TV? Am I somebody?"[61] Hinckley was charged but found not guilty by reason of insanity and was committed to a psychiatric hospital in Washington, D.C. Hinckley has made great progress in his therapy and has recently been granted a brief furlough from the psychiatric hospital where he is confined. In an unfortunate twist for Jodie Foster, a second violent stalker pursued her. In an eerie form of déjà vu, this second stalker made a feeble attempt to kill her, claimed to have left a bomb in her Yale University dormitory room, and also threatened the president of the United States.[62]

Arthur Jackson

Born in Scotland, Arthur Jackson would spend some time in the American military, but most of his life would be spent in Scotland, where he was living when he first saw actress Theresa Saldana in a movie. He became infatuated with her, but he also knew he would never have a relationship with her. This hopelessness led him to plan to kill her so that she would not belong to anyone else. He traveled all the way to the United States to pursue his obsession. Using the services of a private detective, he was able to procure her address through the department of motor vehicles. (After reading this in an article about Jackson, Robert Bardo would find actress Rebecca Schaeffer's address in the same way.) On March 18, 1982, Jackson sat outside Saldana's home. As she walked toward her vehicle, he stabbed her eleven times. A witness intervened, pulling Jackson off Saldana, probably saving her life. After the attack, Jackson was arrested and convicted of attempted murder. While in prison, Jackson made it clear that he intended to kill Saldana when he was released. Years were added to his original twelve-year sentence because of these threats. Jackson was later extradited to England to face charges for a murder committed in the mid-1970s.[63] He would eventually plead guilty to this murder.

COMPLICATIONS INVOLVING STALKING CASES

Analyzing, solving, and prosecuting stalking cases can be very complicated. One issue that complicates analysis and investigation is the victim's fabrication of the stalker. Sometimes stalking accusations turn out to be false, although this happens in fewer than 1% of cases.[64] I have worked in the collegiate environment for many years. During these years, various students have claimed to have been harassed or stalked by an unidentified individual. They have produced letters that they claim to have found on their cars and they have shown me messages spray painted or scratched on the doors of their dormitory rooms, claiming that they have been harassed by telephone and have been followed. Yet in several of these cases, surveillance by video cameras and other means has shown that the students were doing these things to themselves. The telephone calls and other behaviors were simply made up by the "victim" in an attempt to gain attention and sympathy.

This type of incident is not confined to the college campus. In 1996, a trial began in a stalking and harassment case against a grade school teacher. Another teacher in the same school claimed to have been harassed and stalked since 1993. The stalker allegedly made anonymous phone calls to parents and administrators, accusing the victim of sexual harassment, and the victim even claimed to have been physically assaulted when she cut her hand on a razor blade that the stalker left taped to the door handle of her automobile. There was little evidence to prove that the accused teacher had been the perpetrator of the crime; so little, in fact, that the chief of police had a difficult time even making a case to bring to the prosecutor. After two years, the case went to trial and the accused teacher was found not guilty of over 100 counts of harassment, assault, and making terroristic threats when the jury learned that the accusing teacher had made similar allegations in a previous school. The jury's decision did not prove that the accuser was guilty of stalking herself; it merely determined that the accused was not guilty, but the stalking ended with the trial.

Other stalking cases are even more complicated, leaving juries to decide, in part, if stalking ever actually happened. One such case happened in Montgomery County, Missouri. In 1991, Gayle Boone shot and killed her alleged stalker, claiming to have been stalked for months. She was a divorced mother who claimed that someone had left hair in her sink, vandalized her property, called and hung up many times, and even attacked her, trying to strangle her with a rope. During this time, a 20-year-old loner named Patrick Hollensteiner befriended Boone. He involved himself heavily in her life and appeared to be protecting her. She became suspicious of him and eventually came to believe that he, in fact, was the stalker.

One day she found a note on her car that read "tonight, 7:00 P.M." Fearing for her safety, she reported the incident to the sheriff, who promised that two deputies would be parked nearby. She also contacted two friends who agreed to wait outside her home. The three arranged a signal using a telephone if she was in trouble. She was to press the call button twice if she needed help. Hollensteiner did not arrive until 8:00 P.M. Boone let him into the house and as she walked down a hallway, she alleged, he tried to attack her with a knife. He allegedly taunted her as he approached, even making fun of her when she picked up a double-barreled shotgun to defend herself.[65] She pressed the button on the phone, alerting her friends outside who called the police immediately. Unfortunately, the sheriff's deputies were ten miles away when the call came in. As Boone pulled the first trigger on the gun it misfired, but a second pull discharged the weapon and Hollensteiner was hit in the abdomen. He stumbled into the front yard and later died from his wounds.

Boone went to the police station a few days later to make a statement. During six hours of questioning, she had no legal representation. An attorney who had handled her divorce arrived and she assumed he was there on her behalf. That assumption proved false because the attorney was also a local prosecutor. Yet another complication was that Hollensteiner was the nephew of the local sheriff. Boone was charged with first-degree murder. Bail consumed her financial resources and she required help from friends. During the trial, Hollensteiner's ex-wife said he was a nonviolent man, but a police dispatcher remembered domestic violence calls from her during the marriage, asking for protection.[66] At Boone's trial, her lawyer presented no evidence of the stalking. Boone rejected a plea bargain that would have resulted in a fifteen-year prison sentence. The prosecution claimed that she had lured Hollensteiner to her home and that her claims of fearing for her life were motivated by her desire to attract the attention of a deputy that she had dated in 1990.[67] Fearing she would lose, Boone reconsidered the plea bargain and decided to accept it. She has since appealed her conviction saying that she was not adequately represented, but her attorney claims that he provided the best possible defense. One is left wondering if Hollensteiner was, indeed, a stalker who got what was coming to him, or if Boone was a clever, conniving woman who was able to manipulate her friends into helping her set up a murder to look like self-defense.

In yet another complicated stalking case, Guy Ellul killed his ex-wife, stabbing her twenty-one times. Yet when his case went to trial, the jury exonerated him of the murder. Ellul's former mother-in-law, Ruth Williams, claims that Ellul controlled her daughter while they were married and then stalked her after they divorced. Ellul himself admitted that he threatened his ex-wife, Debra, "hundreds of times."[68] The couple met when Debra was 15 and Guy was 25. By the time Debra was 19, they were married. The Canadian couple had a rocky twelve-year marriage in which both spouses allegedly were known to be violent. Guy allegedly threatened that if she ever left him he would kill her.[69] Reportedly he was extremely jealous and did not like Debra being gone. Debra allegedly once threatened to have her husband killed.[70]

Around midnight on February 4, 1989, Debra was home alone when Guy came by her house. What happened next is open to question. According to the prosecution, Guy viciously stabbed Debra twenty-one times. Coworkers had seen Guy sharpening knives some time before the murder and he allegedly told them that the tip had to be sharp because "it goes in first."[71] Debra fought him off as she tried to save her own life, leaving scratches on his face and his hair under her fingernails. During the struggle, she was able to take control of the knife and stab Guy in the arm, but he regained control of the weapon and continued his assault. The prosecution presented experts who said that the stab wounds were consistent with a victim being "immobilized and unable to avoid the thrusts of the knife."[72] The defense countered that it was Debra who first attacked Guy with the knife, explaining the stab wound to his arm. Guy then took control of the knife and in defense stabbed her twenty-one times. Guy claimed that Debra was alive when he left. He said he left in her car and went to a park but later returned to her home to get his own automobile. The jury believed the defense's argument and Guy was found not guilty. The reader is left to draw his or her own conclusions.

CONCLUDING REMARKS

Unfortunately, the best that a stalking victim can hope for is that the stalker will lose interest or realize that the victim is not interested and direct his or her energies and interests elsewhere. Sometimes a visit from police or a restraining order may be the wake-up call the stalker needs to realize that his or her behaviors are inappropriate and therefore, change these behaviors. Some of my clients who were stalked have had this kind of luck. However, as Kristin Lardner's father said, "restraining orders don't restrain."[73] Even stalking laws have their limitations. Ironically, the first person to serve time in a California prison for stalking resumed stalking his former victim while he was still on probation.

Some victims end their nightmares by taking their stalkers' lives. In Detroit, Michigan, 48-year-old Jerry Belanger had been stalked by a woman with whom he had worked at the Ford Motor Company in Detroit, Michigan. She was described as being his ex-mistress, but after their relationship ended, she stalked him until April 25, 1991, when he shot and killed her. Belanger was charged with murder, but the judge in the case said he deserved sympathy because she stalked him "like the character in 'Fatal Attraction.' "[74] Despite the judge's sympathy, the man was still sentenced to eight to twenty years for the murder.

Sabine Tsang was a 27-year-old woman who had been stalked by a coworker. She had complained on several occasions about his behavior and at one point, her stalker allegedly confronted her in a parking lot and tried to force her into her car. Ms. Tsang, however, had a pistol in her possession and used it to protect herself. She fired the weapon at her stalker and hit him twice in the abdomen. The gunshot wounds did not kill her stalker and, as he lay in the hospital, he was charged with attempted kidnapping.[75]

The laws against stalking are improving as time goes on. Unfortunately, they are often improved in response to crimes that result in the deaths of victims. Researchers, writers, and violence experts like

Park Elliot Dietz and Gavin de Becker have contributed greatly to the assessment of the dangerousness of stalkers. Yet there is still much to be learned both in the assessment of risk and in the protection of victims. The formal study of stalking is embryonic. When lawmakers, police agencies, and the public began to realize the crime of stalking was a serious threat, progress was made in the protection of victims. It is my hope that as we learn more about this crime we can hone our laws so that we can protect people before they become victims.

NOTES

1. George Lardner, "No place to hide," *Good Housekeeping*, October 1997, 104.

2. Ibid., 105.

3. George Lardner, "The stalking of Kristin" [book review], *New York Times* (Late New York Edition), December 13, 1995, C21.

4. Ibid.

5. Robert D. McFadden, "Brief romance, growing fears, then 2 deaths," *New York Times* (Late New York Edition), April 9, 1994, 1.

6. Ibid.

7. Ibid.

8. Patricia Tjaden and Nancy Thoennes, "Stalking in America: findings from the national violence against women survey research in brief," U.S. Department of Justice, available at FTP: *www.ncjrs.org/txtfiles/169592.txt*, April 1998, 14.

9. Robert I. Simon, *Bad men do what good men dream* (Washington, DC: American Psychiatric Press, 1996), 48.

10. Tjaden and Thoennes, "Stalking in America," 4.

11. "Intimate partner violence fact sheet," Centers For Disease Control and Prevention, available at FTP: *www.cdc.gov/ncipc/dvp/ipvfacts.htm*, 1998, 4.

12. Ibid.

13. Doris M. Hall, "The victims of stalking," in J. Reid Meloy, ed., *The psychology of stalking: clinical and forensic perspectives* (San Diego, CA.: Academic Press, 1998), 118.

14. Ibid.

15. Simon, *Bad men do what good men dream*, 50.

16. Hall, "The victims of stalking," 125.

17. Ibid., 128ff.

18. Simon, *Bad men do what good men dream*, 50.

19. Robert L. Snow, *Stopping a stalker: a cop's guide to making the system work for you* (New York: Plenum Trade, 1998), 29.

20. Ibid., 30.

21. Hall, "The victims of stalking," 132.

22. Ibid.

23. American Psychiatric Association, *Diagnostic and statistical manual for mental disorders, 4th edition* (Washington, DC: American Psychiatric Press, 1994), 297.

24. Snow, *Stopping a stalker*, 27.

25. Ibid.

26. Hall, "The victims of stalking," 121.

27. Bob Trebilcock, "I love you to death," *Redbook*, March 1992, 103.

28. Michael Kelleher, "An obsession with Laura," *Sartore Township*, available at FTP: *www.svn.net/mikekell/farley.html.*

29. Ibid.

30. "Accused slayer of seven tells of obsession," *Los Angeles Times*, August 21, 1991, A/20.

31. Trebilcock, "I love you to death," 103.

32. Ibid.

33. Kelleher, "An obsession with Laura."

34. Ibid.

35. Trebilcock, "I love you to death," 103.

36. Kelleher, "An obsession with Laura."

37. Ibid.

38. Ibid.

39. "Accused slayer of seven tells of obsession," A/20.

40. Trebilcock, "I love you to death," 103.

41. Ibid.

42. Kelleher, "An obsession with Laura."

43. Trebilcock, "I love you to death," 112.

44. "Jury urges death penalty for man who killed seven," *Los Angeles Times*, November 2, 1991, A27.

45. "Accused slayer of seven prepared for massacre, prosecutor says," *Los Angeles Times*, July 9, 1991, A18.

46. "Jury urges death penalty for man who killed seven," A27.

47. Kelleher, "An obsession with Laura."

48. Trebilcock, "I love you to death," 112.

49. Kelleher, "An obsession with Laura."

50. "Trebilcock, "I love you to death," 114.

51. "Death sentence decreed for man who killed seven at defense firm," *Los Angeles Times*, January 18, 1992, B6.

52. Mike Tharp, "In the mind of a stalker," *U.S. News and World Report*, February 17, 1992, 29.

53. Ibid.

54. Ibid.

55. Chris Verner, "Newsmaker: slaying of actress haunts accused fan," *Atlanta Journal/Constitution*, July 19, 1990, A02.

56. "Obsessed fan who killed actress sentenced to life without parole," *Atlanta Journal/Constitution*, December 21, 1991, A13.

57. J. Reid Meloy, "The psychology of stalking," in J. Reid Meloy, ed., *The psychology of stalking: clinical and forensic perspectives* (San Diego, CA: Academic Press, 1998), 27.

58. "Obsessed fan who killed actress sentenced to life without parole," A13.

59. Verner, "Newsmaker: slaying of actress haunts accused fan," A02.

60. Simon, *Bad men do what good men dream*, 61.

61. Snow, *Stopping a stalker*, 6.

62. Buddy Foster and Leon Wagener, "The real story behind Jodie Foster's haunting ordeal," *McCall's*, June 1997, 48.

63. Meloy, "The psychology of stalking," 26.

64. Michael D'Antonio, "The strangest stalking case ever," *Redbook*, June 1996, 127.

65. Claire Safran, "Was justice done?" *Good Housekeeping*, March 1995, 95.

66. Ibid., 156.

67. Ibid.

68. Claire Safran, "Justice for Debra," *Good Housekeeping*, March 1994, 136.

69. Ibid.

70. Ibid.

71. Ibid., 214.

72. Ibid.

73. Melinda Beck, Debra Rosenberg, Farai Chideya, Susan Miller, Donna Foote, Howard Manly, and Peter Katel, "Murderous obsession: can new laws deter spurned lovers and fans from 'stalking'—or worse?" *Newsweek*, July 13, 1992, 61.

74. "Fatal attraction," *Atlanta Journal/Constitution*, August 17, 1997, A15.

75. Beck, Rosenberg, Chideya, Miller, Foote, Manly, and Katel, "Murderous obsession," 62.

Homicide by Children, Part I

In Portland, Oregon, on June 23, 1995, 9-year-old Brandon Roses retrieved his father's hunting rifle and then went to his brother's room where his brother kept cartridges that would fit the weapon. Brandon, his 6-year-old brother, and his 5-year-old sister were playing alone. When his sister annoyed him, Brandon loaded the hunting rifle and shot her. The child died as a result of the gunshot wound. Brandon was charged with her murder, the second youngest child in the state of Oregon to be charged with that crime. He would later plead guilty to the charge of manslaughter.

There is no doubt that children are capable of killing. Our image of childhood aggression is limited to petty arguments, and the "violence" perpetrated by most children is consistent with this perception, even though some children may take the life of another by accident. For example, playing with a firearm may lead to a fatal gunshot wound or experimentation with matches may lead to a fatal fire. However, a limited number of disturbed children are not only capable of killing someone intentionally but have done so. These are frightening children whose disturbances are evident to both parents and therapists. A combination of access to weapons, lack of supervision, and a violent culture is contributing to the increased seriousness of violence perpetrated by children. Over the past decade, I have analyzed many children, some for the court system and others for parents or guardians. Many of these children have been as mentally healthy as their parents. In fact, in a few cases they have been healthier. A small number of these children, however, have shown clear signs of serious dysfunction indicative of the potential to engage in violent behavior.

Young children are incapable of masking their feelings and their thoughts. It is not until children are in grade school that they begin to develop an ability to hide their thoughts and emotions, but even then their ability to do this is weak. Even children practiced at deception have difficulty hiding the powerful emotions in their hearts and minds. If a child is angry, he will throw a tantrum regardless of where he is. If he is excited he will dance and sing, again, with no attention to place, time, or context. Therefore, when a child is deeply disturbed, he or she cannot help but exhibit symptoms of that disturbance. The cause and treatment of such disturbances vary, but I am confident they are no secret to anyone who interacts at any depth with these children.

Children who commit calculated, cold-blooded murder may suffer from an attachment disorder. When babies are born their first cognitive processes regarding social interactions involve an assessment of the safety of the world. In essence, they develop a perspective of the world as either a safe place or a frightening and unpredictable place. Parents teach the infant that the world is safe and predictable by meeting her needs. When the child is hungry, she is fed. When she is afraid, she is cuddled. When she is in discomfort, the problem is alleviated. Through this process, the child learns that the world is predictable and that there is an individual responsible for ensuring that these needs are met. It is to this person that the baby bonds, in a process called attachment.

In cases of severe abuse or neglect, the infant perceives that the world is not a place to be trusted and that people are not to be trusted. These infants grow up distrusting others and they depend solely on themselves to meet their needs. It is said that these children lack a conscience, a statement that is not totally inaccurate. Because of their egocentric and hedonistic perceptions, they lie, steal, cheat, or hurt others without remorse because life to them is about the survival of the fittest. A side effect of their failure to bond is aggression. These children resent compassion and loving relationships. They have never received love and compassion and they resent anyone who tries to give it to them as well as others they see receiving it. They will not allow themselves to feel love, compassion, or sympathy for others. As they get older, they may learn to pretend to feel compassion or remorse, but their hearts are stone cold. These are among the most seriously disturbed children; they have significant potential to rape, molest, torture, and kill.

Not all children who kill are attachment disorder children. As you will see in this chapter, some children kill because they have learned dysfunctional means for coping, just like many of the adults I have discussed in previous chapters. Imitating what they have seen, heard, or read is one dysfunctional coping skill that can lead children to murder. Children have copied murders from movies like *Scream*, books like *Rage*, songs, and violent games like *Doom* and *Dungeons and Dragons*, and they have even copied real-life events like school shootings. I have always been frustrated by musicians and moviemakers who take no responsibility for modeling aggressive behavior. They say children recognize that their material is fantasy; therefore, they say, there is no reason to suppose children will copy the behaviors these musicians and others describe or even instruct the listener/reader/viewer to perform. Advertisers know quite well the power of suggestion. They pay millions of dollars for just minutes of advertising time on television because they know that even brief encounters with their product can influence the viewer's behavior. Psychologically healthy children can differentiate between fantasy and make-believe, but some children are not mentally healthy. These make no distinction between reality and fantasy; to them, behaviors from "make-believe" scenarios in movies and on TV are plausible behaviors and coping strategies.

Other children kill when they make impulsive decisions. Their worldview includes violence as a strategy for dealing with disagreements. Their stage of development makes it difficult or even impossible for them to understand the ramifications and permanence of their actions. These children may commit mass murder thinking it will be fun or exciting, or that it will elevate their status among their peers, without regard to the long-term consequences of their actions.

JASON McCLENDON

In Forsyth, a middle-Georgia town just north of Macon, 13-year-old Jason McClendon had led a difficult life. His mother, 32-year-old Nancy Powell, was reportedly a drug user and she had lived with several men during Jason's thirteen years. Powell herself had been raised in difficult circumstances. Her mother was Japanese, her father was in the military. According to Powell's ex-husband, her mother had tried to kill her on more than one occasion and she had been passed back and forth from one family to another after that.[1] Jason never knew his real father and Powell married Fred Tingle when the boy was young. At that time he appeared to be a good child doing well in school. Powell's marriage proved difficult when Tingle discovered that Powell was using drugs. They separated and reunited several times over the following months. Eventually, the moving, the drugs, and the disruption in his life took its toll on Jason, who began to lie and steal. After Jason complained to teachers that Tingle had abused him, Tingle lost custody of him and he was returned to his mother.

Friends and their parents said he was a respectful, polite, and quiet boy, but he was, in fact, deeply troubled. Even though his record included only minor offenses, it was evident to some that his life was headed in an unproductive direction. In an attempt to redirect him, he was admitted to the Sheriff's Boys Ranch in Hahira, Georgia, the year before the murder. However, he was expelled because he ran away several times.

On Friday, September 22, 1995, Jason bet three school friends $50 that he would kill his mother who, at the time, was working as a barmaid. He told them that he had other victims in mind as well, saying that he also planned to kill his mother's boyfriend and that he wanted to kill his math teacher.[2]

The next morning, Saturday, September 23, 1995, Jason said he smoked marijuana in his bedroom and decided he no longer wanted to live. As his mother slept, he shot her three times in the head. After shooting his mother, he walked through the woods to a friend's house. There he told 15-year-old Chad Ingle what he had done and asked him not to call the police. Ingle said he did not believe McClendon had really killed his mother because he "treated it like a joke."[3] But it was no joke when, around 4:30 P.M. that day, the 32-year-old woman was found dead on her couch.

Jason returned to his house after the murder and left the shotgun under the house, but then he disappeared. Using bloodhounds and helicopters, police searched for him in the rain for three days. While on the run he survived by breaking into several residences. First he broke into a hunter's cabin, spending the night there, and then he broke into the home of a neighbor he knew was in the hospital. There, he showered, washed and dried his clothes, and spent the night. The next day, he broke into another home, this one occupied by 66-year-old Twyla Tharpe, a retired schoolteacher. She was asleep on the sofa when she realized someone was in her house. Calling her husband on the phone she told him of her suspicions. Her husband, in turn, contacted the police. She called out to the unknown intruder and said, "Jason, is that you?" to which he replied, "yes, ma'am."[4] He asked her not to call the police, but she told him they had no choice. Listening to a police scanner in the home, he heard that police were arriving at the residence. Tharpe calmed him as the police arrived at the house, saying, "Now, I'm going to put my arms around you, and you put your arms around me, and we'll walk out there and I'll make certain nobody hurts you."[5] She did exactly this, and the boy was taken into custody.

He told police that he was not sure how the murder happened. He said, "The next thing I knew . . . I shot her."[6] McClendon initially confessed to the crime, but in court he pleaded innocent. At his trial he argued that his mother abused him.[7] After he was tried as an adult, the jury convicted him of voluntary manslaughter and he was sentenced to twenty years in prison. His rage did not abate with the murder of his mother or with his conviction. He has reportedly threatened to kill Powell's boyfriend if he is ever released from prison.[8]

JONATHAN MILLER

On Monday, November 2, 1998, a 13-year-old middle school student named Josh Belluardo had been arguing with his 15-year-old neighbor, Jonathan Miller, as they rode the school bus home. The bus pulled into the cul de sac where both boys lived and as Belluardo got off the bus, Miller punched him in the back of the head. Miller then kicked him in the stomach, hit him in the face, and then laughed and held his hands above his head like a football player scoring a touchdown. The school bus driver immediately used her radio to call for help. Josh's mother, also a bus driver, heard the call for help and raced home. Just minutes later, she arrived and found her son unconscious and mortally wounded, lying in a neighbor's yard. Josh's sister, who was home at the time, had rushed to Josh's aid just minutes after the attack. She watched him turn red, then purple, then blue. After two days in a coma, he was removed from life support and he died. The attack had caused a microscopic hole in an artery at the base of his brain.

After the attack, Miller left the scene, went home with a friend, and began preparing for a campout they were going on that night. Miller realized he was in trouble when he heard someone yelling. Initially, he hid in the woods nearby, then he went to a friend's house to hide, but then he decided to confess what had happened. On his way, he was detained by a sheriff's deputy.

The two boys were students at different schools. Jonathan was a sophomore at Etowah High School and Josh was a student at E. T. Booth Middle School. Students who knew Miller described him as a bully who called other children names and picked on them. Alan and Robin Miller, however, claimed they did their best to raise their son right. They said that they ate dinner together, went camping, and talked routinely.[9] But there was more to the story. Miller had been suspended nineteen times while a student at the middle school; eleven times he received out of school suspension and eight times in-school suspension. He had been in trouble a total of thirty-four times and had a history of cursing at teachers, making threats, and intimidating other students. The principal said that his parents were uncooperative, defensive, and always blaming someone else. The father of another boy that Jonathan had hit complained to Jonathan's father the year before this murder. Jonathan's father told him that his son probably deserved it.

In court, Miller's lawyer argued that a fall from a bicycle the summer before the attack had caused the injury to Josh's brain. Josh had suffered a head injury in the fall, but testimony from his doctors concluded that this did not contribute to his death.[10] Miller was convicted of felony murder and sentenced to life in prison.

Two specific behaviors after the attack provided a glimpse of the life and thoughts of this young man and his family. Miller was granted bail as he waited for his trial. A condition of his bail was that he was to have no contact with any of the children who had witnessed the attack. After he was released on bond, however, his parents hosted three overnight parties at their home and invited several of the children that Miller was specifically told not to contact. His bail was revoked and he was returned to jail. Both he and his parents argued that they thought that it would be acceptable to have the parties. The

Millers' lawyer said that he had told them it would be acceptable, but the words of the judge had been clear—have no contact with any potential witnesses. For some reason, the Millers were able to justify in their minds a behavior that was directly forbidden by a court of law.

The second behavior came in an interview after Miller was sentenced. Even though he showed great remorse, given his reputation as a bully and his failure to accept responsibility, one might wonder whether his remorse was for his victim or for the trouble in which he found himself. Miller apologized for his actions but said the system was too harsh on him. "I wish the sentence would be lowered a little and that the charge could change because I'm not a murderer. I don't see myself as a murderer."[11] Miller's parents made similar statements, saying their son did not commit murder.[12] As the law is stated, however, a person commits felony murder if he causes someone to die because of his actions, even if he did not intend to kill. One might believe that Miller did not intentionally cause Belluardo to die, but regardless of Miller's intentions, Belluardo died. Yet the Millers reframed the incident just as they did the parties. They may have disagreed with the wording of the law, but to say that their son did not commit murder is to deny the obvious. One would have to wonder if these two incidents were typical of the way the Millers approached life, excusing and reframing their son's behaviors and allowing him to do what he wanted.

The Belluardos, who filed a $2.5 million lawsuit against the Millers, saying they "failed to curb their son's 'violent behavior,' " said they were pleased with the verdict and the sentence.[13] Just after this murder, Georgia passed anti-bullying legislation.

JOSHUA PHILLIPS

Joshua Phillips was 15 years old when a Florida jury sentenced him to life in prison without the possibility for parole for the death of his 8-year-old neighbor. He was 14 at the time of the murder. He was tried as an adult; the judge told him, "I do not perceive you to be a child. Your monstrous acts made you an adult."[14]

When Madlyn Rae Clifton, a spunky 8 year old, was discovered missing on November 3, 1998, in Jacksonville, Florida, a massive campaign was launched in an effort to procure her safe return. Leaflets with the girl's picture were printed and distributed, a billboard appeal for her return was organized, and volunteers raised $100,000 in hopes that she was still alive. The last person known to have seen her alive was her 14-year-old neighbor, Joshua Phillips. Police questioned Joshua and even searched his house three times, but they found no sign of the missing child. Joshua himself had participated in the search for the child, although the child was already dead and concealed in the boy's bedroom. During one search by police, the boy's parents, who were unaware that the child's body was hidden in their home, explained that the faint odor in the house was caused by their pets.[15] Police accepted the explanation and did not pursue their search any further. In fact, the odor came from the child's body, which had already begun to decompose.

The truth of his actions could not escape Joshua, who had killed the child, taped her in a fetal position to a piece of plywood, and hidden her under his waterbed, inside the frame. Each night as he slept on this very bed, the odor grew stronger. Joshua tried to hide the smell by using air fresheners and by stuffing clothing around the corners of the bed, taping it tight. Despite his attempts to conceal the body, seven days after "Maddie" had disappeared, Joshua's mother became suspicious of the odor and saw a liquid coming from beneath her son's bed. She then moved the bed frame. To her horror she saw the child's feet and she alerted the police.

Joshua and Maddie had played together in the past with no sign of trouble between the two. Neighbors described Joshua as a polite, nice boy, and police had no record of any trouble with him. On November 3, the two were playing together in Phillip's yard, at which time he dealt the first blow to the girl. Neither the defense nor the prosecution denied that Joshua hit Maddie in the head with a baseball bat while they were in the yard. But the defense would argue that Joshua acted in panic, killing her after he accidentally hit her. The prosecution would counter that the boy's actions were premeditated and might have been sexually motivated, because he had discussed sex with the girl before and when she was found she was not wearing any underwear.[16]

According to court testimony, after Joshua hit her with the bat, Maddie began screaming and, fearing that his father would be angry, Joshua dragged the little girl into his bedroom where he again struck her with the bat in an attempt to silence her screams. When the child continued to moan, Joshua stabbed her in the neck with a knife and then pushed her body under his bed. Joshua went to clean himself up, but he then heard her moaning again. Pulling her dying body from beneath the bed, he stabbed her repeatedly until he was sure she was dead.

Joshua then bound the child with tape and put her body under his waterbed in an attempt to hide any evidence of the crime. That night Joshua helped in the search for the missing girl, and his parents fully cooperated with police as they did a routine search of the home. Chillingly, the boy slept over the dead girl's body for six nights. After his mother discovered the body, the boy was arrested and charged with murder after he confessed. Both weapons, the bat and the knife, were recovered. An autopsy showed no signs of sexual assault even though the girl's underpants had been removed. She had suffered numerous blunt trauma injuries to the head, nine stab wounds to the chest, and two stab wounds to the throat.

The trial lasted only two days. The defense did not call any witnesses at the trial, but Joshua's attorney, Richard Nichols, said Joshua's actions began as an accident and got out of hand. He agreed that Joshua panicked and beat the girl with the bat, cut her throat, and stabbed her. According to Joshua's attorney, the murder was not premeditated. The jury believed otherwise and, after only two hours of deliberation, they found Joshua guilty of first-degree murder. Joshua received nearly the harshest penalty allowed under Florida law. Even though he was tried as an adult, he was spared the death penalty because he was under 16 years of age at the time of the crime.

Joshua showed no emotion when the verdict was read in the courtroom, though his attorney said he had cried during a meeting about the case.[17] Whether his tears fell because of his future in prison or because he was remorseful for his actions, only Joshua knows.

SCHOOL SHOOTINGS

Few events in the past two decades have captured the attention of our nation like the shootings in our schools. Seeing the bodies of dead schoolchildren on the evening news, the randomness of these tragedies has left most parents across the nation wondering if it could happen to their own children. These crimes have happened in all parts of the country, in both rural and suburban schools. The affluence of the areas where these shootings have occurred had created a false impression of safety. This impression is violently disturbed when boys enter cafeterias and hallways with firearms.

Table 6.1
School Shootings/Assaults

Perpetrator	City	Date	School	Deaths	Injuries	Status
Unknown	Blackville, SC	10/12/95	high school	1	1	suicide
Jamie Rouse	Pulaski, TN	11/11/95	Richland HS	2	1	incarcerated
Unknown	St. Peters, MO	12/18/95	Ft. Zumwalt SHS	hostages/no injuries		incarcerated
Barry Loukaitis	Moses Lake, WA	2/2/96	Frontier JHS	3	1	incarcerated
Thomas Hamilton	Dunblane, Scot.	3/13/96	Dunblane Primary	17	17	suicide
Horrett Campbell	Wolverhampton, Eng.	7/9/96	St. Luke's Church	0	7	incarcerated
Evan Ramsey	Bethel, AL	2/19/97	Bethel Regional HS	2	2	incarcerated
Luke Woodham	Pearl, MS	10/1/97	Pearl HS	3	7	incarcerated
Michael Carneal	West Paducah, KY	12/1/97	Heath HS	3	5	incarcerated
Mitchell Johnson	Jonesboro, AR	3/24/98	Westside Middle	5	10	incarcerated
Andrew Golden	Jonesboro, AR	3/24/98	Westside Middle	5	10	incarcerated
Andrew Wurst	Edinboro, PA	4/24/98	J. W. Parker Middle	1	0	incarcerated
Jacob Davis	Fayetteville, TN	5/19/98	Lincoln Co. HS	1	0	incarcerated
Kip Kinkel	Springfield, OR	5/21/98	Thurston HS	2	25	incarcerated
Dylan Klebold	Littleton, CO	4/20/99	Columbine HS	13	23	suicide
Eric Harris	Littleton, CO	4/20/99	Columbine HS	13	23	suicide
T. J. Solomon	Conyers, GA	5/20/99	Heritage HS	0	6	incarcerated

The youngest person to attempt a school shooting that I am aware of was detained by police in May 1998. A 5-year-old kindergartener was a student at a Tennessee grade school. The boy brought a loaded .25 caliber pistol to school in his book bag. According to the child's statement to authorities, his intent was to kill several students as well as his teacher. He was angry at the students because they had "beaten him up," and he was angry with the teacher because she had sent him to the office for misbehaving. The child's mother and grandfather admitted that the boy had acquired the weapon from his grandfather's dresser, but they deny that he intended to kill anyone.

The boy and his mother lived with the grandfather, and the mother had a series of charges in her past. Among them were charges of firing a gun at her ex-boyfriend's car, reckless driving resulting in her son (then 3 years old) being thrown at the windshield, stabbing one person and punching another, and vandalizing another woman's car. Based on his mother's history, perhaps we could speculate as to where this young boy learned violence as a means to solve his problems.

Table 6.1 outlines a number of incidents that have occurred over the past few years at schools where students were held hostage, injured, or died. Unfortunately, these are not the only murders on school grounds. Every year there are assaults and killings in school parking lots, on athletic fields, and at other school functions both on and off campus. In addition, this sample does not include shootings at colleges and universities.

Michael Carneal

On December 1, 1997, 14-year-old Michael Carneal arrived at Heath High School in West Paducah, Kentucky, with an armload of rifles and ammunition. An adolescent desperate for attention and respect from his peers, he would shoot into an early morning gathering of students, leaving three children dead and five injured.

Disparate reports were presented on Michael Carneal. Even though Michael was not thought to have been close to his parents, he had never been in any significant trouble at home or at school. His older sister was the valedictorian of her class and his father was a respected attorney. Unlike many of the children who have killed at school, Michael was a regular attender at his local church, and he was not involved with violent movies, video games, or guns. His parents said they never saw any signs of mental illness in their son, and they described him as a very sensitive boy. As an example of his sensitivity they related a time when he was so distraught over accidentally hurting a student in his karate class that he dropped out of karate class altogether.[18] According to some people who knew him, he was a social, friendly boy who got along well with others. He played baritone horn in the high school band and his principal said that he was very intelligent and had never been suspended. The only infractions he had been disciplined for at school were accessing a pornographic Internet site and a minor act of vandalism.

But there was another side to this boy, who was described by friends as a "jokester." Michael seemed to be a healthy boy to many people, but based on his own words he was a thief and a con artist. In postarrest interviews, Michael said that he sold parsley to classmates telling them it was marijuana, he stole CDs, and he distributed at school pornography that he had downloaded from the Internet.[19] A variety of pornographic images were found on his home computer after his arrest. Despite his church attendance, among his school friends he was a self-proclaimed atheist and he and his friends would stand near a daily prayer circle at school and mock the participants.

It is unclear to what degree his shooting spree was prepared in advance, but prosecutors would argue that he had discussed shooting classmates and taking over the school as much as a year earlier.[20] He also wrote a violent story, discovered after his arrest, in which a boy named "Michael" was picked on by friends. His brother in the story saved him using a gun, and "Michael" presented the resultant corpses to his mother as a present.[21] Michael was a small boy who was frequently teased about being gay, a derogatory term that he resented. Carneal's true character, on the one hand well-liked and funny, and yet on the other hand dishonest and willing to do anything for attention, is open for debate, but the shooting itself tips the scales in favor of the latter description.

Carneal's motive for the shooting is not clear. Like Luke Woodham and other perpetrators of school shootings, it is possible that Michael was motivated by a failing romance. He was fond of a classmate named Nicole Hadley. Her mother said that Michael liked Nicole, but his affections were unrequited. Even though Michael would later say he did not target any students specifically, Nicole would be the first person he shot. Therefore, one theory as to his motive was that he was angry with Nicole because her affections were beyond his reach.

A second possibility was that he was mimicking a movie. Originally, Michael would tell investigators that he got the idea of shooting students by watching a movie called *The Basketball Diaries*, in which a group of teenagers with guns take over their school.[22] He told investigators that he had spoken with his friends about the movie and said he "might do something like that."[23] Later, however, he would retract this statement and say that the movie played no role in his decision.[24] He would provide a third possible reason for the shooting.

By Thanksgiving 1997, Michael Carneal was a frustrated young man, tired of being picked on and ignored, desperate to be popular with his peers and to be perceived as "cool." The Wednesday before the shooting was the last day of class before the Thanksgiving holiday. Michael apparently had some plan at least by this day, even though he told investigators that he had not planned to shoot students until just moments before it happened. On this day he told his friend, Ben Strong, not to attend his usual prayer meeting in the halls of Heath High School on the following Monday. Carneal told Strong not to be there "because, you know, we're friends."[25] Strong was a senior, a defensive tackle on the football team, the son of a minister, and the leader of the daily prayer group. Because of Michael's reputation as a jokester, Strong did not take the threat seriously. Carneal himself said that he had a "habit of making empty threats to annoy people."[26]

The next day, Thanksgiving Day, Carneal broke into a neighbor's garage. According to a friend who lived there, Carneal knew where the key for the gun cabinet was hidden. He took several weapons and 700 rounds of ammunition and pushed them through the window of his bedroom. The owner of the guns did not even realize they were missing until police contacted him after the shooting. Referring to his theft of the guns, Carneal said, "I was feeling proud, strong, good, and more respected. I had accomplished something. I'm not the kind of kid who accomplishes anything. This is the only adventure I've ever had."[27] On Friday, he took some of the guns to a friend's home and they fired them. He said he made the decision on Sunday to take them to school on Monday and show them off to his friends. He wrapped two rifles, two shotguns, and the ammunition in a blanket and loaded the bundle into the trunk of his sister's car on Monday morning. He stowed a .22 caliber Ruger pistol in his backpack.

When he arrived at school that Monday morning, some students asked him what he was carrying in the blanket and he told them props for a science project. He proceeded to the hallway area where students routinely gathered before school. There he met with his friends while, a few feet away, Strong's group had gathered for their daily prayer meeting. When Carneal showed the guns to his friends he thought that they would be impressed, but their reaction was less strong than he had expected. They discussed the guns for a few minutes, but the boys quickly turned their conversation to other things and Michael felt he was being ignored. He said later that he thought he decided to shoot into the crowd because his friends were ignoring him. "I had guns . . . and they were still ignoring me," he said.[28]

In a desperate attempt to get his friends' attention, Carneal put his backpack down and put earplugs in his ears. He withdrew from his backpack the .22 caliber Ruger with ten rounds in the clip and one in the chamber. About that time, the nearby prayer meeting was just concluding. Because of Carneal's reputation as a practical joker, even when fellow students saw the pistol, they thought it was a stunt. Carneal pointed the weapon in the direction of the prayer group and pulled the trigger. Nicole Hadley fell to the floor. After a second and third round he paused, but then he began quickly pulling the trigger, letting bullets fly indiscriminately through the halls. After hearing the first shot, Strong turned to Carneal, asked him what he was doing, and told him to put the gun down. As Carneal continued to fire, Strong rushed toward him and pushed him against the wall, where Michael dropped the weapon with one round still in the clip.

In a nearby office, Principal Bill Bond was sitting at his desk. It was about 7:40 A.M. when he heard three shots, a pause, and then what he described as the distinct sound of a series of gunshots. When he came into the hallway, he saw Strong and Carneal face-to-face near the wall with the Ruger lying on the floor at their feet. Bond approached the two boys and kicked the gun away as the hallway filled with screams from injured and frightened students.

Carneal left three students dead, among them Nicole Hadley. Of the five injured students, one would be paralyzed from the waist down. Carneal told investigators that he did not think the Ruger was powerful enough to kill anyone and he did not think he would get into trouble, but when he realized what he had done, he begged for someone to kill him.[29] As police investigated they began to find evidence of a boy who was less well rounded than he appeared to be on the surface. Pornographic and violent materials, both downloaded from the Internet, were found in his room.[30] Michael described his action to the McCracken County sheriff as "just a random shooting."[31]

Carneal was charged with three counts of murder and five counts of attempted murder. The parents of the three slain children filed a $100 million lawsuit naming forty-five defendants. Among them were Michael's parents, teachers and administrators at the school, Time Warner, Polygram Film Entertainment Distribution, Inc., Palm Pictures, Island Pictures, New Line Cinema, game producers Nintendo of America, Inc., Sega of America, Inc., Sony Computer Entertainment, and the Internet sex sites Network Authentication Systems, Inc., and Meow Media, Inc.[32] Carneal pleaded guilty of murder but claimed to be mentally ill. He was sentenced to life in prison and will not be eligible for parole for twenty-five years. This young boy who wanted to be popular is now incarcerated at a juvenile detention center. Perhaps a clue to his motive can be seen in his statement, "people respect me now."[33]

Luke Woodham

By all accounts Luke Woodham was teased and picked on from his earliest school days. In spite of the teasing, Woodham was described as a quiet boy who just absorbed the insults, never even responding, concentrating on his grades and his job at a Domino's Pizza restaurant where he had aspirations of entering an assistant manager's program. Luke, heavyset and bespeckled, was often in the company of his divorced mother, even when he was on a date. Because of his poor vision, his mother normally drove him to school. As he began his high school career, he was a solid A-B student, but he began associating with other "outcasts" known as Kroth. Even though none of the seven boys in this group was ever in any trouble, their activities were less than productive. They would gather at Woodham's home while his mother was working at her job as a secretary. During their gatherings they discussed Hitler and the German philosopher Nietzsche, and they engaged in a fantasy game involving threats to blow up the school. Even more troubling, Woodham was heavily influenced by one member of this group, Marshall Grant Boyette, Jr. Woodham had briefly dated a girl, Christina Menefee, who had later broken up with him. When he discussed this with the group, Boyette told Woodham that he "should just kill her and be done with it so he wouldn't have to see her again."[34]

A year prior to the shooting, Woodham had dated Christina Menefee for a mere three weeks. After four or five dates, Menefee, a gracious and kind young girl, wanted to break off her relationship with Woodham, whom she called "Luke Skywalker." She discussed the situation with her father, explaining that she felt sorry for Woodham and did not want to hurt the sensitive young man because she recognized that he had few friends and was an underdog. With her father's encouragement, she gently explained her feelings to Woodham and then disengaged from the relationship. On the surface, Woodham appeared to have accepted the breakup, but the relationship would stay alive in his mind. After the shooting he said, "I only loved one thing in my whole life and that was Christina Menefee. But she was torn away from me."[35]

Woodham's hate was building during the year following his breakup with Menefee. The years of ridicule were taking their toll on him and the violent influence of his friends was pushing him in an unhealthy direction. He came to believe that Boyette was the only person who cared about him, and the group began engaging in activities that Woodham described as Satanism. His first violent behavior was the killing of his own dog. Woodham and Boyette beat the dog nearly to death. Then they put the dog in plastic bags, set fire to the bags using lighter fluid, and threw them into a lake. Killing the animal was bad enough, but Woodham's alleged written description of the event in a diary was chilling. "On Saturday last week, I made my first kill. The victim was a loved one, my dear dog Sparkle. I will never forget the howl she made. It sounded almost human. We laughed and hit her more."[36] Woodham allegedly went on to describe the sight of the sinking bags as "true beauty."[37] Even though in his writings Woodham took responsibility for the killing, in his court testimony, he would blame this event on Boyette.[38]

As Woodham's rage grew, it was fed by his friends, who encouraged him to seek revenge. He believed he had endured enough rejection and ridicule. According to Woodham, even his mother told him he was "fat, stupid and lazy."[39] He said he began to see "demons that urged him to kill."[40] His writings reflected his hatred of those who had mistreated him. Woodham wrote, "I have suffered all my life," and he instructed others to "hate the accursed god of Christianity."[41] "I am the epitome of Evil!" he said. "I have no mercy for humanity for they created me, they tortured me until I snapped and became what I am today."[42]

Woodham did not compile a formal list of people against whom he wanted revenge, but he apparently had some specific people in mind. The son of Pearl's mayor, Kyle Foster, was one possible target. During his attack at the high school, Luke apologized to a student for shooting him, saying, "the bullet was meant for Foster."[43] Fortunately for Foster, he was late for school on the day of the attack and was not in the courtyard when the shooting occurred.

On October 1, 1997, Woodham decided to take action. He awoke early while his mother was still asleep, and he crept into her bedroom carrying a baseball bat and a butcher knife. In court, he would say he did not remember what happened next, but the evidence showed that he beat and stabbed his mother to death as she slept in her bed. He then drove his white Chevy Corsica to Pearl High School. Carrying a hunting rifle under his coat, he walked into the school courtyard at 7:55 A.M. He handed a student a written note that he described as his "manifesto" and walked toward Christina Menefee, who was talking with friends. As he approached, he took out the hunting rifle and shot Christina in the neck. Then, as 17-year-old Lydia Dew tried to escape, he shot her in the back, killing her. For eleven minutes Woodham terrorized the students and faculty of the school.

Assistant Principal Joel Myrick said that he saw Woodham walking along "thumbing fresh rounds" into the weapon and he knew he had to do something to stop the attack.[44] Myrick ran to his car where he kept a .45 caliber pistol. As he was returning to the school building, he saw that Woodham was leaving. Myrick yelled at him to stop, but Woodham ignored the demand and got into his automobile. As he attempted to escape, he lost control of the car and stopped. Myrick ran up to the car, put his gun to Woodham's neck, and ordered him out of the automobile. Woodham said, "Mr. Myrick, I was the guy who gave you the discount on the pizza the other night."[45] As the two waited for the police to arrive, Myrick asked Woodham why he had done what he did. Woodham said, "Mr. Myrick, the world has wronged me."[46]

Woodham, 16 years old at the time, was arrested and charged with murder and aggravated assault. Police went to his home and discovered the body of his mother just as Woodham had left her. He was then charged with her murder as well. As the residents of Pearl tried to make sense of the tragedy, police announced that Woodham had not acted alone. They arrested the other members of Kroth for conspiracy to commit murder. The boys, Justin James Sledge, Delbert

Shaw, Wesley Brownell, Daniel Thompson, Donald Brooks, and Boyette, ranged in age from 16 to 18. The charges against them were later dropped. Woodham cried as he explained that he was not in control of himself. He said that the demons and voices he experienced told him to commit the murders. He would testify that he had no memory of killing his mother, that after entering his mother's room the next thing he knew was that she was dead.

Yet his "manifesto" showed deliberate forethought. In this document he wrote, "I killed because people like me are mistreated every day. I did this to show society push us and we will push back."[47] Two separate juries rejected Woodham's insanity defense. In his first trial, he was convicted of the murder of his mother and in his second, he was convicted of the murders of Menefee and Dew as well as seven counts of aggravated assault. He was sentenced to life in prison for each of the three murders as well as twenty additional years for each count of aggravated assault.

Some would argue that society pushed Woodham toward his drastic behavior. Fellow Kroth member Justin Sledge disrupted a candlelight service, yelling, "Woodham went mad because of society."[48] But the evidence does not support such a claim. People all over the country are ridiculed, but they choose more appropriate means of coping with their frustrations. A more likely cause was that Woodham, as well as his friends, considered revenge a reasonable method for dealing with discontent. In fact, conspirators Brooks and Boyette were later accused of plotting to kill Brooks's father.[49] Woodham, perhaps, got just what he wanted—publicity. After being arrested Woodham expressed "morbid appreciation" for his infamy.[50] In his mind, he was finally somebody important.

Andrew Golden and Mitchell Johnson

Andrew Golden, a boy barely four feet tall, was raised in a close-knit family. The 11-year-old boy had never been in trouble before March 1998 when he and Mitchell Johnson killed four classmates and a teacher at West Side Middle School in Jonesboro, Arkansas. Golden had been around guns since his earliest days, getting his first rifle when he was only 6 years old. His grandfather was a gun collector and his father was the founder of a local gun club committed to "practical pistol shooting" involving shooting pop-up targets and silhouettes. There was little in Andrew's background that might have warned about the plan he and Mitchell Johnson would hatch, a plan that would lead to the most deadly school shooting in U.S. history before the Littleton, Colorado, incident.

Unlike Golden, Mitchell Johnson had grown up in a less than desirable home. While living with his biological father and mother in Minnesota, he existed in deplorable conditions. According to his mother, animal feces littered the floor, rotting food covered the counter, and the yard was unkempt.[51] His mother divorced his biological father in 1994 and she and her son moved to Arkansas. Despite the conditions of the Minnesota home, Mitchell's mother said the divorce was difficult for Mitchell. Eventually, though, she met an ex-convict named Terry Woodard, and they married, making Woodard her third husband. "Mitch" got along with the tattooed Woodard and even seemed to romanticize his stepfather's prison past. Woodard said that Mitchell was a "gang banger wannabe" who thought prison was "cool."[52] Friends of Mitchell also described a boy who glorified gang behavior. They told of Mitchell flashing "Blood" signs and telling them he "had a lot of killing to do."[53] He was said to have pulled out a knife in the locker room the Monday prior to the attack on the school.

How Mitchell was perceived depended on who was asked. Some said he was a romantic and a choirboy while others said he was a bully.[54] He played basketball, baseball, and football, and he seemed to get along with his classmates. At the time of the shooting, Mitchell's mother said the family was the happiest they had ever been. But Mitchell harbored secrets. Unknown to his mother, Mitchell had allegedly been repeatedly sexually abused over a four-year period by a boy in his neighborhood.[55] Mitch himself had also sexually molested a child. He admitted to sexually touching the 2-year-old granddaughter of his father's fiancé and was ordered to undergo counseling.[56]

It is not clear how the two boys ever got together. They were in different grades because Johnson was two years older than Golden. Andrew's family said that Johnson had never been to their house and they had never even heard his name until after the shooting. The boys apparently only knew each other from the school bus on which they shared an assigned seat. However this unlikely pair came together, they most definitely concocted their plan as a team.

There is evidence that some people should have known what Mitchell and Golden were planning.[57] Mitchell was thought to have been angry about a student, Candace Porter, with whom he wanted a relationship. After the breakup with this girl, he told other students before the shooting, "tomorrow you will find out if you live or die."[58] Other students heard his threats to Candace. Mitchell told a classmate that he was angry at Candace for her rebuff and that he was going to shoot her and then "kill everybody else in the building."[59] As is often the case, these students all thought Mitchell was joking. His threats were not limited to students, however. Mitchell told someone that he wanted to kill English teacher Shannon Wright because "she was mean and gave him too much work, and was nice to everyone but him."[60] He would, in fact, carry out this threat.

It is not clear who actually hatched the idea to shoot students at the school; both boys would claim that the other one had been the mastermind and they themselves had simply gone along with the plan. Whatever the truth, on March 24, 1998, both boys put their plan into action with military precision. That morning, Johnson told his mother that he was not feeling well and he did not feel he could go to school. Just before she left for work, he told her that her husband needed her to leave the keys to the family's minivan so that he could take it to the repair shop later in the day. At school, Andrew skipped his first class. The two then tried unsuccessfully to break into a steel gun cabinet in the Johnson home using a blowtorch and a hammer. They collected several unsecured handguns from the home and then broke into Golden's grandfather's house. In the home of this gun collector, they had no trouble finding weapons. There the boys stole three rifles, seven handguns, and 3,000 rounds of ammunition. Dressed in camouflage uniforms they loaded the minivan with sleeping bags, food, a crossbow, hunting knives, and other survival gear. They planned to drive to a cabin in the woods owned by the Goldens after the shooting. However, they ran into a problem almost immediately. Three different gas stations refused to serve them because of their ages.

Undaunted, they drove the van back to the middle school where 250 of their classmates were studying. Loading themselves with the stolen weapons and ammunition, they set up a makeshift camp just inside the woods seventy-five meters from the school. Andrew returned to class at 12:30 P.M., but as an excuse to return to where Johnson waited in the woods he said he needed to go to the bathroom. As he left the building and in accordance with the plan, he set off the fire alarm and rushed to where his firearms were waiting in the woods. When children exited the building as they had done many times for fire drills, Johnson and Golden opened fire. When the children saw the blood of their classmates on the sidewalks, they realized someone was shooting at them, but when they tried to reenter the building they discovered that the doors had automatically locked behind them. Realizing they were trapped, they screamed for someone inside to open the doors. In the meantime, Johnson and Golden continued to fire. Shannon Wright pulled a child close to her in an effort to shield the child from the gunfire. Two rounds hit the 32-year-old teacher, one in the chest and one in the abdomen. The child she protected remained uninjured, but Mrs. Wright was fatally wounded.

Within minutes the shooting was over. Some children had found their way into the gymnasium. Outside, the ground was covered with the bodies of injured and dying children and teachers. Golden and Johnson packed up their weapons and sprinted through the woods toward the parked van. Police had been summoned and one officer on the way to the scene saw the two boys exiting the wooded area, still dressed in camouflage, Johnson carrying a 30-06 hunting rifle and Golden carrying a .30 caliber carbine. The officer arrested the boys without incident. At work, Johnson's mother, Gretchen Woodard, learned of the attack from two phone calls, the second from her 11-year-old son who said, "Mom, you have to come get me. Mitchell shot some kids."[61]

Golden was reported to be deeply upset about the attack and was said to be crying for his mother shortly afterward, while he was detained at a juvenile detention center. He had little memory of the attack, telling his grandfather that he did not target anyone specifically and he only remembered shooting at a car. His father, a trucker who learned of his son's involvement in the attack while he was on the road, has said that he visits his son every week and his son is deeply remorseful, agonizing over the way he terrorized a community. As for Mitchell Johnson, he showed little remorse. His lawyer said Mitchell told him he wanted to "hurt people who had hurt him and to teach everybody a lesson."[62] In the course of the attack, the boys fired twenty-seven times, killed four classmates as well as Mrs. Wright, and wounded ten others, including a second teacher.

If they had been tried as adults, they could have received the death penalty, but because the two boys were under the age of 15 at the time of the crime, they were tried in juvenile court. They were convicted of their crimes, but because they were tried as juveniles, the state can only hold them until they are 21 years of age. However, because of a crowded juvenile system the two will most likely be released even earlier. The chances are good that they will be freed by age 18.

Kipland Kinkel

May 21, 1998, began like any other day at Thurston High School in Springfield, Oregon. The summer break was approaching and students were preparing for student government elections. About 400 of the 1,700 high school students gathered in the cafeteria that morning following an honors assembly. Eating breakfast, chatting about the school year, and preparing for their classes, several students saw 15-year-old Kipland ("Kip") Kinkel enter the cafeteria wearing a trench coat and a cowboy hat and carrying a gun. Thinking it was a student government campaign prank, many of the students paid no attention to him. Even after the shooting started, some expected another student to arrive to save the day, completing the theatrics, but Kinkel's actions were not theatrics. The students did not know that two of their fellows students had already been shot outside a choir room and that before Kinkel was finished two students would be dead and twenty-five injured.

When I first heard about this incident, some of my students asked me if it could be true that Kip came from a "good home" as had been said in the news at the time. I very much doubted it, but as I investigated this case myself, I found it an anomaly. Even though one could have seen this behavior coming, it appears that the Kinkel family was, indeed, a very loving family who did everything they could to prevent the tragedy that occurred.

Kip was the second child of Bill Kinkel, a 59-year-old son of a Baptist minister, and 57-year-old Faith Zuranski. Both of Kip's parents were Spanish teachers. His father, though officially retired, taught Spanish at Lane Community College near their home, while his mother taught at Springfield High School. Their oldest child was 21-year-old Kristin, six years older than Kip. Kristin, a spunky 100-pound cheerleader, was a scholarship student at Hawaii Pacific University studying speech pathology. By all accounts, the Kinkels were good parents. They invested time, money, and energy in their children. Vacations, camping trips, outdoor educational trips, and other family activities were common. Despite his parents' good intentions, however, Kip seems to have been a difficult child from early on. Even though his grades were acceptable and he had no trouble with his parents until about three years before the shooting, a family friend described him as an "obnoxious brat" when he was younger.[63]

A few years before the shooting, Kip's parents began to see a disturbing change in their son. He seemed obsessed with violence, expressing an interest in explosives, guns, and violent television programs. Initially, his parents restricted his TV viewing, but when they caught him violating this restriction they disconnected the TV altogether. Kip began associating with some young men that his parents believed were a bad influence. In an effort to improve his grades and to change the violent course he seemed to be following they withdrew him from the public school. Home school, however, did not solve his problems and Kip was back in public school the next year.

Kip and some of his friends pursued an interest in bomb making. They once tried to order some bomb-making books through the Internet, but the material was mistakenly sent to the bank where they had purchased their money order, so they never received it. Later, they would succeed in purchasing books on the subject and they constructed a variety of explosive devices. Kip then began asking his father for guns. His father rejected the idea initially because he was concerned about Kip's violent interests, but he later relented. He thought that if he exposed his son to guns under his authority, he would have more control and perhaps lessen his son's interest in guns. This hope would not be realized. Bill first bought Kip a .22 caliber Ruger semiautomatic rifle. The clip for this weapon held fifty rounds—the number Kip would eventually unload on his classmates. Later his father purchased a 9mm Glock pistol for Kip.

During this time, he seems to have led two lives. He was popular with girls and nearly all of his teachers said they liked him, although they said he did not apply himself. Others called him a "trustworthy Boy Scout–type of kid."[64] Yet many of his friends also noted that he had difficulty with authority. Even though he was a member of the football squad team he rarely played because he routinely lost his temper and swore at coaches. Because of his temper, friends said they would let him win basketball games in order to avoid seeing him get angry. Kip was a purple belt in karate; he was suspended in the seventh grade for karate kicking a boy in the head. Even his parents had difficulty dealing with his temper. Bill told a friend that Kip had threatened him and his wife and that "any refusal of his demands resulted in tantrums, threats, and increasingly outlandish behavior until they gave in."[65]

Kip bragged about his guns and about the explosive devices he constructed. Allegedly he once brought a pipe bomb to school and showed it to some of his friends. He was never caught with any such device at school, but he claimed to have blown up a variety of things including mailboxes, bushes, and trees. All the while, Kip was becoming more violent. He told his friends stories of torturing animals, claiming to have killed cats and tortured and dissected live squirrels.[66] Some might suppose that these conversations were purely braggadocio, especially when he claimed to have blown up a cow. However, the fact that torturing animals was on his mind and he thought such behavior humorous was a disturbing sign.

Even though Kip was well-liked by his teachers and classmates, even his friends recognized his disruptive nature when they jokingly voted him "Most Likely to Start World War III." Others found him temperamental and frightening. He seemed to delight in describing the gory details of skinning animals, and he frightened others by describing his thoughts about putting a bomb under the bleachers during a school assembly then figuring some way to trap the students inside. A student once asked him why he liked guns so much. Kip answered, "Because when I snap, I want to have all the firepower I can."[67]

As I studied this case I came across numerous statements from people who knew this boy. In interview after interview they related instances where Kip alluded to killing, threatened to kill, or threatened specific individuals. For instance, he was said to have read from his journal in literature class about his plans to "kill everybody."[68] Another time when a boy called him a derogatory name, Kip said, "I want him dead."[69] A statement from a classmate summarized what I have come to know of this boy when he said that Kip simply talked "way too much about killing."[70]

As his parents attempted to find solutions to Kip's behavior, they consulted various experts. Kip was diagnosed as hyperactive and prescribed Ritalin, but the drug had no effect on his aggression. He was sent to a counselor who worked with him on anger management, but Kip hated the therapy. He was also diagnosed as depressed and was prescribed Prozac. None of these interventions worked. Bill and Faith became frustrated and felt hopeless. Several observers noted that if the Kinkels began talking about their son they would simply be over-whelmed with frustration and discouragement. Bill even engaged an expert in deliquent youth in a conversation about Kip when they chanced to meet in an airport. Bill reportedly told the counselor at the airport that he was "terrified of his son."[71]

Even though his behavior was frightening, Kip managed to stay out of legal trouble. Only two incidents are recorded. In one, he and several friends were caught when they toilet papered a house using over 450 rolls of toilet paper. On another occasion, Kip was on a ski trip with a friend. The boys left their hotel one night and pushed a rock off an overpass. A car was grazed by the rock but not seriously damaged. The driver chased the boys back to the hotel where they were caught. Bill was called at home and drove to the hotel to retrieve his child. After the toilet papering incident, Bill found a sawn-off shotgun, a .22 pistol, and bomb-making books in a trunk in Kip's room. Kip claimed to have purchased the two guns at school for $100 each. Even though Bill had discovered the bomb-making books, he would never discover the extent of Kip's involvement with explosives. Kip kept his bombs hidden in a crawl space in the garage and after the murders, police would find twenty devices, some sophisticated and prepared to explode. They also found a hand grenade and chem-icals that could be used to make explosives, along with instructions for making bombs.[72]

Kip seemed to be calming down in the weeks prior to the shoot-ings, but friends said that he had simply learned to "put on a good show."[73] The day before the shooting, Kip purchased a handgun from a classmate for $100. The classmate had stolen the weapon from the father of another student. Unfortunately for Kip, the owner discov-ered the weapon was missing and notified police, who quickly pieced the facts of the theft together. While the boys were still at school, police came and searched several lockers, including Kip's, where they found the .32 caliber pistol. Police arrested Kip and the student who had stolen the weapon.

Bill Kinkel arrived at the police station and Kip was released into his custody. On the way home they stopped at a fast-food restaurant and ate a late lunch. It was about 2:00 P.M. when they arrived back at the Kinkel house. Around 3:00 P.M., Bill received a phone call from the father of one of Kip's friends and they discussed the gun incident. This man was the last person to speak to Bill Kinkel. About thirty minutes later, Kip's English teacher called and spoke with Kip.

Ten minutes after that a school counselor tried to reach Kip by telephone to encourage him and discuss his suspension and the credit he was to receive for his coursework, but there was no answer. It is speculated that between 3:00 P.M. and 3:40 P.M., Kip shot his father once in the back of the head, killing him. By 4:30, students from Bill Kinkel's Spanish class began calling. Kip answered the phone and told them Bill would not be coming in because of family problems. About two hours later, Faith Kinkel returned home after having done some grocery shopping. Unaware that Bill was dead in another room, she carried the groceries into the house with Kip's help. After the groceries were put away he said, "Mom, I love you," and then shot and killed her.

Sometime after he had killed his father, but before his mother came home, Kip spent time on the phone with two of his friends. He allegedly told them he was "considering violence to punish educators responsible for his suspension."[74] His friends said that Kip several times commented about when his mother would get home. He also told them that as he waited in jail for his father to come and get him, he had considered hanging himself with his shoelaces in his cell because he felt his life was over. After killing his mother, he left his house and spent the night with his friends.

Around 8 A.M. the next morning, Kip taped a .22 caliber bullet and a 9mm bullet to his chest. He planned to use these to commit suicide if he ran out of ammunition. He then dressed in a trench coat and loaded himself down with two knives, two pistols, a .22 caliber rifle, several fully loaded clips, and other ammunition. Then in his family's Ford Explorer he drove the ten miles to the school of 1,700 students, parked a few blocks away, and climbed through a fence. Inside the building, he walked past the choir room, where he shot two students, one of them in the face. He then went to the cafeteria, where a crowd of about 400 students had gathered to eat breakfast and chat before class, and began shooting. Students ducked for cover and fled toward the exits as bullets shattered a large plateglass window. During the shooting, one witness said that Kip "put his foot on the back of one kid and shot him four times."[75] Another student, Mikael Nickolauson, was shot once in the torso and once point-blank in the head.

Jacob Ryker, a member of the wrestling team, was celebrating his seventeenth birthday that day. When Kip began shooting, Ryker saw that his 17-year-old girlfriend, Jennifer Alldredge, had been shot.

About this time, Kip's .22 ran out of ammunition, but he continued to pull the trigger. Hearing the clicking sound of the dry-firing weapon, Ryker decided to rush Kinkel and attempt to subdue him. He told reporters later, "I saw she [Alldredge] got hit, and I went for it. Enough's enough."[76] As Kip tried to reload, he saw Ryker charging him. Kinkel pulled one of the pistols and shot Ryker in the hand, but too late to avoid being tackled. Other students assisted Ryker in pinning Kinkel to the floor as he yelled at his fellow students, "Just shoot me. Shoot me now."[77] When it was all over, he had fired fifty rounds from the .22 Ruger in less than a minute. He left two dead and twenty-five injured in the cafeteria. After he was arrested he told officers "it might be a good idea if they went to his home."[78] An hour and a half later, police entered the Kinkel residence and discovered Bill and Faith dead of gunshot wounds.

As if the tragedy at his home and the shooting at the school were not enough, Kip was not done with his aggression. After he was arrested, he was searched, but officers failed to find a hunting knife that was taped to his leg. At the police station, Kip was left alone in a detention room while an officer left to secure his weapon. While the officer was gone, Kinkel moved his handcuffed hands from behind his back and retrieved the knife from beneath his pant leg. When the officer returned, Kinkel jumped at him with the knife, forcing the officer to subdue him with pepper spray.[79]

Back at the Kinkel residence, investigators evacuated the neighborhood when they discovered numerous explosive devices in and around the home. After the house was cleared of explosives, forensics investigators were allowed in the house, but another device was found and they were again forced out.[80]

Kip was charged with numerous offenses including four counts of aggravated murder, twenty-six counts of attempted aggravated murder, six counts of first-degree assault, eighteen counts of second-degree assault, unlawful possession of a firearm, unlawful manufacture of a destructive device, possession of a destructive device, and first-degree theft.[81] Initially, his lawyers claimed he suffered from mental illness that rendered him incapable of understanding his conduct as criminal, he couldn't form the intent to commit the crimes, and he suffered from an extreme emotional disturbance. But after pleading not guilty by reason of insanity and just three days before his trial was set to begin, he changed his plea to guilty of four counts of murder and twenty-six counts of attempted murder. During his sentencing hearings, experts testified that he suffered from mental illness as well as brain damage. This damage involved reduced activity in certain areas of the brain resulting in violent behavior. Regardless of the cause of his behavior, Kip was sentenced to 111 years in prison.

Jake Ryker was hailed as a hero both by the media and by law enforcement.[82] One of the boys who talked with Kinkel on the phone, even as Bill Kinkel lay bleeding in the Kinkel house, believed that Kip killed his parents because he knew how embarrassed they would be by his arrest on the gun charge. This student believed Kip killed them to protect them.

An extensive article on Kip Kinkel was published in *Rolling Stone* magazine. This article, in part, paints a picture of Kinkel as a very "cute, funny, and smart kid with an active social life" who did not match the profile of this type of killer. When one looks at the whole picture, it seems to me that this heavily armed, destructive, vindictive, and angry boy was anything but cute.

CONCLUDING REMARKS

It is obvious from the cases described in this chapter that no single thing causes children to kill. In a haunting preview of things to come, one of the articles that reviewed the case of Kipland Kinkel contained a picture and an interview with a teacher from Heritage High School in Conyers, Georgia. Little could she know that just months later a similar incident would befall her own students.

Whether they murder at home, at school, or both, their motives, mental states, and upbringings are varied. Likewise, whether these children kill one person or several people, the cases are always tragic. However, the shooting at Columbine High School in Colorado is among the most tragic cases in history, partly due to the magnitude of the crime. Twelve children and one teacher lost their lives, and estimates of the damage caused by the perpetrators of the attack ran into the millions. Yet, for me, the tragedy of Columbine is related more to the amazing cruelty of the two perpetrators. Chapter 7 is devoted exclusively to this case.

NOTES

1. Jack Warner, "Drugs blamed for Forsyth family tragedy: youth, 13, pleads not guilty to killing his sleeping mother," *Atlanta Journal/Constitution*, December 19, 1995, C02.

2. Jack Warner, "Teen bet friend he'd kill mother," *Atlanta Journal/Constitution*, September 27, 1995, C1.

3. "No bond asked as teen, 13, is silent in Monroe court," *Atlanta Journal/Constitution*, September 28, 1995, C02.

4. Ibid.

5. Ibid.

6. Warner, "Teen bet friend he'd kill mother," C1.

7. "This week in Georgia," *Atlanta Journal/Constitution*, September 22, 1996, D02.

8. Ibid.

9. Mark Bixler, "Tearful apology: 'I wasn't thinking,' says bus stop killer," *Atlanta Journal/Constitution*, September 19, 1999, D1.

10. Cheryl Crabb, "Community 'touched and broken,' " *Atlanta Journal/Constitution*, November 7, 1998, D2.

11. Bixler, "Tearful apology," D1.

12. Ibid.

13. Ibid.

14. "15-year-old gets life in neighbor's slaying," *Atlanta Journal/Constitution*, August 21, 1999, A11.

15. "Missing girl's body found under neighbor's bed," *CNN On-Line*, *www.cnn.com/US/9811/10/missing.girl/index.html*, November 10, 1998.

16. "Florida teen guilty of killing 8-year-old neighbor," *CNN On-Line*, *www.cnn.com/US/9907/08/fla.child.murder.03/index.html*, July 8, 1999.

17. "Boy, 14, charged with stabbing death of Jacksonville girl," *CNN On-Line, www.cnn.com/US/9811/11/11/jacksonville.murder.ap/index/html.* November 11, 1998.

18. "Parents of Kentucky school shooter say they never knew son could be violent," *CNN On-Line, www.cnn.com/US/9905/17/paducah.school. shootings.ap/indext.html*, May 17, 1999.

19. Jonah Blank, "The kid no one noticed," *U.S. News and World Report* (Internet Edition), October 12, 1998.

20. Jonah Blank and Warren Cohen, "Prayer circle murders," *U.S. News and World Report* (Internet Edition), December 15, 1997.

21. Blank, "The kid no one noticed."

22. Mike Williams, "Violence goes to high school," *Atlanta Journal/Constitution*, December 7, 1997, G01.

23. "Movie 'factor' in school shootings: more students are being questioned as Kentucky town prepares to bury three young victims," *Atlanta Journal/Constitution*, December 5, 1997, A03.

24. Blank, "The kid no one noticed."

25. "3 dead, 5 hurt in Ky. school attack," *AP On-Line, headlines. prodigy.com/sd/AP/src_html/nm00gnky.htm*, December 2, 1997.

26. Blank, "The kid no one noticed."

27. Ibid.

28. Ibid.

29. Ibid.

30. "Parents of Kentucky school shooter say they never knew son could be violent."

31. "3 dead, 5 hurt in Ky. school attack."

32. James Prichard, "Media sued in fatal rampage at school," *Atlanta Journal/Constitution*, April 13, 1999, A3.

33. Blank, "The kid no one noticed."

34. Sue Anne Pressley, "A bloody morning casts pall on town," *Atlanta Journal/Constitution*, October 26, 1997, A14.

35. Ibid.

36. Bill Hewitt, Joseph Harmes, and Bob Stewart, "The avenger," *People Weekly* (Internet Edition), November 3, 1997.

37. Ibid.

38. "Teen in Mississippi killings 'saw demons,' " *CNN On-Line, www.cnn.com/US/9806/04/woodham.trial.pm/index.html,* June 4, 1998.

39. John Cloud, "Of arms and the boy," *Time* (Internet Edition), July 6, 1998.

40. "Teen in Mississippi killings 'saw demons.' "

41. Pressley, "A bloody morning casts pall on town," A14.

42. Ibid.

43. Howard Chua-Eoan, "Mississippi gothic: in a dramatic turn, an alleged one-man rampage may have become a seven-pointed conspiracy," *Time*, October 20, 1997, 54.

44. Hewitt, Harmes, and Stewart, "The avenger."

45. Chua-Eoan, "Mississippi gothic," 54.

46. Hewitt, Harmes, and Stewart, "The avenger."

47. "Teen passed note before shooting," *AP On-Line, headlines.prodigy.com/sd/AP/src_html/nm00gnzj.htm,* October 2, 1997.

48. Pressley, "A bloody morning casts pall on town," A14.

49. Chua-Eoan, "Mississippi gothic," 54.

50. Cloud, "Of arms and the boy."

51. Nadya Labi, "Mother of the accused," *Time* (Internet Edition), April 13, 1998.

52. Sylvester Monroe, "A boy and his lawyer," *Time* (Internet Edition), April 27, 1998.

53. Jonah Blank, Jason Vest, and Suzie Parker, "The children of Jonesboro," *U.S. News and World Report* (Internet Edition), April 6, 1998.

54. Labi, "Mother of the accused."

55. Cloud, "Of arms and the boy."

56. Labi, "Mother of the accused."

57. Monroe, "A boy and his lawyer."

58. Andrew Phillips, "When children kill," *Maclean's* (Internet Edition), April 6, 1998.

59. Blank, Vest, and Parker, "The children of Jonesboro."

60. Ibid.

61. Labi, "Mother of the accused."

62. "Anger behind shooting at school, lawyer says," *Atlanta Journal/Constitution*, April 18, 1998, A10.

63. Randall Sullivan, "A boy's life," *Rolling Stone* (Internet Edition), September 17, 1998.

64. "Suspect called short-tempered, fascinated with explosives," *CNN On-Line, www.cnn.com/US/9805/22/oregon.suspect.profile/index.html*, May 22, 1998.

65. Sullivan, "A boy's life."

66. Patrick Rogers, Michael Haederle, Elizabeth Leonard, and Johnny Dodd, "Mortal lessons," *People Weekly* (Internet Edition), June 8, 1998.

67. Sullivan, "A boy's life."

68. Jeff Barnard, "Bombs found at boy's home; death toll rises," *Atlanta Journal/Constitution*, May 23, 1998, A08.

69. Sullivan, "A boy's life."

70. Rogers, Haederle, Leonard, and Dodd, "Mortal lessons."

71. Ibid.

72. Barnard, "Bombs found at boy's home," A08.

73. Sullivan, "A boy's life."

74. Leon Stafford, "Area schools now act on threats," *Atlanta Journal/Constitution*, May 24, 1998, A01.

75. "Suspect showed signs of trouble; second student dies of head wounds," *Atlanta Journal/Constitution*, May 22, 1998, A08.

76. Rogers, Haederle, Leonard, and Dodd, "Mortal lessons."

77. Patricia King and Andrew Murr, "A son who spun out of control: an Oregon teen is charged with killing his parents and his classmates. The road to the cafeteria," *Newsweek*, June 1, 1998, 32.

78. Ibid.

79. Jeff Barnard, "Police: boy lunged at officer with knife," *Atlanta Journal/Constitution*, May 24, 1998, A7.

80. Barnard, "Bombs found at boy's home," A08.

81. "Trial date set for teen in school shooting," *Atlanta Journal/Constitution*, June 17, 1998, A10.

82. Sullivan, "A boy's life."

Homicide by Children, Part II: Columbine

The tragedy at Columbine High School was the worst school shooting in U.S. history. Two troubled bullies, cowards without their homemade explosives and semiautomatic firearms, ruthlessly took the lives of twelve innocent children and a teacher who was a loving father, grandfather, and husband before taking their own lives. One of the potential problems of books like this one is that they can either intentionally or unintentionally elevate criminals onto some perverse pedestal of infamy. In no way do I want my words here to glorify the terroristic behavior of these two demented young men. I do not want anyone to read my account of this tragedy and interpret it in any way except as it is intended—as a portrayal of two pathetic bullies who brutalized innocent children for their own selfish, distorted pleasure. I feel compassion for these boys in their hopelessness, but their behavior is among the most heartless I have ever seen. Two young boys with immense potential chose to squander it at the expense of others.

I have committed an entire chapter to this incident, in part, because this case was so complicated, involving hundreds of people. Parents, teachers, students, law enforcement officers, and others were witnesses, investigators, and victims. This case also presented some of the most difficult questions I have ever had to address. Why did two seemingly ordinary boys feel it necessary to commit such an act?

Could someone have known what was going on in the lives of these troubled teens and prevented this crime? Perhaps an equally important question is *should* someone have known? Detailed accounts of the lives of these two perpetrators in the year leading up to this episode and the event itself are necessary to enable me to address these questions.

ERIC HARRIS AND DYLAN KLEBOLD

Littleton, Colorado, a well-to-do community near Denver with a population of 35,000 people, was 18-year-old Eric Harris's last stop on a long list of moves. His father, a decorated military pilot, moved the Harris family from Ohio to Michigan, to New York, and finally to Colorado. Eric's mother worked for a catering company and his older brother had been a successful athlete at Columbine High School. Harris's friend and classmate Dylan Klebold, at 6'3" and 17 years of age, was a year younger than his more dominant friend. Dylan's father was a former geophysicist and a collector of vintage BMWs who had changed careers and founded a home-based mortgage management company. Dylan's mother, Susan, worked as an administrator at a local community college assisting disabled students with job placement. Dylan and Eric both worked at Blackjack's Pizza. Neither boy seemed to be a problem either at work or in their neighborhoods. Neighbors said the boys were quiet and no trouble, but I interpret this to mean that neither one bothered the neighbors personally. My suspicions are validated by comments from other neighbors who said that nobody in the neighborhood really knew either of them very well. Their character and distorted views may not have been obvious to the neighbors, but they were far from being secret.

Klebold and Harris met each other at Columbine High School, in Littleton. In 1994, the City of Denver had invested $13.4 million in renovations to the high school—upgrading the athletic fields and the school building as well as constructing a new auditorium. Ironically, in 1999, at the time of the shooting at Columbine, the Colorado State legislature was considering a concealed gun law. However, no firearms legislation under consideration at the time would have prevented the tragedy. Even as Harris and Klebold were still in control of the high school, a reporter asked a law enforcement officer if this event changed his mind on gun legislation. The man responded, "Ma'am, these boys are already breaking the law."[1]

GROWING RAGE

In order to fully understand the events of April 20, 1999, one must understand the social hierarchy at Columbine High School. Many of the students at this high school, including Klebold and Harris, came from financially secure homes, but none of the interviews I have reviewed implied in any way that the high school social structure was based on socioeconomic status. Many of the people interviewed after the tragedy at Columbine argued that the athletes and the athletic program were at the top of the social order.

Teachers, parents, and school administrators allegedly maintained a bias in favor of athletes at Columbine, giving them special privileges. Numerous stories have been told of the privileges that the athletes, called "jocks," were allowed. For example, one athlete was reportedly allowed to park his $100,000 Hummer all day in a fifteen-minute parking space. Other athletes were accused of bullying and sexually harassing students and were allegedly left undisciplined or minimally disciplined. In one case, a female student pressed charges against an athlete for sexual harassment, and an administrator from Columbine tried to talk the mother out of the charges because it would "ruin [the athlete's] possibilities of playing on the football team."[2] Other students said that teachers gave privileges to athletes and yet were harsh in their approach to other students, especially the members of Harris and Klebold's group. Evidence of the offense that other students took to the athletes was displayed in bathroom graffiti that read, "Columbine will explode one day. Kill all athletes. All jocks must die."[3]

Both parents and students perceived a school-wide indulgence of athletes. They believed that criminal convictions, physical and sexual abuse and harassment, and racial bullying were allowed to exist without consequence. One athlete was said to have harassed a Jewish student, reportedly singing songs about Hitler in the boy's presence. This athlete and another student assaulted the Jewish boy and threatened to set him on fire. Even though the offending student had a history of aggression, having been expelled from another school for fighting, the guidance office refused to act. The Jewish student's parent then approached the school board with the problem. The board called police and the boys were charged with harassment, but even though they were sentenced to probation, they were still allowed to play football.[4] Even the sheriff's department was aware of possible problems with the prestigious and seemingly untouchable athletic groups. Several months before the shooting, the sheriff's department warned the Jefferson County Board of Commissioners about growing violence in the Columbine area, including fighting by gang-like groups of athletes, but school officials believed that the reports exaggerated the problem.[5]

Klebold and Harris were "undesirables" because they did not participate in the athletic program in any way. They resented the privileges that they perceived the jocks enjoyed both from teachers and school administrators. As the jocks continued to pick upon Klebold, Harris, and other students with whom they associated, these teens solidified themselves into a recognizable clique. The athletes began calling the group the "Trenchcoat Mafia" because they dressed in trench coats and dark clothing, and they favored the "Goth" look. The athletes routinely wore white hats and shirts with sports insignias and, by their dark style of dress, the Trenchcoat Mafia became the visual antithesis of the jocks. Even though the jocks did not intend the label as a compliment, in an act of defiance and solidarity, the students of the "Trenchcoat Mafia" adopted the label for themselves, formalizing their unity. Living at the bottom of the social hierarchy did not *cause* Klebold and Harris to commit their atrocities, but it probably acted as a catalyst for their rage as well as providing confirmation that they would always be outsiders.

TROUBLE BREWING

Whether all members of this group participated or not, at the very least the behavior of some of the members of the Trenchcoat Mafia mimicked neo-Nazism. Harris and Klebold wore steel-toed combat boots with red laces, consistent with neo-Nazism and, along with their fellow trenchcoats, bragged about guns and hating blacks, student athletes, and Hispanics. They glorified Hitler and greeted each other with Nazi phrases such as "Sieg Heil!" and "Heil Hitler!"[6] Participation in a group like this is disturbing in itself, but some have said that the boys were even on the fringe of this extreme group.[7] Klebold told people that he did not like Harris's pseudo-Nazisms, but it did not stop his association with Harris or his own behavior, dressing in neo-Nazi fashion, nor did it prevent his participation in the trenchcoat group and the planning and execution of the attack.

About a year before the shooting, Harris and Klebold were arrested for breaking into a van from which they stole $400 worth of electronic equipment. They were assigned to a program in which the charges would be expunged from their records after ten months of counseling and community service. Both boys successfully completed the program and convinced their court officers and the judge that they were remorseful and repentant. Though they claimed to be remorseful, even as they stood before a judge, Harris's diary showed that they were silently planning their revenge on the Columbine students. The day of the shooting, when Klebold and Harris entered the library, they told all jocks to stand up and said, "anyone with a white hat or shirt with a sports emblem on it is dead."[8]

The Web Site and Indications of Problems

One of the most overt signs of the boys' violent perspective was evident on the web site that Harris maintained on the Internet. The site has long since been removed by America Online, but reports have indicated that the site contained both general and specific threats. Harris claimed to have made and detonated bombs with a coconspirator he identified as "VoDKa," a nickname associated with Klebold.[9] The site also provided instructions for bomb building and said that pipe bombs were "the easiest and deadliest way to kill a group of people. You can use screws, BBs, nails of all kinds."[10] On the site, Harris reportedly said he wanted to "kill everyone in Denver."[11] "I will rig up explosives all over town," he said. "I don't care if I live or die."[12] Harris, claiming to hate Jews and blacks, expressed his rage in the text of the web site. "LIARS!!! OH GAWWWWWWWD I HATE LIARS," he proclaimed.[13] "Well, all you people out there can just die. You all better hide in your houses, because I'm coming for everyone soon, and I will be armed to the teeth, and I will shoot to kill, and I will kill everything," he warned.[14]

At least one student was specifically mentioned on the web site. Brooks Brown, a classmate of the boys, had crossed paths with Harris in the year prior to the shooting. Harris had broken the windshield of Brown's car by throwing a chunk of ice at it. When confronted, Harris said it was an accident, but Brown's mother believed neither his explanation of the episode nor his apology. The Browns later discovered Harris's web site. I'll "blow up and shoot everything I can," it said. "Feel no remorse, no sense of shame. . . . I don't care if I live or die in a shootout, all I want to do is kill and injure as many of you [expletive] as I can, especially a few people. Like Brooks Brown."[15] This specific threat, in conjunction with and in the context of the vile tone of the rest of the web site, frightened the Browns. They took the threat seriously, searched their property for bombs, and then copied pages from the site and took them to the sheriff's department. Unfortunately, the sheriff's office said there was little they could do. Brown's parents warned neighbors to watch out for Harris and Klebold.[16] They also filed a complaint with America Online, the web site service provider, but their concerns were ignored. Parents of other students were also concerned about Harris and Klebold. The father of one student, Isaiah Shoels, had complained to authorities about the two boys, saying that he thought they were dangerous racists.[17]

Their pattern of aggressive behavior was widespread and clearly visible even beyond the web site. The boys watched the violent movie *Natural Born Killers* over and over again.[18] Throughout this film the main characters senselessly slaughtered helpless people. The boys engaged in violent computer games like *Doom* and *Quake*, among the most graphic and violent computer games on the market, in which players can set the level of gore they desire. The boys liked "industrial music," a style that glorifies antiauthoritarian behavior.[19] The summer before the shooting, the boys allegedly waved a pistol at a classmate with whom they were angry.[20] Even Harris's parents recognized problems in his behavior and, after they sought help for him, he was prescribed the antidepressant Luvox. According to a videotaped message that the boys left for police, Harris deliberately discontinued taking this medication in order to allow his rage to grow.

Classmates were aware of troubling signs in the boys' behavior. One classmate said Klebold "didn't behave very well in class, was disrespectful to the teacher, and he would never listen to anybody." Others said he sometimes lost his temper.[21] Another student said in creative writing class, "their poems were always about plants dying and the sun burning out. Whenever I heard them, I would just plug my ears because I can't stand stuff like that."[22] Another student said, "They always wrote about how killing people was good. They had sick minds."[23]

The boys' violent thoughts were evident to teachers and to a counselor at the school. They produced essays for an English class that were of such a violent nature that the teacher talked to their parents. In one essay, Harris portrayed himself as "a shotgun shell."[24] A school counselor became involved with one of the boys over this writing project but discounted its significance after talking to the boy's father. The boys produced videos of a violent nature as well. One of these videos was presented in class and showed Harris and Klebold with toy guns shooting helpless classmates in the halls of the school. A friend of the boys said that the two had produced other videos on the same theme. In summary, the boys were described by others as anti-everything, obsessed with death, despising God, and impossible not to notice.[25] Yet the most significant symptoms of their troubled minds were ignored, discounted, or completely missed by many of the people that had the opportunity to observe and interact with these boys.

Preparations

The preparation for the attack was incredibly detailed. The boys purchased weapons, constructed various kinds of explosive devices, and gathered information on school schedules so that they would know where students would be gathered and when. Harris's diary, found after the assault on Columbine, showed that he and Klebold had planned their attack for nearly a year. The diary described the plans for the shooting and included maps, cafeteria schedules, and details of which rooms would be most crowded at various times. The explosives the boys would use in the attack were made from just $200 worth of materials easily available from hardware and sporting goods stores, and police said the bombs they constructed could have been built in an afternoon.

Even more chilling than the diary were five videotapes that were discovered after the killings. In these videotapes, filmed with a home video camera at Klebold's home, the boys portrayed themselves as outlaws, sipping whiskey, toting guns, and practicing drawing their weapons from beneath trench coats. In these tapes, the boys claimed that their plan was "the real McCoy," not like those of the amateurs in other school shootings. They said on tape that they hoped to "kill 250 of you." In reference to the video game, Klebold says, "It's going to be like [expletive] *Doom*. Tick, tick, tick, tick. . . . Ha!" and "Directors will be fighting over this story."[26] Klebold said on tape that the moment of the attack would be the most "nerve-wracking of my life, after the bombs are set and we're waiting to charge through the school. Seconds will be like hours. I can't wait."[27]

In January 1999, Harris and Klebold purchased a TEC-9 assault pistol from an acquaintance for $500. Robyn Anderson, Klebold's 18-year-old girlfriend, would purchase the other three long guns—two shotguns and a rifle—that the boys would carry into the high school in April. The barrel of one of the shotguns was sawn off and left lying on top of Harris's dresser in his bedroom as were bomb-making materials. The week before the shooting, neighbors said they heard breaking glass and other noises from Harris's garage. They assumed the boys were doing something for a class project. Instead, the boys were probably preparing the shrapnel for their explosive devices. Pipe bombs and devices utilizing propane cylinders were also constructed. It was reported that Harris had a key to the school because he was a member of the audio-visual program.[28] However, it is unknown if the boys used this key to enter the school prior to the shooting. The boys had computer modeled their crime by customizing the game *Doom* to make the shooters fight people that could not fight back.[29] It is amazing to me that any two adolescents could have kept such detailed plans secret for such a long time.

The boys were nearly caught at one point when a gun shop clerk called their home. The boys had ordered clips for their weapons. When the clerk called the Harris household, Harris's father answered the phone. When Mr. Harris was informed that his clips were in, he told the clerk that he had not ordered any. However, he did not investigate any further. Harris commented on this incident in the videotapes he left for police, saying that they would have been caught if his father had checked into it.

By April 1999, Harris's life was a succession of failures. The marines had rejected him because of his psychotropic medication, and no college had accepted him. While Dylan Klebold took his girlfriend, Robyn Anderson, to the prom three days before the attack, Harris had been turned down by his prospective date for the prom. The apparent leader in the attack, Harris had his submissive follower behind him, his plans in order and weapons in place, he had practiced his attack through a computer game, and his rage was ripe for the attack. On the morning of the attack, the boys filmed their last videotape. Harris closed the tape saying, "That's it. Sorry. Goodbye."[30]

THE DAY OF THE SHOOTING

April 20, 1999, would have been Hilter's 110th birthday, perfect symbolism for the neo-Nazi wannabes. Klebold began the day bowling with friends, wearing a shirt that labeled him "Serial Killer." By 11:10 A.M., he and Harris had arrived in the parking lot of the Columbine school wearing fatigues and ankle-length black trench coats. They were loaded down with pipe bombs, other explosive devices, ammunition, and four firearms—the TEC-9 assault pistol, two shotguns, and a rifle. As Harris pulled a duffel bag from his trunk he spoke to Brooks Brown, the boy he had previously threatened on his web site. The two had settled their differences and become friends. Brown told Harris he had missed a philosophy test that morning. "Doesn't matter anymore," Harris said. "Brooks, I like you. Now get out of here. Go home."[31] Some have questioned Harris's motive for letting Brown go. He may have allowed Brown to leave because they were friends, but others have speculated that killing Brown in the parking lot might have alerted students in the cafeteria to the attack, allowing many of them to escape.

The boys carried the duffel bags filled with explosives into the cafeteria and then returned to their car. There, they loaded themselves with weapons and ammunition and donned their trench coats. Across the parking lot, Klebold's girlfriend, Robyn Anderson, was in her car. When the shooting started, she crouched down in the front seat and remained there throughout the episode.

Their original plan involved three stages of explosives. "Judgment Day," as they called it, would begin at 11:17 A.M. with an explosion several miles away. After police were drawn to that location, a second device would explode in the cafeteria, forcing the students into the parking lot where Klebold and Harris would shoot them. Finally, a third set of devices would explode after the shooting; these were intended to kill rescue workers. This elaborate plan failed from the beginning. When the boys realized their bombs were not exploding, they improvised.

Pandemonium

At the same time that Brown and Harris were talking in the parking lot, about forty-five students had gathered in the library, on the second floor of the school directly above the cafeteria. The end of the semester was looming and research papers were due. Isaiah Shoels, Patrick Ireland, and Cassie Bernall were among the many students who had chosen the library as the place to study and read during the lunch period. Within hours, their sanctuary would become a morgue.

Outside, some students resting at a hillside picnic area not far from the cafeteria saw Harris and Klebold in the parking lot. One of the two boys removed his coat, revealing devices that looked to some like hand grenades. Detonating a string of firecrackers, the boys approached 17-year-old Rachel Scott and shot her in the leg. As she lay bleeding, the gunman asked her if she believed in God. When she replied, "yes," he said, "Then go be with him now."[32] She was then shot in the temple, the first to die at Columbine. Quickly the two boys moved toward the cafeteria where they came upon 15-year-old Danny Rohrbough. He was shot in the back and died in a pool of blood within a few feet of the cafeteria where his body lay for the next twenty-four hours.

At first, the students at the picnic area near the parking lot thought that Klebold and Harris were filming a video, as they were accustomed to do. They realized this was not the case when one of the boys pointed a weapon in their direction. As they scattered, one boy was shot in the knee and another in the chest. As this was happening, a sheriff's deputy received a distress call from a school employee saying a girl had been wounded. When he responded to the scene outside the cafeteria, he exchanged shots with Harris and then called for assistance.

One of the boys lobbed an explosive device into the parking lot before entering the cafeteria where hundreds of students had gathered to take advantage of "free cookie" day. Students flocked to the window when they heard the gunshots outside and then they saw an explosion in the parking lot. Some of the students realized something was wrong and began to seek cover, but most of them were not fully aware of what was taking place. As the gunmen entered the cafeteria, surveillance video showed them on one knee firing into the crowd of students and throwing explosives. Even as this was happening, a few students still thought it was a prank, but as a janitor yelled at them to get down, they dropped their books and other possessions and scattered in panic. As the gunmen detonated explosive devices and fired into the crowd, one student cowered under a table in the cafeteria. One of the gunmen was standing so near her that the ejected shells from his weapon were falling on her back, but she was not injured. Almost immediately after the shooting began, calls began to flood into 911 operators. Students with cellular phones and others using school phones called police, parents, bosses, and relatives begging for help.

Even though police arrived quickly, it was not clear who the shooters were or how many perpetrators were in the building. The police on the scene were not prepared with the proper equipment to storm the building, they did not want to raid the building and mistakenly shoot students, and they did not want to allow the gunmen to escape among the fleeing victims. They decided to take up positions outside the building and organize a plan for containment and assault. As they secured the outer perimeter of the building, the police began to discover explosive devices around the school, a fact that would complicate their rescue attempts. By 11:30, approximately twenty minutes after the first call, SWAT personnel were on the scene.

Students fled the dining area and sought refuge in various places, trying to make sense out of what was happening. One student said he saw a boy with a shotgun. "Finally, I started figuring out these guys shot to kill for no reason. . . . They wanted to shoot to have fun. They're sick people."[33] Some students escaped the building while others ran toward the library believing they would be safe there. A few students found a hiding place in a storage room in the kitchen. Barricading the door with anything they could find, they called police. During the conversation, the policeman on the phone could hear the gunman trying to get into the storage room. The policeman instructed the callers to be ready to attack the shooters if they got in.[34] The gunmen, either frustrated or bored with their attempt to enter the storage room, went on to another area leaving these students uninjured.

As parents began to arrive on the school grounds, police instructed them to go to nearby Leawood Elementary School and wait for their children there. By noon, only minutes after the shooting began, some of the wounded were already being taken to area hospitals, but inside Columbine School, the carnage had only just begun.

Dave Sanders, a business teacher and girls' athletics coach, was in the teachers' lounge when he heard the commotion. He ran to the cafeteria. Helping students there as they tried to escape the gunfire, he then moved to the second floor of the building, attempting to herd students to safety. Looking out into the hallway from a classroom, a student said that he saw Sanders running down the hall then suddenly he was shot twice from behind, bullets destroying his chest. Mortally wounded, Sanders stumbled into a classroom and collapsed. Blocking the door to prevent the gunmen from entering, the students in the room began to treat the injured teacher using their shirts as pillows and bandages. "I can't breathe. I've got to go," he told them.

In an attempt to keep him conscious and to divert his attention from his injuries, they removed pictures of his daughters from his wallet and asked him to talk about them. Other students in the room wrote out "HELP, BLEEDING TO DEATH" on a board and placed it in front of the window.[35] In a bathroom off one hallway, two girls climbed on top of the toilets so their feet would not show, while in the hallway just outside the door, they heard one gunman yell, "I'm guarding the stairs."[36]

Two male students, who had also sought refuge in a bathroom, decided they should try to escape. They knocked a hole in the ceiling and climbed along a ventilation shaft. The shaft gave way and they fell into the teachers' lounge.[37] Uninjured by the fall, they ran out of the building. Other students hiding in closets and classrooms could hear the macabre laughter of the gunmen as they heckled fleeing students, saying, "Oh, you f——ing nerd. Tonight's the night you die."[38] "They were just shooting. They didn't care who they shot at. They just kept shooting," said one student who escaped.[39] Outside, parents and media began to gather as word of the attack spread throughout the community. At a nearby public library, officers had established a command center. An off-duty police captain and SWAT team member whose son was a student at the school led a team of officers to the front of the building. When they approached the main entrance, they could see one of the gunmen, but they did not enter the building, fearing the boys had laid a trap for them.[40] Confusion among law enforcement personnel mounted as hundreds of officers from city, county, state, and federal agencies arrived on the scene. They were still uncertain how many perpetrators there were and who they were, and some law enforcement officers had heard that the gunmen had changed clothing in an effort to disguise themselves and slip out of the building. SWAT team members were aware of explosive devices in the building so they were forced to carefully check for explosives as they proceeded inside. This slowed their progress.

Students had locked themselves in classrooms. Several students relayed accounts of the gunmen trying to force their way into their locked and barricaded hiding places. Other students who were stranded in the hallways futilely attempted to enter locked classrooms as they tried to find a place to hide. Whether students who heard someone trying to enter rooms were hearing the shooters or actually hearing desperate students trying to hide is unknown, but in many cases it was clearly Harris and Klebold who were just outside the doors. One student said, "They were so close. They shot the window of the classroom next door. They tried to get into our classroom. They were playing with the handle and then went on. We could hear people pleading for their lives."[41]

A 38-year-old science teacher managed to hide about fifty children in his classroom. As they lay on the floor in his room, a bullet came through the door and embedded itself in the wall. Next door was his wife, who also taught science. In her room she attempted to calm the twenty-five students who sought refuge with her by giving them paper and having them write letters. Yet another science teacher barricaded students inside his classroom and they hid in the darkened room waiting to be rescued. Students trapped throughout the building watched live news coverage of the event on TV monitors and could see law enforcement officers encamped outside as well as hordes of parents who had rushed to the scene.

As the attack continued, police determined the probable identities of the shooters. They sent officers to the Klebold home and forced its occupants to leave. Dylan's parents were still not fully aware of the role their son was playing in the drama unfolding at the high school. As they waited outside their home, they were informed of their son's involvement by a friend who had heard a news report.[42] Around this time, the Klebolds' lawyer called police at the high school and offered Mr. Klebold's assistance in negotiating with Dylan, but police declined the offer, saying there was nothing the father could do.

The father of the young Jewish boy that athletes at the school had tormented heard about the shootings while in his car. Using his car phone he called the school. The answering machine in the office picked up his call and recorded him as he screamed, "I knew something like this in this school could happen."[43]

The Choir Room

Across the hall from the science rooms was the choir room. According to one witness, as the shooting began most of the male students fled, leaving mostly female students behind. About sixty of these students, without a teacher or administrator present, hid in a small room at the back of the choir room, blocking the door with furniture. They had just finished barricading the door when the gunmen began shooting through the doors of the choir room.[44] The students used a phone in the small room to call for help. As the siege continued, the air became thin and the students had difficulty breathing. While they were hiding, the telephone rang. Answering the phone, they found that the caller was from a grade school, asking why the scheduled concert was being delayed.[45]

The Library

A 35-year-old mother and part-time art teacher, Patricia Nielson, was in a hallway not far from the library as the gunmen came up the stairs to the second floor. Standing near her was 16-year-old Brian Anderson. She heard the shooting and started toward the exits, but she was stopped by what she saw. "Just as we got to the second set of doors, [Harris] turned around and looked straight at us. . . . He smiled at me and pointed the gun."[46] The round broke a pane of glass in a nearby door and Anderson was hit in the chest. Rushing into the library, Nielson realized she, too, had been injured. Glass and fragments from the gunshot had damaged her shoulder. Her frightened pleas were recorded by 911 operators. Screams for the children to get down and gunshots were audible on the recorded 911 call. "Oh, God, oh, God . . . I've got kids under the table here," she said in her panic. "They're in here. They're killing kids. I need to go now."[47]

Student Makai Hall was working in the library when he saw Nielson come into the room yelling for the students to take cover. Minutes later, Harris and Klebold entered the library, shouting that they wanted revenge. As students hid under tables and desks, Klebold and Harris commanded all "jocks" to stand up. The two would spend their last minutes on earth in the library, terrorizing staff and students. It was in the library that twelve of the dead were found, including the gunmen. In an attempt to conceal their identity as athletes, several students were said to have removed their shirts and caps.

Guns blazing, Harris and Klebold began shooting students with abandon. Makai Hall was shot in the knee by a shotgun blast. As he lay injured on the floor with multiple fragment wounds to his leg, one of the gunmen threw an explosive device in his direction. Disregarding his injury, Hall grabbed the device and threw it away from the area where he and other students were lying.[48]

Mrs. Nielson had found a hiding place under a desk. Unable to see anything, she could hear Harris and Klebold as they tormented and killed the helpless students. "Look at that head blow up. I didn't know brains could fly," one cruel gunman boasted.[49] At one point bullets came through the desk where she was hiding, but she was not hit. In a back room off the library, two library workers took refuge. The gunmen overlooked this hiding place and the two workers were not harmed.

One of the gunmen put his gun to Bree Pasquale's head but he did not pull the trigger. "He put a gun in my face and said, 'I'm doing this because people made fun of me last year.' "[50] The boys went through the room asking people why they should be allowed to live. "We've waited to do this a long time," "Oh, I know you—you can go," and "We're out of ammo . . . gotta reload" were among their comments while they terrorized students in the library, as if they were playing some vulgar video game.[51]

One of the shooters looked under a desk and found 17-year-old Kacey Ruegsegger cowering there. He said "Peek-a-boo" and shot her at nearly point-blank range. The gunman put a pistol to the head of another student, but then he noticed Isaiah Shoels, a black student. "Hey, I think we got a n_____ here," he said.[52] "I hate n_____," he said as he turned his gun toward Shoels and shot him once in the head and then twice in the face.[53] Laughing at his destruction, he said, "Hey, I always wondered what a n_____ brains looked like."[54] Shoels, who as a baby had survived a heart defect, died on the spot. Students were shot if they made any sounds. One injured girl begged a gunman for her life, but he simply shot her again.[55] The gunmen sauntered throughout the library wearing ammo belts, shooting students at their leisure.[56] "Who's next? Who's ready to die?" they asked. Some students covering the bodies of their classmates, friends, or siblings escaped injury while others were executed.

One athlete in the library removed his white cap and hid it, but he was shot anyway. Initially, he pretended to be dead, but after saying a prayer, he decided that God wanted him to run. Helping other students as he ran, he found his way outside, where he informed police what the shooters looked like and where they were.[57]

Cassie Bernall was praying when the gunmen confronted her. Just two years before, she had been a rebellious teenager, heavily involved in witchcraft and drugs, running with the wrong crowd and on the verge of suicide. Yet after a conversion experience at summer camp, she became a committed Christian. Known to other students as a religious girl, she had asked her parents to remove her from a Christian school because she believed she could make a difference among the students of Columbine. Cassie looked the gunman in the face and told him, "There is a God and you need to follow along God's path."[58] He asked her, "Do you believe in God?" When she said, "Yes," he said, "There is no god," and shot her once in the head.[59]

One wounded student, 16-year-old Evan Todd, seized an opportunity to escape and fled the building. Once outside, he told police what he knew. Having some experience with guns, he described the weapons and told the police where the gunmen were. For some reason, however, the police told him to calm down and "take his frustrations elsewhere."[60]

At some point during the rampage in the library, multiple gunshot wounds to the head and foot seriously wounded Patrick Ireland. Sensing an opportunity, he stumbled toward a broken window, dragging his useless leg and arm, and cleared the broken glass from the window frame. Outside, SWAT members saw him and realized he was planning to jump to the ground two stories below. Rushing to the window, they caught him as he helplessly dropped into their waiting arms. Later, when asked what his plan was, he said he went out the window because it was the shortest way out and he was confident someone would catch him.[61]

The two killers left the library around 11:30, about the time the SWAT teams arrived. The killers made their way to the cafeteria where surveillance videos show them drinking from the cups left on the tables by students. About thirty minutes later, they returned to the library. By this time, nearly all of the students and teachers had escaped. Harris shot himself in the head as Klebold lit one last explosive device. As the fuse burned, Klebold, too, took his own life. However, the smoke from the device set off the sprinkler system and extinguished the bomb. Their last bomb failed just as their first had.

The Siege Draws to a Close

By 2:30 P.M., the first large group of students were freed from classrooms and other hiding places by law enforcement officers while the gunmen were still thought to be holding the second floor. The students were taken to a holding area where they were searched, questioned, treated for their injuries, and debriefed. Then they were sent to Leawood Elementary School where some of their parents were waiting. Back inside the high school, the library quieted. Even when students began running from the room, Mrs. Nielson was too afraid to leave. She moved from her hiding place under the bullet-riddled desk to a cupboard, where she tried to find a pencil to write a good-bye note to her family.[62] SWAT members continued their progress through the building, freeing terrified students. The fire alarms were so loud that rescue personnel said they could not even hear the gun-shots. In some cases, students would not leave until school staff assured them that the SWAT team members were not the gunmen. Yet law enforcement was still unsure how many shooters there were and did not want them to escape among the crowd of students being rescued. Therefore, as rescuers assisted students from the building, they told the students, "If any of you take your hands away from your head, we're going to pull you away immediately. Get up and put your hands on your head. Run! Run!"[63] The air was filled with the smell of gunpowder and smoke as the students fled the building, stepping over the bodies of fellow students as they went. Sprinklers that had gone off at the beginning of the shooting spree because of the explosions had left water six inches deep throughout the building. SWAT teams liberated students in the classroom where students were attending to Dave Sanders's injuries in a desperate attempt to save his life. They did not want to leave him, but they were assured that paramedics were on their way and they were forced to leave him there.

When they finally reached the library at 3:30 P.M., nearly four hours after the attack began, law enforcement officers found Harris and Klebold dead amid a "sea of explosive devices." According to the coroner, one of the boys had shot himself in the mouth and the other one in the side of the head. Unfortunately, the police were not fin-ished yet. The boys had apparently wired their bodies with explo-sives.[64] Other explosive devices were found throughout the building, including a duffel bag found in the kitchen containing a propane tank, gasoline can, nails, BBs, and glass.[65] Authorities declared the school safe by 4:30 P.M., but around 6:30 P.M. they found an explosive device in the parking lot. The scene was cordoned off and the bodies remained where they had fallen until the next day.

Paramedics did finally reach the mortally wounded Sanders, but he died just minutes after they arrived. Outside on a basketball court, a sign was erected on the backboard saying, "Prayer corner: Please join us." Volunteers assisted the wounded on the school lawn as parents searched among the throng of students leaving the building, their hands on top of their heads, hoping to catch a glimpse of their own children. Bruce Beck watched for his stepdaughter, Lauren Townsend, aged 18, while her mother waited by the telephone. Sadly, Lauren was one of the casualties in the library. Parents who had convened at nearby Leawood Elementary School were reunited with their children. At 10:30 P.M., the last of Harris and Klebold's bombs exploded in the building, but no one was hurt.

THE AFTERMATH

The nation was paralyzed by the events of April 20, 1999. As the media broadcast live pictures, people from coast to coast watched the tragedy unfolding at Columbine. Forever etched in our minds are the images of law enforcement officers herding children from the Columbine school with their hands on top of their heads as panicked parents strained their necks in hopes of seeing their children. As investigators swept through the war-torn building, students were found dead and injured beneath desks and tables while others, physically unharmed, were found hiding in a walk-in freezer, in closets, and in classrooms. In the parking lot at Columbine High School, Rachel Scott's car became a shrine for several days. Flowers, stuffed animals, and cards decorated the automobile as a memorial to her and to the other victims of the shooting. For months, headlines in newspapers across the country updated readers on the investigation, the progress of the injured, and new arrests. The image of Patrick Ireland dangling from the library window, helplessly falling into the arms of waiting SWAT team members, will rank among the most indelible photographs of the century.

The carnage was so widespread that, initially, investigators believed the boys must have had help. The numerous explosive devices placed in the parking lot and the building added credibility to this theory. Also fueling the theory of coconspirators was a gun dealer's claim that Klebold and Harris had tried to buy guns from him along with three other teens. Videotaped records from the store, however, showed that this was not the case. During the attack, a "third" gunman had been reported, but it was later concluded that one of the boys had shed his coat and the "third" gunman was simply a second description of the same boy. Three other boys were also detained as possible suspects, but they were quickly eliminated as conspirators. In the subsequent weeks, over eighty investigators followed 4,000 leads, interviewed 8,000 individuals, and cataloged thousands of pieces of evidence. Unbelievably, all the ammunition rounds were accounted for. In the end, the investigators unanimously concluded that the two boys had acted alone. By themselves, these boys inflicted damage to 23,000 square feet of the building's carpet, walls, ceilings, and windows, using bombs, water, and bullets. An estimated 900 to 1,000 bullet and shrapnel holes pockmarked the building. The investigation of the crime scene and repairs to the school would take months. The public library that served as a command post throughout the episode was reopened to the public on May 8, but Columbine students completed the remaining weeks of their semester at a sister high school. Columbine High School was renovated and reopened in time for fall classes to begin. The school system claimed that the cost of replacing the bloodstained carpeting and repairing the damaged walls, broken windows, and other damage to the building would exceed $8 million by the fall of 1999.

The arrests that were made in conjunction with this event left the parents and loved ones of the victims feeling hollow. The person who supplied the TEC-9 was arrested for unlawfully providing or permitting a juvenile to possess a handgun and for illegal possession of an assault weapon, and a second man was arrested on similar charges.[66] The first man was sentenced to six years in jail. Multiple lawsuits were filed within six months of the shooting. Victims' families sued the Harris and Klebold families, as well as the sheriff's department, the school district, gun makers, and others. Even Klebold's family sued the sheriff's department, saying they were not appropriately informed about Harris's violent tendencies. One report said that "just about everyone [was] a potential defendant.[67]

Patrick Ireland is recovering his speech, but he is paralyzed on the right side of his body and confined to a wheelchair. Rachel Scott and Daniel Rohrbough, who were shot on the sidewalk outside the cafeteria, died in the attack. Teacher Dave Sanders was also killed, shot as he helped students through the hallways. All the other deceased victims, Cassie Bernall, Isaiah Shoels, Lauren Townsend, Steven Curnow, Corey DePooter, Kelly Fleming, Matthew Kechter, Daniel Mauser, John Tomlin, and Kyle Velasquez, were killed in the library. Kacey Ruegsegger, the girl to whom the cruel gunman had said "Peek-a-boo" before shooting her, survived. Several of the defenseless students and teachers were shot in the back.

One injured student, Anne Marie Hochhalter, was shot in the chest and paralyzed. In the months since she was shot, she has regained some movement in her legs. Tragically, six months after the April shooting, Anne Marie's mother walked into a pawnshop and asked to see a .38 caliber revolver. As the clerk was processing paperwork for the purchase, Carla June Hochhalter, aged 48, loaded the weapon with ammunition she had apparently brought with her, fired a round into the wall, and then in front of nearly a dozen witnesses, fired a round into her head. She died as a result. The reach of Harris and Klebold's violence extended even six months beyond their deaths.

Even though the boys indicated they were angry with "jocks," only six of the students killed were athletes and none of them were among the crowd who had tormented the boys and their group. Toxicology reports indicated that neither Harris nor Klebold had drugs or alcohol in their systems at the time of their deaths. As for the families of the gunmen, a spokesperson for the Klebold family said, "This is a conscientious, normal family that's done everything right. This came as a bolt out of the blue."[68]

CONCLUDING REMARKS

The answers to the questions I posed at the beginning of the chapter are not very satisfying. Could someone have known? I believe so. I address this issue in more detail in Chapter 10. Should someone have known? Perhaps, but no single individual had access to all aspects of these boys' lives. Without that information, these prolific and accomplished liars were able to erect a façade that made it difficult to get beyond the surface of their lives. One might suppose that at least their parents should have known, but as Sheriff Stone told a *Time* magazine reporter, "You want to go after them [the parents]. How could they not know? Then you realize they are no different from the rest of us."[69]

Why did these boys feel the need to cause such devastation? Athletes, unfair school administrators and teachers, Hitler, or society did not drive them to this act. Moving from place to place with his military family did not cause Harris to kill. Neither do I believe Harris's videotaped claim that his family (except for his parents) had treated him like the "runt of the litter" and that people were making fun of him had driven him to his state of fury. I do not believe Klebold, who said that the two of them would have settled their differences "with their fists," but they knew they would be suspended.[70] This ridiculous claim holds no credibility. It supposes that they would rather kill innocent people and die themselves than be suspended from school. None of these excuses caused their actions that April day in 1999.

Sadly, the answer may simply be that they had a hedonistic, perverse desire to be famous. Each of the boys wanted to be somebody important. In their videotapes, they claimed that the boys in Jonesboro, Arkansas (whom they misidentify as being from Kentucky), were just seeking acceptance from others. I believe that Klebold and Harris sought the same thing. Despite their claim of originality, they used a strategy similar to that of the boys in Jonesboro, originally planning to flush the students from the building with a bomb and then shoot at them as they flooded the parking lot. Their purpose was tragically simple. It reminds me of a scene from the James Bond film *GoldenEye*. As the movie nears its conclusion, the villain, who will make billions of dollars if his plan of worldwide destruction succeeds, and Bond are face to face. Bond tells the villain that without the glitter and the elaborate plans, it all boils down to the fact that he is nothing more than a common thief. Klebold and Harris did not feel a part of society and decided that they would gain importance at the expense of others. In spite of all their elaborate planning, their delusions of grandeur, their arrogant claims of control, and their dime-store psychoanalytic nonsense blaming everyone but themselves, it all boils down to two ruthless boys throwing a gigantic temper tantrum to get attention. It would be easier to cope with this tragedy if the answers were more profound. Unfortunately, they are not. The world in which the two boys lived during the year preceding the shooting was very small. It did not include family, friends, or school. The circle of their lives included only each other and their plot of destruction. They stepped beyond this circle only when necessary, pretending to be functional at school, in court, at work, and at home, but rushing back into their circle of hate and destruction at every opportunity. They purposefully fueled their hate and deliberately sought ways to make it grow. Fortunately, however, their ineptitude in executing their plan resulted in far fewer deaths than they had planned.

Both boys tried to assure their parents, through their vile and hate-filled videotapes, that they were not to blame for the massacre. Their feeble apologies to their parents, however, could not overshadow their amazingly cruel and heartless premeditation. They said they hoped to create nightmares and flashbacks that haunted their victims and "drove them insane." While nightmares may not have driven survivors "insane," haunting the survivors may be the only part of their plan that they actually accomplished.

Our nation was stunned by the cruelty and carnage that was perpetrated by these two young men. I cannot help but empathize with my minority brothers and sisters as newscasters said what a tragedy it was that this should happen in such an affluent area. Even though I know this was not the intent of these reports, the implication is that this tragedy would have been more acceptable if it had occurred in a less affluent area. The sad truth of the killings at Columbine, West Paducah, Jonesboro, Pearl, and Springfield is that these are not isolated events. Children die every week at schools around our country. Three things set events like Columbine and Jonesboro apart from these other shootings. First, episodes like Columbine seem to be completely random. Innocent children have died or been wounded in these incidents simply because they are in the wrong place at the wrong time. Other shootings at high schools around the country involve drug deals, rival gang activity, or domestic issues that have a clearer motive. Many people are not surprised if young men kill each other over drugs, stolen property, or escalated disagreements, things that happen with some regularity both on and off school property. Second, the attacks are perceived to have come with little warning, although as I have shown, this perception is not supported by the facts. Third, and perhaps most tragic, some people in our nation are bigoted enough to suppose that the killing of black, Asian, or Hispanic children is not as significant as the killing of white children.

Columbine is not the last school to see this type of tragedy. Unfortunately, it has happened again in Conyers, Georgia, where T. J. Solomon opened fire on a crowded commons area of Heritage High School, injuring six students, but his actions were far from the level of destruction at Columbine. In the winter of 1999, a 13-year-old Oklahoma student allegedly fired fifteen rounds from a 9mm handgun at his classmates, wounding five of them. We can pray that we are finished with this type of tragedy, but as these two incidents show us, Columbine was not the last. Several events make me doubt that we have seen the end. First, although America Online quickly removed Harris's web site from their system, the damage was done. Even before the smoke had cleared from the hallways of the high school, perverted Internet users were glorifying the event. One America Online user even claimed to be Eric Harris, writing, "Shut up and shoot it. . . . quit whining, it's just a flesh wound. . . . Kill Em Aallll!!!!"[71] That behavior is bad enough, yet in October 1999, police in Colorado arrested a 17-year-old Columbine student, a friend of Harris and Klebold, for inciting destruction of life or property. Unbelievably, this student threatened to carry out another shooting at Columbine, telling a classmate that he wanted to "finish the job Eric Harris and Dylan Klebold had begun on April 20."[72] He pleaded guilty to threats and was ordered to participate in a juvenile diversion program for a year. Ironically, this was a similar court-ordered program to the one Klebold and Harris had been ordered to participate in after breaking into a van. There have been other threats, as well. In December, using an Internet chat-room, an 18-year-old man in Florida told a Columbine sophomore that he needed to finish the job at Columbine and warned her to stay away from school the next day. The man was arrested for this threat. Sadly, there apparently is no shortage of ill-minded potential perpetrators.

A suicide note was allegedly found, demonstrating the unending egocentric and hedonistic attitude that dominated the lifestyles of Eric Harris and Dylan Klebold. According to police, Harris allegedly said, "This is the way we wanted to go out."[73] The videotapes left for police to find made it obvious that the boys wanted to be seen as cult heroes.[74] They apparently felt the need to communicate their personal desires even after their deaths. Both the Harris and the Klebold families submitted public statements of apology for the devastation caused by their sons. Even after studying dozens and dozens of homicides, I have emotional difficulty dealing with the reality of Columbine. The amazing cruelty of these two boys makes my heart ache. We can only pray that this event was an anomaly and that parents and children across our nation will be spared any such event in the future. In summary, I must agree with one writer who said the boys "gave evil a face."[75]

NOTES

1. Heard while listening to local news coverage of the Columbine incident.

2. Lorraine Adams and Dale Russakoff, "Dissecting Columbine's cult of the athlete: in search for answers, community examines one source of killers' rage," *Washington Post* (Internet Edition), June 12, 1999, A01.

3. Nancy Gibbs, "The Littleton massacre," *Time* May 3, 1999, 29.

4. Adams and Russakoff, "Dissecting Columbine's cult of the athlete," A01.

5. Eric Pooley, "Portrait of a deadly bond," *Time*, May 10, 1999, 30.

6. "Portrait of school killers," *CNN On-Line, www.cnn.com/US/9904/29/BC-CRIME-SHOOTING-PORTRA.reut/index.html*, April 29, 1999.

7. "Columbine investigation turns to parents' role: police: 'trenchcoat mafia' members advised by lawyers," *CNN On-Line, www.cnn.com/US/9904/25/school.shooting.04/index.html*, April 25, 1999.

8. Adams and Russakoff, "Dissecting Columbine's cult of the athlete," A01.

9. Pooley, "Portrait of a deadly bond," 26.

10. Gibbs, "The Littleton massacre."

11. Patricia Chisholm, "Teens under siege," *Maclean's* (Internet Edition), May 3, 1999.

12. Gibbs, "The Littleton massacre."

13. Adams and Russakoff, "Dissecting Columbine's cult of the athlete," A01.

14. "Portrait of school killers."

15. Pooley, "Portrait of a deadly bond," 26.

16. T. Trent Gegax and Matt Bai, "Searching for answers," *Newsweek*, May 10, 1999, 33.

17. Matt Bai, Daniel Glick, Sherry Keene-Osborn, T. Trent Gegax, Lynette Clemetson, Devin Gordon, and Daniel Klaidman, "Anatomy of a massacre," *Newsweek*, May 3, 1999, 31.

18. Amy Dickinson, "Where were the parents?" *Time*, May 3, 1999, 40.

19. Chisholm, "Teens under siege."

20. Bai, Glick, Keene-Osborn, Gegax, Clemetson, Gordon, and Klaidman, "Anatomy of a massacre," 27.

21. Jim Hughes, "Descriptions vary of suspects," *Denver Post Online www.denverpost.com/news/shot0420d.htm*, April 21, 1999.

22. Pooley, "Portrait of a deadly bond," 30.

23. Angie Cannon, Betsy Streisand, and Dan McGraw, "Why? There were plenty of warnings, but no one stopped two twisted teens," *U.S. News and World Report*, May 3, 1999, 16.

24. James Brooke, "Teacher of Colorado gunmen alerted parents," *New York Times* (Late New York Edition), May 11, 1999, A14.

25. Cannon, Streisand, and McGraw, "Why? There were plenty of warnings," 16.

26. "Teen killers had message for parents," *Atlanta Journal/Constitution*, December 12, 1999, A11.

27. Ibid., A1.

28. Gibbs, "The Littleton massacre."

29. Pooley, "Portrait of a deadly bond," 32.

30. Nancy Gibbs and Timothy Roche, "The Columbine tapes," *Time*, December 20, 1999, 51.

31. Pooley, "Portrait of a deadly bond," 28.

32. David Van Biema, "A surge of teen spirit," *Time*, May 31, 1999, 58.

33. "Quotes from Columbine High School shootings," *CNN On-Line*, *www.cnn.com/US/9904/20/AM-SchoolShooting-Quotes.ap/index.html*, April 21, 1999.

34. Bai, Glick, Keene-Osborn, Gegax, Clemetson, Gordon, and Klaidman, "Anatomy of a massacre," 25.

35. Gibbs, "The Littleton massacre," 30.

36. Bai, Glick, Keene-Osborn, Gegax, Clemetson, Gordon, and Klaidman, "Anatomy of a massacre," 28.

37. Gibbs, "The Littleton massacre," 30.

38. Ibid.

39. "Two suspects among possible 18 dead in Colorado School rampage," *CNN On-Line*, *www.cnn.com/US/9904/21/school.shooting.01/index.html*, April 21, 1999.

40. Bai, Glick, Keene-Osborn, Gegax, Clemetson, Gordon, and Klaidman, "Anatomy of a massacre," 30.

41. "Bodies remain inside school as police check for bombs: 15 people, including gunmen, dead in Colorado massacre," *CNN On-Line*, *www.cnn.com/US/9904/21/school.shooting.03/index.html*, April 21, 1999.

42. Gegax and Bai, "Searching for answers," 33.

43. Adams and Russakoff, "Dissecting Columbine's cult of the athlete," A01.

44. Bill Hewitt, Vickie Bane, Ron Arias, Karen Bates, et al., "Sorry and outrage," *People Weekly* (Internet Edition), May 3, 1999.

45. Gibbs, "The Littleton massacre," 31.

46. "Art teacher talks for the first time about Columbine shooting," *CNN On-Line*, *www.cnn.com/US/9906/13/ColumbineSurvivor.ap/index.html*, June 13, 1999.

47. Mike Williams, "Terror resounds in frantic 911 calls: gunshots boom in background of phone conversations recorded during Littleton attack," *Atlanta Journal/Constitution*, April 24, 1999, A1.

48. "Wounded student: shooter 'an all-right guy,'" *CNN On-Line*, *www.cnn.com/US/9904/23/victim.released/index.html*, April 23, 1999.

49. "Art teacher talks for the first time about Columbine shooting."

50. Hewitt, Bane, Arias, Bates, et al. "Sorry and outrage."

51. Gibbs, "The Littleton massacre," 31.

52. Bai, Glick, Keene-Osborn, Gegax, Clemetson, Gordon, and Klaidman, "Anatomy of a massacre," 31.

53. "Bodies remain inside school as police check for bombs."

54. Bai, Glick, Keene-Osborn, Gegax, Clemetson, and Klaidman, "Anatomy of a massacre," 31.

55. "Bodies remain inside school as police check for bombs."

56. Matt Labash, "The power of Cassie Bernall: to evil, she made the perfect answer," *Reader's Digest*, August 1999, 53.

57. Gibbs, "The Littleton massacre," 20–36.

58. Ibid., 25.

59. Ibid.

60. "Columbine shooters documented their rage on home videos," *CNN On-Line*, *www.cnn.com/1999/US/12/12/columbine.tapes/index.html*, December 12, 1999.

61. "Columbine student rescued from window making 'incredible' recovery," *CNN On-Line*, *www.cnn.com/US/9905/07/school.shooting.02/index.
html*, May 7, 1999.

62. "Art teacher talks for the first time about Columbine shooting."

63. Gibbs, "The Littleton massacre," 32.

64. Hewitt, Bane, Arias, Bates, et al., "Sorry and outrage."

65. Gibbs, "The Littleton massacre."

66. "Colleague of Columbine shooters arrested," *CNN On-Line*, *www.cnn.com/US/9906/17/columbine.arrest/index.html*, June 18, 1999.

67. "Parents suing each other, school district over high school massacre," *CNN On-Line*, *www.cnn.com/US/9910/19/columbine.aftermath.ap/index.html*, October 19, 1999.

68. "Columbine investigation turns to parents' role."

69. Gibbs and Roche, "The Columbine tapes," 50.

70. Robert Weller, "Columbine tapes full of 'hate,' " *Atlanta Journal/Constitution*, December 14, 1999, A15.

71. Susan Greene, "Killers quickly gain internet cult status," *Denver Post Online*, *www.denverpost.com/news/shot0420bb.htm*, April 20, 1999.

72. "Columbine student charged after allegedly making threat to 'finish the job,' " *CNN On-Line*, *www.cnn.com/US/9910/21/columbine.threat.01/index.html*, October 21, 1999.

73. Bai, Glick, Keene-Osborn, Gegax, Clemetson, Gordon, and Klaidman, "Anatomy of a massacre," 31.

74. "Columbine gunmen made videotapes leading up to massacre," *CNN On-Line*, *www.cnn.com/US/9911/11/columbine.videos.ap/index.html*, November 11, 1999.

75. Nancy Gibbs, "Noon in the garden of good and evil: the tragedy at Columbine began as a crime story but is becoming a parable," *Time*, May 17, 1999, 54.

8

Assessment of Risk for Homicide

Assessment of the likelihood of violent behavior is perhaps one of the most elusive goals in mental health. When evaluating the likelihood of future violence for the courts and for the prison system, psychiatrists must use accepted standards. When they are considering the early release of a prisoner, parole boards want to know how likely the convict is to be violent. In clinical practice, therapists must assess the probability that their client might act violently toward another patient, a spouse, or even therapists themselves, to protect and/or warn all possible parties.

In my early clinical days, as I have already stated, I was convinced that there had to be some indicators that, when present, would indicate a client more likely to be violent and, when absent, would indicate a client less likely to be violent. This chapter is the result of several years of reviewing the literature, summarizing the research, applying my conclusions, and refining my theory on risk assessment variables.

PROBLEMS WITH PREDICTION AND ASSESSMENT

I rarely use the word "prediction." The term itself presents problems for the clinician. If I were to predict that a patient would act violently, the patient would, indeed, have to commit some violent act in order for me to be proven correct. My goal in assessing risk is to provide intervention so that the client will not, or cannot, commit the act that I believe to be imminent or likely. Therefore, if I use the term "prediction" and my choices for intervention are effective, I will always be wrong.

It is for this reason that I address this process as assessment of risk for violence rather than prediction for violent behavior. Everyone has the *potential* for nearly any behavior, but the likelihood of some behaviors is greater than the likelihood of others. Similarly, all of us are potentially violent, but most of us will never behave violently. Gavin de Becker has said that "the source of violence is in everyone; all that changes is our view of the justification."[1] When our level of risk for violence is low, clinical intervention is unnecessary. However, when the level of risk is very high, intervention is critical. The patient does not have to engage in violence to be classified as a high risk.

Consider this example. A psychologist has a patient that he believes is a potential threat to the patient's spouse and he *predicts* that the patient may attempt to harm the spouse. The psychologist uses his chosen therapeutic techniques to address the patient's issues. Therapy has the desired effect on the patient's decision-making and behavior and he never attacks his spouse. We can say that the prediction was wrong because the patient was predicted to act violently, but he did not. This is called a *false-positive*.

When assessing the level of risk in a potentially violent individual, I look for risk factors that increase or decrease the probability of violence. I then provide an indication of the person's level of risk on a low-to-high continuum. The purpose of risk assessment is to determine the need for intervention and to provide due warning to potential victims. When the assessed risk is high enough as determined by the evaluator, the clinician intervenes. With "prediction" no intervention is implied unless the patient is predicted to be violent. Assessment of risk provides a wider margin of safety than prediction because the clinician determines, according to both objective and subjective evaluation, when intervention is necessary.

The process of assessing risk is not without problems, however. Often the information I need is unavailable. The more I know about the person I am assessing, the more holistic my conclusions will be. However, some information about the person may be impossible for me to acquire or may be unavailable. Invaluable information may be inaccessible to me for legal or pragmatic reasons. For example, juvenile records could provide a great deal of information on an individual's coping skills and decision-making, but these records are usually sealed by the court.

Likewise, information from spouses, former spouses, coworkers, or others who know the individual can be of tremendous help as I try to understand a client and his way of thinking, but I may not have access to these sources. Even when it is theoretically possible to access sources, it may not be prudent. If the company for which I am doing an assessment is sued, this type of information might present problems during litigation. Lawyers could argue bias in information I received from acquaintances that may have led to a person's dismissal from a job, and this could compromise the entire case. For these reasons I am limited in the type of information I can acquire and use in the assessment process. In theory I would consider a wide variety of sources, but in practice I cannot.

Assessing risk also presents the possibility of self-fulfilling prophecies. A self-fulfilling prophecy occurs when an individual lives up to the expectations of another. This problem has existed in the educational system for years. A child is incorrectly identified as a slow learner and placed in the educational system based on that diagnosis. However, although the diagnosis was incorrect, the student lives down to the prophecy, thus fulfilling it. Likewise, an individual may be identified as a high risk, but the process of determining that the person might harm others may, in fact, provide him with the idea of doing so. Hence, the prophecy concerning violence is fulfilled.

In order to prevent self-fulfilling prophecies, I never imply to my client that I believe he or she is a high risk for violence and I certainly never provide him or her with any ideas. When interviewing an individual, I might reflect allusions to violent behavior that I have picked up in our conversation. I might say, "I've heard you imply you have considered acting aggressively. What do you think about that?" If the subject confirms my fears I would respond by asking him or her to elaborate. It would be unethical to lead a client by asking, "Have you ever thought of taking your gun to work and shooting your boss?" or any other such question that could provide ideas where none existed previously.

Keeping the above discussion in mind and acknowledging that the assessment process is not free from pitfalls, I believe that the process of assessing risk of violent behavior has integrity for both children and adults. Even though the process is not flawless it can provide us

Table 8.1
Hierarchy of Risk Variables for Violent Behavior

1. history of violent or aggressive behavior
2. subjective fear of the individual by others
3. threats of intent to do harm
4. social isolation (loner)
5. antisocial behavior
6. absent or weak social support system
7. lack of or weak social skills
8. substance abuse
9. clear feelings of being wronged by the target
10. poor self image
11. suicide attempts/ideation
12. fantasies of violence
13. job instability
14. severe situational stress
15. presence of aggressive models
16. specific victim
17. frequent divorce
18. loss of a job
19. poverty
20. available weapon
21. male
22. age 23–45

with information that may protect the health and welfare of our clients, coworkers, and others.

RISK FACTORS IN ADULTS AND CHILDREN

Currently, the checklist of risk factors in Table 8.1 contains a hierarchical list of twenty-two items. The more factors at the top of the list present in the individual, the higher the risk for violence. One must keep in mind, however, that even if every item on this list is present in an individual, it does not guarantee that the person will be violent. A critical differentiating factor in assessing risk is the coping skills of the person. In my experience, no perpetrator has presented all twenty-two items, but many have presented most of the top ten. Likewise, even if very few of these factors are present, that does not preclude the possibility that one will act violently. It only implies that the risk for such behavior is low. Of course, the context in which the subject exists must be considered in the assessment process.

In an in-depth review of twelve homicide cases (currently unpublished), my coauthors and I were able to clearly identify triggering mechanisms in ten of the twelve. It is our belief that if these perpetrators had been properly identified as high risks, and if the triggering mechanisms had been foreseen, these ten homicides could have been averted. We also found that in all twelve cases, the perpetrators presented at least one clear indication prior to the event of their intent to do harm. Furthermore, all twenty-two items were present in at least one of the twelve cases. Of even more importance was that nearly all the top ten items were present in all cases, lending credibility to the hierarchical nature of the list. The discussion that follows outlines and describes these twenty-two items.

History of Aggressive Behavior

One of the few things in regard to the assessment of risk for violence on which most psychologists and researchers agree is that a history of violent behavior is one of the best predictors of future violence. If the patient has exhibited a particular method of dealing with frustration and aggressive drives, there is no reason to suppose he or she will not select similar methods in the future. Therefore, a history of aggression is one of the most important risk factors in this list.

Originally, this item read "history of violent behavior," but I changed it to read "history of aggressive behavior." The reason for this change lies in the definition of the term "violent." As we have seen, what one person perceives as violent another may not. For example, Robert Helfer had clearly engaged in verbally aggressive and intimidating behavior toward a coworker. He had been heard yelling at his family by neighbors, and yet one acquaintance was surprised at his violent outburst on the day he shot his coworkers. Many of his behaviors could easily have been classified as violent or aggressive but at the time were not identified as such by the acquaintance. Describing someone as aggressive is broader and perhaps less threatening to the one reporting the behavior than describing someone as violent, yet in the process of assessment, both terms address the same process.

Aggressive behavior could include, but is not limited to, domestic violence, fighting, aggressive language, aggression against inanimate objects (punching walls, throwing dishes, etc.), tantrums, and deliberate intimidation.

Subjective Fear of the Individual by Others

In Gavin de Becker's book, *The Gift of Fear*, he develops an argument that as we have evolved, we have developed a gift of fear that warns us and protects us from harm. According to de Becker, we have the ability to perceive clues to threats to our safety that we do not always process in our conscious thoughts, even though we could. These clues produce our fear. Therefore, even when we cannot be sure why we are afraid, we can trust that our fear is justified. After researching dozens of homicides, I have become convinced that there is something instinctive in our assessment of others and de Becker is on the right track. In nearly every homicide case I have reviewed, before a perpetrator ever committed a murder, at least one person was afraid of him. Often many people were afraid of him. In some cases they kept their thoughts to themselves until after the homicide, but in other cases they openly discussed their concerns long before anything ever happened. Sometimes they could link their fears to specific behaviors. For example, Robert Helfer had deliberately intimidated one of his coworkers. She openly expressed her fear of the man because of his clearly intimidating behavior. In cases where people have kept their fears to themselves until after a murder occurred, they have made statements like "I always felt like something like this could happen, but I don't know why." In cases like these, the person's fear is subjective, but it is not inappropriate, as revealed by the perpetrator's actions.

For this reason, it is significant when people express fear of a person that I am assessing. Of course, I would never suppose that someone should be fired from a job or arrested due solely to another person's subjective fear, but I trust such fear as a risk factor. In the process of assessing risk for violence by an employee, I always ask if other employees, bosses, or acquaintances have expressed any concern about or fear of the individual.

One of the businesses that I serve as a consultant for has a twenty-four-hour hotline that employees can call if they are concerned about a coworker. They can express their concerns anonymously. Certainly, this could be abused, but it has been very successful for this business. Once a concern is logged with the security office, an investigation is undertaken. If the investigation turns up no further evidence of risk, the matter is dropped. On the other hand, if other risk factors are present, the business decides on a plan for intervention.

Threats of Intent to Do Harm

I take all threats seriously, whether someone threatens to kill himself or someone else. While it may be unlikely that the subject will actually carry out his or her threats, I know it is at least on his or her mind. I encourage businesses to adopt a zero tolerance policy toward threatening behaviors. The most obvious example of this philosophy is the airport. If, while walking through an airport magnetometer, I were to make a threat to blow up an airplane, I would be immediately detained. Even if I was laughing as I said it, it would not be taken as a joke by the airport security staff. Likewise, if I "joked" that I had a gun and was going to hijack a plane, I would be detained.

We accept zero tolerance in the airport even though, of the hundreds of people who have been detained for such threats, maybe none have actually intended any violence. Employees in a business must be made aware that any threat will be taken seriously. Therefore, when such a policy exists, and a threat is made, supervisors do not have to try to decide if the person is serious or not. It is assumed the person is serious, based on the policy.

When I first began work in the counseling field, I and others were trained to consider any statement of finality or other information implying suicide as a cry for help. We were instructed never to assume the client did not mean what he or she said or implied. In my fifteen years in the field, I have adhered to this advice. I always address statements and actions that indicate suicidal ideation. Usually, I stop the session at that point and address this issue with the client. I have done this many times, but I have never had a client say that he or she was not at least thinking about suicide. I cannot know if the client would have committed the act if I had not intervened. The point is that these clients were at least considering it among other options. None of my apparently suicidal clients have ever followed through and committed suicide. Does this mean I was I wrong in my assessment and intervention? Were they low risk from the start? I do not think so. I believe the process of identification of risk and subsequent intervention prevented at least some of them from following through with an act that was being seriously considered. It is this same process that I encourage clinicians and others to use as they assess the risk for violence. If a subject says or implies that he is thinking of violence, violence is likely.

Social Isolation

Social isolates are individuals who have either a very weak or a nonexistent support network. These are people that the media call "loners." Some loners are quite odd and stand out in a crowd. They may be socially incompetent and, therefore, find it difficult to achieve and maintain relationships.

This is not always the case, however. Some social isolates have casual friendships. What distinguishes these friendships from normal social relationships, though, is depth. Some social isolates that I have studied have been described by friends as normal. When asked about their interactions with an isolate perpetrator, friends might say they fished together or were on the same softball team. What I always find to be true in these cases, however, is that the friendships were very shallow. When I ask what kinds of things they talked about when they were fishing or playing softball, the answer is always shallow small talk. Acquaintances of social isolates could not tell you much about the isolate's *personal thoughts* on matters of substance. Discussion of deep personal issues would be rare or nonexistent. Deep personal thoughts are different from personal opinions. For example, a social isolate may share his opinion of the government, but he will not express his personal anxieties or his hopes and dreams for his own future.

Mentally healthy people have a few very close friends. In these relationships, healthy people can discuss deeply personal subjects. They can talk about their fears, their goals, and their dreams. Social isolates never broach these subjects because they do not know how, they do not know what their goals and dreams are, or they are fearful of sharing their thoughts.

Antisocial Behavior

Even though there is a specific clinical definition of antisocial personality disorder, I use the term here in a nonclinical way. A person is antisocial if he or she deliberately violates social rules in his or her conduct. People are antisocial when they *refuse* to adhere to culturally expected social graces and expected behaviors and patterns of dress according to gender, and when they consistently and deliberately violate both written and unwritten social rules. Antisocial behavior manifests itself as sexual harassment, lewd conversation, inappropriate expressions of emotion in a given context, consistently inappropriate dress, invasion of personal space, and so forth. It may also include lying, cheating, stealing, vandalism, and other illegal activities.

The critical issue in identifying antisocial behavior is that the subject is *deliberately* violating social rules and norms. This is distinguished from weak social skills (addressed below) in that subjects with weak social skills may violate social rules and norms, but their failures are the result of ignorance or confusion, not deliberate attempts to violate social norms that they know exist.

Absent or Weak Support System

Our social network joins with us in celebration when we experience successes and helps us hold our lives together when we experience failures. I liken social support systems to the legs of a table. The more legs there are, the more stable the table will be. In a furniture store, I once saw a waterbed completely supported by ordinary paper cups. The weight of a filled waterbed is roughly similar per square inch to that of a refrigerator. Yet when the weight of the bed was distributed over the dozens of cups beneath it, each cup was able to bear a portion of the load, carrying a weight that did not exceed its limits. The stress was distributed across a broad support system.

Most people have a support system made up of many legs. They have immediate family, extended family, social groups (e.g., softball teams, fishing buddies, women's clubs), religious groups and activities, jobs, and hobbies. Some people also have formalized support systems such as counselors or ministers whose main task is to assist persons with stresses. When a person experiences life stress, he or she looks to one or more of these support systems for encouragement, empathy, and solutions. The more pieces the support system includes, the more broadly the load can be distributed, thus providing more stability in the life of the individual.

These systems can also be proactive in preventing individuals from engaging in inappropriate behaviors. The social pressure to conform as well as the drive to avoid embarrassment within the group helps a community maintain order and provides impetus for the individual to avoid antisocial, immoral, or illegal behavior. (An exception would be when one's social system encourages dysfunctional behavior—i.e., gang behavior.) For example, a healthy individual has many reasons not to commit an armed robbery. Even if he really needs the money, potential embarrassment to his family and other social groups, fear of prison, and resources within the support group that provide options for meeting financial needs will lessen the likelihood that he will commit such a crime.

As the number of supporting structures decreases, the more weight each remaining structure must carry. Eventually, there is too great a load for the systems to support, and the individual collapses. It should be no surprise that people often choose the workplace for violent behavior. For a person who has few friends, an estranged or absent family, no hobbies, and poor coping skills, life may be precariously balanced on one's job—the one remaining leg. When it is removed, the table collapses. The subject then has nothing to lose by shooting colleagues and self. It is for this reason that the development of a support network is critical in the treatment of potentially violent individuals.

Lack of or Weak Social Skills

A person has weak or absent social skills if he or she violates social rules because he or she knows no better. One of my students many years ago was an annoyance to many people in the administration and the faculty. He would come by our offices unannounced and stay an inappropriately long period of time with no apparent purpose. He was a very gentle, malice-free individual, but socially he was extremely awkward. I realized at some point that the reason he stayed so long in our offices is that he did not have the social skills necessary to begin and end a conversation. He simply did not know how to do it.

Therefore, when he came by my office I taught him this skill. When he arrived, I would make small talk for a few minutes as is common in our culture. Then I would say, "Tim [not his real name], you came to see me for some reason. I am wondering what that reason was."

Tim would think for a minute and then he would address the topic that brought him to my office. After discussing that topic, I would say, "Tim, we have discussed the thing you came here for. I am wondering if there is anything else I can do for you?" He would think and then either say "no" or go on to the next topic. If he had no other business I would say, "Tim, since we have done the business you came for I suppose you can go now and I'll get back to work. Thanks for coming in." He would smile and say "OK" and go about his business. He was a very kind young man, but for some reason he had never developed the normal social graces that most of us acquire along the way, either formally or by observation.

Examples of weak social skills include violation of personal space, inappropriate social comments, and awkward behavior and remarks in both formal and informal settings. People who have weak social skills probably have poor coping skills as well. The same processes that allow one to learn social graces also allow one to learn coping strategies.

Substance Abuse

Chemical use has been present in about half of the homicides I have reviewed. Sometimes it is cocaine, marijuana, or some other illegal drug, while at other times the drug involved is alcohol. Drugs alter our decision-making processes. Because alcohol and other drugs of this classification slow our reflexes and lower our inhibitions, people who are drinking say and do things they would never say or do when they are sober. The normal inhibitive cognitive processes are slowed or turned off.

As a therapist working with children, I know that if alcohol is present in the home, the risk of child abuse goes up. Research has demonstrated a relationship between physical abuse and alcohol abuse.[2] A parent who may be relatively passive while sober may become aggressive when the disinhibiting effects of alcohol begin to affect the cognitive processes. Therefore, the presence of alcohol or drugs increases the risk for violence.

Clear Feelings of Being Wronged by the Target

One common attitude among the murderers that I have researched is failure to take responsibility for their circumstances in life. While it is true that the world can be an unfair place, healthy individuals take things as they come and deal with them as best they can. Unhealthy people place the blame for most or all of their troubles upon others and refuse to take any responsibility for their circumstances and difficulties. They perceive themselves as victims, blaming their problems on spouses, employers, coworkers, and friends.

These people will steal from their workplaces, pilfering cash, office supplies, and other items. They may sabotage computer systems and databases. They will stay home from work claiming to be sick when they are not, and they will file a variety of grievances with their employers including discrimination allegations, sexual harassment charges, and workmen's compensation claims. At home, these subjects will justify marital infidelity, defend the selfish use of family money, and fail to engage in a share of the workload, claiming they have been mistreated in some way. Instead of viewing these behaviors as dishonest, illegal, and/or immoral, the subject believes he is getting what he deserves because of some wrong that exists either in reality or in his mind.

Poor Self-Image

As humans, we share the need to feel worthy. We want people we care about to be proud of our accomplishment and we want to feel needed. A person's bad feelings about who he is exhibit themselves as one of several behaviors. One response to a poor self-image is overachievement. Overachievers compensate for their poor self-image by attempting to prove their worth through productivity.

A second response to a poor self-image is to internalize bad feelings. These individuals may overeat, drink excessively, or engage in other indulgent, unhealthy, and self-destructive behaviors in an attempt to abate or mask their bad feelings. For example, a person may perceive that she is unattractive because of her weight. Instead of trying to lose weight, ironically she may overeat. In this way she creates in herself a reflection of how she perceives herself. She also eliminates the disappointment of failing to live up to the unrealistic expectations of others. At its extreme, internalized disappointment in the self may result in suicide.

A third response to a poor self-image is to externalize disappointment and anger through aggression. This manifests itself through vandalism, tantrums, and other destructive behaviors. This third type of person is most likely to act aggressively toward others. I might add, however, that some research indicates that those who internalize their poor self-image can also redirect their anger outwardly.[3] Therefore, one who may be at risk for suicide at one point in the assessment process may be at risk for violence toward others in the future.

Suicide Attempts/Ideation

It is not uncommon for people to make feeble attempts at suicide. I have worked with patients who attempted suicide by taking antacids, scratching on their wrists in ways that barely caused bleeding, and using other methods that caused almost no injury. When one attempts suicide in a half-hearted way, others may not take the attempt seriously. The patient very likely may not have been serious at that time, but that does not mean that he or she might not become serious later. Similarly, some people succeed at suicide by accident. They place their head in an oven and turn on the gas, expecting a roommate to come home and find them before it is too late. However, the roommate gets delayed in traffic and arrives when the other is already dead.

Thinking about suicide, called "ideation," is expressed in suicidal attempts. Ideation can also be demonstrated in statements of finality, suddenly paying off all debts, mending relationships, and giving away prized possessions. As a clinician I may ask my client about his or her suicidal thoughts and I may administer a suicidal ideation psychometric instrument. If someone is contemplating suicide, we might assume a poor self-image, poor coping skills, and a high level of stress. Therefore, for reasons that have already been discussed, one is also at greater risk for homicide.

I must add one caveat to this discussion. Suicidal ideation is not uncommon. Many mentally healthy people have considered suicide at one time or another in life. The distinguishing factor is how seriously one considered the act and how much thought-energy was invested. Even in healthy people, suicide is one of many options that may be briefly considered, but it is quickly dismissed. For example, my clients have told me they thought about killing themselves at some point. When I probe the issue, if they say they never considered it seriously or they assure me they would never do it because they have too much to live for, I usually do not worry about them very much. On the other hand, if they have made specific plans, with detailed ideas on committing the act (when, where, and how), I am very concerned.

Fantasies of Violence

On a rainy, unpleasant day many years ago in a crowded hospital parking lot, a woman took a parking place that I was obviously waiting for. As the person in the space backed out, the woman drove into the space ahead of me. I was so angry I considered how satisfying it would be to flatten her tires, but of course, I did not act on my aggressive fantasy. I would suppose that most of the readers of this book have fantasized about revenge at one time or another but have never acted upon it. Like suicidal ideation, fantasizing at some level about violence is not unusual.

Just as I do with suicidal ideation, sometimes I must determine the level of detail in violent thoughts by directly asking the client what he or she thinks about. A person who provides little detail and who has few thoughts of violence is a lesser risk than one who has many violent thoughts and detailed notions of executing those fantasies. I once evaluated a very angry child. He was 8 years old and had expressed violent thoughts many times in our sessions. When I asked him about his vengeful thoughts about a relative, he provided incredible detail about how he wanted to kill this person. Fortunately for the relative, the boy, because of his age, had developed plans that were impossible to complete. They involved fantastic, nonexistent killing machines. However, I was very concerned about this child's rage, despite the fact that he could not execute his plan as he had planned. He obviously had invested a great deal of energy in feeding his anger.

It is not the fantasies themselves but the pervasiveness of fantasies of violence that determines potential problems. A subject who constantly surrounds himself with violent images, books, movies, art, and so forth, is demonstrating how he sees the world and his place in the world. While violent movies can be cathartic for some of us, they can feed an aggressive passion for revenge in others. I am most concerned when I am evaluating a subject if he or she is heavily involved in violent activities (i.e., martial arts), fascinated by violent images, and surrounded by violent systems (friends, movies, weapons, etc.). Involvement in martial arts by itself, as with any single variable, is never a predictor of violent behavior. In fact, I sometimes encourage my clients to participate in martial arts if it interests them, because of its therapeutic, health, and cathartic value. But in the context of other risk factors, the clinician can distinguish between a normal level of aggression and obsession with violent thoughts.

Job Instability

There are many reasons why people lose their jobs. The businesses they work for may close, they may be laid off for reasons totally unrelated to them personally, or they may have been hired as temporary employees. However, when assessed in the context of other variables, moving from job to job may be an indicator that one is unable to function productively in a social context.

Severe Situational Stress

Most of us have had to deal with severe situational stress at one time or another. We have found ways to cope with our losses, difficulties, and disappointments. Severe situational stress could include the death of a loved one, a house fire, being fired or laid off (see "Loss of a Job"), an arrest, financial trouble (e.g., an audit or bankruptcy), or other stressful circumstances. But it is not just tragedies that generate stress. Thomas Holmes and R. H. Rahe have found in their research on stressful life events that even events we consider positive can produce significant stress.[4] Three of the top ten most stressful events, according to Holmes and Rahe's Social Readjustment Rating Scale (SRRS), are events that we normally think of as positive—getting married ranks at number seven, marital reconciliation ranks at number nine, and retirement ranks at number ten. Pregnancy, vacations, and Christmas are other positive events that can generate stress.[5]

We all live with stress, but the high-risk individual has few effective ways to cope with it. Therefore, a spouse packing to move out may be the final stressor that leads to her murder at the hands of a husband who has few effective coping skills. What may be severe situational stress to one person may be less stressful to a person with effective coping skills. The stressful event can act as a triggering mechanism, giving the impression that a normal person just "snapped." However, the potential for violence was there all along.

Presence of Aggressive Models

Much of our behavior is learned by observation, called "vicarious learning." We learn to be fathers by watching how our fathers raised us, and we learn to be spouses by watching how our parents interacted. It is for this reason, for example, that people who are abused as children are more likely to become abusers themselves and why male children raised in a home where a father abuses his wife are more likely to become wife abusers. One may find this odd, but girls who grow up seeing their mothers abused are more likely to be abused by their husbands, even when they tell themselves that they would never allow a spouse to do what they saw their fathers do to their mothers. Our perception of how the world operates is largely determined by observational learning. We pursue what we know.

Likewise, we learn to cope by watching how those around us cope. If we are surrounded by aggressive models or if we were raised in homes where aggression was a means of dealing with frustration, we may behave that way ourselves. Of course, people have choices and they are capable of breaking these cycles, but remember that the focus of this book is on people who kill other people. I am not addressing subjects who are healthy and have highly developed coping skills. Those who become murderers are dysfunctional in more ways than one, including the adoption of unproductive behaviors.

Specific Victim

When one identifies a specific victim, the risk for violent behavior increases. The specific victim could be a single individual (a spouse, a coworker, an attorney, etc.) or it could be a place (a business, a department, a family, or a house). Murderers who have identified an individual as the specific victim in a work environment will pass over other individuals in the hall while they search for their chosen victim. They will calmly talk to other workers, advise them to leave the building, and so forth, while they brutally kill someone else. Yet people who have identified a place as the specific victim, rather than an individual, will kill anyone they come across in the hallway, parking lot, or conference room.

Identifying a specific victim involves listening during open-ended conversations with the subject for specific threats against a place or person. I must consider how often potential victims are identified. I also listen for comments expressing seemingly exaggerated frustrations about specific people or places.

Frequent Divorce

This variable is very similar to "job instability." Just as they change jobs, people divorce for many reasons. Sometimes people marry and divorce several times for reasons largely beyond their control. However, when one has been unsuccessful in numerous relationships, in combination with other risk factors, it is possible one has difficulty maintaining social relationships. An inability to get along with others, especially a spouse, provides evidence of social isolation, absent or weak social skills, absent or weak social support systems, and poor coping strategies.

Loss of a Job

Loss of a job can act as a triggering mechanism because it is a form of severe situational stress. Those of us who have careers invest heavily in our work. In part, our work often defines who we are. When we introduce ourselves, one of the first facts we provide about our identity is our career. A job is especially critical as a part of a man's identity. A successful career says that he can take care of himself and his family. When a man loses a job, even if it is for reasons beyond his individual control (such as a layoff based on company losses) he sees it, in part, as a personal statement about his identity and his ability to take care of himself and those he loves. Men, more than women, personalize this loss and attach to it feelings of failure. If the subject has poor coping skills and weak or absent support systems, violence is more likely when facing this type of stress.

Poverty

Being poor does not make one violent. Poverty, however, can create desperation, and desperate people do desperate things. Victor Hugo's *Les Misérables* provides a poignant example of how an ordinary citizen can commit a crime when pushed by the desperation of poverty. At the beginning of the French Revolution, Jean Val Jean, an otherwise respectable citizen, chooses to steal a loaf of bread when he sees his family sick and starving to death. This desperate act changes his life. While stealing bread is a far cry from committing murder, the process is much the same.

Available Weapon

Gun control is a volatile issue in our culture. Many people support the right to keep and bear arms, regardless of the type of weapon. Others argue for strict gun control laws that would disarm our nation. It is a fact that most homicides committed in the workplace are committed with firearms. However, anything can be a deadly weapon. I have reviewed homicides committed with crossbows, spears, spear guns, knives, hammers, rocks, cinder blocks, automobiles, clubs, plastic wrap, poisons, rope, string, pencils, machetes, screwdrivers, gasoline, bricks, shotguns, machine guns, pistols, explosives, and bare hands. This list provides only a few examples. The point is not to say that gun control would help or hinder. The point is to demonstrate that when one chooses to kill, any weapon may accomplish the task.

Many individuals have weapons in their possession. In some states, like Georgia, it is not difficult to obtain a license to carry a concealed weapon. One of my FBI friends once summarized my description of Georgia's gun laws by saying, "So I might assume that any person I encounter in Georgia could be carrying a firearm?" He was right. But the incidence of homicide is not significantly higher in Georgia than it is in New York, where gun laws are extremely restrictive.

It is a reductionist overreaction to suppose that disarming all individuals would end or even reduce the homicide problem. Many people own guns and never use them. Others use their guns for hunting and recreation. Still others use their weapons to protect themselves. The presence of any specific weapon is simply one of many risk factors. A person intent on committing a homicide will use any weapon available. Firearms are efficient and easy to use and they allow distance between the perpetrator and the victim.

When assessing an individual for risk of violent behavior, if a number of other risk factors are present and the person has ready access to a firearm, I am more concerned than if access to a firearm is one of only a few risk factors present. If the subject is obsessed with weapons and has many at his disposal, I am even more concerned. A business manager once asked me about a man under her authority who was so stressed that he "had to" go to the firing range at lunchtime to work off his stress by shooting targets. On the one hand, cathartic behavior shooting targets is certainly more productive than shooting coworkers, but the fact that he had a weapon at work (which was against company policy) and he chose weapons as a means for catharsis gave me reason to be concerned.

Male Gender and Age 23–45

These final two factors are based on statistical probability. It is a statistical fact that men are perpetrators of violence more often than women. People in the 23 to 45 age range also make up the majority of the violent individuals I have identified in this book.

In Chapters 1 and 2 I stated that mental illness does not cause violent behavior, but many of the cases I have discussed involve people who were diagnosed with mental illnesses. However, correlation does not prove causation. In other words, the fact that two variables are related (homicide and mental illness) does not mean that one causes the other. For the same reason, even though most murderers are male and most of them fall into this age range, maleness does not *cause* one to commit a homicide nor does falling into this age range *cause* one to commit murder. They are correlated variables.

Even though these two variables do not cause one to kill, I do not think it is an accident that men are more likely to kill than women. Part of the reason is biological. Testosterone, the principal male hormone, is much more abundant in the male system than in the female system (even though both males and females have both male and female hormones in their systems), and testosterone has been directly linked to aggression. It is for this reason, among others, that boys tend to be more aggressive than girls. However, as logical human beings, we are not completely bound to our biological nature. We have the ability to reason and to overcome biological drives.

CONCLUDING REMARKS

There is no flawless system for assessing risk for violent behavior. In fact, there is no problem-free system for assessing anything in the mental health field. Some measurement instruments claim to be more effective at assessing risk for violence than others, but I see several problems with psychometric instruments. First of all, there is a lot of money to be made in their sale. I always question claims when the one making the claim is trying to sell the instrument. The process I have described in this chapter is free.

Second, many instruments claim to be comprehensive. I believe that the human psyche is much too complicated to be reduced to anyone instrument, even when it is a valid instrument. One of my graduate interns asked for help in interpreting a personality profile that had been administered to one of her clients. She had worked with the client for six months. I asked her to put the results of the test away for a minute and to tell me what she knew about her client. After she had spent several minutes describing him to me, I asked her if that was what the personality profile said about him. She said it was. This instrument was a highly respected measurement tool in mental health. I asked her what she would have believed if the instrument said something that contradicted her experience. Would she have maintained the opinion formed by her clinical experience and interaction with the client or would she have abandoned all that for the conclusions of the measurement tool? Since she said she would have leaned more heavily on her experience, I suggested that an appropriate use for the conclusions of that tool would be to consider them as one of many pieces of information that she needed to use in assessing her client—not the only piece of information. Therefore, even the assessment process described in this chapter must be considered as providing only a partial picture of the person within a given context—as one of many facets.

Finally, psychometrics can be very expensive, they may require professional administration, and they may be difficult to interpret. Especially for the clinician in private practice or the small business owner, acquiring the expertise for psychometric instrument administration and interpretation may be impractical. My purpose in the development of the process described here was to provide a means of assessment that did not require professional administration or interpretation. It is simple and easy to use.

I must provide one more cautionary note. This process is not the end of the process of risk assessment—it is the beginning. Once a high risk for violent behavior has been established, the assessor must then decide on intervention. The intervention process may take weeks, months, or years. The process of assessing for risk launches the process for intervention that will save lives and help people be more fully functional.

NOTES

1. Gavin de Becker, *The gift of fear: survival signals that protect us from violence.* New York: Little, Brown & Company, 1997, 44.

2. Charles L. Thompson and Linda B. Rudolph, *Counseling children, 4th edition.* New York: Brooks/Cole Publishing Company, 1992, 404.

3. Gerald D. Oster and Janice E. Caro, *Understanding and treating depressed adolescents and their families.* New York: John Wiley & Sons, 1990.

4. Dennis Coon, *Introduction to psychology: exploration and application, 8th edition.* New York: Brooks/Cole Publishing Company, 1998, 468.

5. Thomas H. Holmes and R. H. Rahe, "The social readjustment scale," *Journal of Psychometric Research, 11* (1967), 213–218.

9

Intervention and Prevention of Homicide

Prevention of homicide involves three major arenas—intervention with potential perpetrators, prevention by organizations, and prevention on the individual level. In the first arena, one must identify high-risk individuals, perhaps even in childhood, long before they consider killing. Once identified, interventions change the individual's course, making violence less likely. Clinicians, however, do not always have access to high-risk individuals early in their lives. Therefore, they also intervene when homicidal behaviors seem imminent, to interrupt the emotional digression that leads to homicide. A second preventive arena involves careful preparation by schools, hospitals, and businesses in the development and implementation of violence prevention plans and policies. These policies address identification of potential perpetrators, escape plans, and policies on threats and aggressive behaviors. Through these plans, potential victims know what to do if they are threatened, and a culture that lessens the likelihood of homicide is developed. Finally, prevention involves things we can do as individuals when a violent incident is threatened or is in progress, in order to protect ourselves.

INTERVENTION—THERE IS HOPE

Most of my work with the mentally ill is interventive. Even with very young children, the purpose of my therapy is to pave the way to a more productive future and to help my clients avoid problems. I have invested heavily through my education, research, and practice in an attempt to find the most effective interventions. As a graduate student I was skeptical about some therapies. My skepticisms proved to be well-founded as I tried some therapeutic approaches in practice, but occasionally approaches I had dismissed as impractical or theoretically problematic have proven to be quite useful. Therefore, the conclusions I present in this chapter have developed during the course of my education, research, and practice. Without any one of these three pieces, my conclusions and suggestions might be less than credible.

In this section I address measures that can be taken culturally, in the workplace or community, therapeutically, and medically to prevent violent behavior. When these arenas are working in harmony, successful intervention is more likely. Even though some interventive strategies may seem more practical than others or may be preferred by some clinicians over others, there is no single method or strategy that is always the only appropriate choice.

Intervention is not limited to professional counselors and physicians. This section contains ideas for everyone regardless of occupation or social position. Even outside the clinical context, those untrained in the psychological or social sciences can provide hope, mentoring, and direction to those who are lost and without hope.

HOME-Safe Project

Currently under development is an intervention and preventive strategy for violent behavior, called the "HOME-Safe" project. The purpose of this project is to ensure that schoolchildren, employees, and others return home safely. "HOME" is an acronym that stands for hope, observation, mentoring, and empowerment.

It is undoubtedly as frustrating for you as it is for me when I see news of a homicide and then I hear someone say, "I knew this was going to happen." I always wonder what was done to prevent the occurrence or to help the perpetrator deal with his or her issues. I concede that sometimes interventions were attempted and yet they failed. Often, however, nothing was done. I believe that the HOME-Safe project will provide a comprehensive intervention, both early intervention and crisis intervention, which can be applied in a wide variety of contexts and which involve multiple segments of an individual's environment.

Hope. Desperate people do desperate things. Suicide is an act of hopelessness and desperation in which a person sees no reasonable alternative. When addressing this clinically, I must find a way to help the client see other alternatives and find hope in circumstances that appear hopeless to the client.

Sometimes we can find hope by looking to the future. In the midst of crisis, people often cannot see any further than their immediate circumstances. For example, financial troubles may be overwhelming to an individual. He receives numerous late notices from creditors, the mortgage company is on the verge of repossessing his house, and the bank is preparing to repossess his automobile. He realizes he will seem like a failure to his family and friends. Overwhelmed with feelings of failure and hopelessness, he is unable to see beyond the immediate crisis. To see a future where one can rebuild a broken financial life and to realize that many people have fallen on hard times and overcome them, later to reestablish their former lifestyles, is part of healing and coping.

In the midst of crisis, the person involved cannot see that things are not really as bad as they seem. The man struggling under tremendous financial pressure may believe that his wife and friends will disown him because of his bad financial choices. Yet often the opposite happens. During times of stress, people with a reasonable support system find that those who love and care for them rally around and support them.

Family members and friends can provide hope for desperate people. Family members are on the front line and have the best opportunity to see despair as it is developing. Assuring the loved one that he or she is not alone and that, together, they can overcome troubling circumstances provides the hope that helps in overcoming the emotional turmoil of a crisis.

Formal religious organizations certainly can provide hope. I have found that people gravitate toward religion when they have nowhere else to turn. Family tragedies, personal crises, and so forth may push people away from a higher power, but they may also draw people closer to it. Those who draw closer to a higher power are grasping for hope when their other strategies have failed. Ministers and lay persons can provide hope for the hopeless by addressing the promises of their various faiths and looking beyond this world for strength and for answers.

Counselors can offer hope through the therapeutic process. They can help the client organize his world into manageable pieces. If you have ever been on the scene of a car accident, you may be able to relate to the crises I see in my office. The person involved in a traumatic event like an automobile accident is unprepared for the emotions that follow. She is full of questions. Was it my fault? Will I get a ticket or have to go to court? How do I take care of this car? How much will this cost me? Will my insurance be affected? How will I get around until my car is fixed or replaced? She is also plagued with emotional and existential questions. What if I had died? Who would have cared for my children? Have I done what I wanted to do in life? Was God trying to tell me something?

Most of these questions are not overwhelming by themselves, but when they all come at once, as they do in a crisis, one may have difficulty prioritizing issues and dealing with the stress of the event. The counselor helps the client organize events and thoughts so that the client can address them in a reasonable order. Once the client realizes that her problems are manageable, she calms down and sees hope for a productive future. Even though she may still be haunted to some degree by the event and she may still have unanswered questions, she can cope with the issues by addressing them in manageable doses.

Observation. The second step of the project is observation. My grandfather committed suicide when I was about 12 years old. Even now, more than a quarter of a century later, I still have questions. Did we miss something? Did he look to us for help and did we fail to see it? These questions are common after a tragic event like a suicide and they are also common after a homicide. Unfortunately, many times there were signs of what was coming, but people who had the opportunity to see these clues missed them.

I must take a moment to address a tangential issue. It is imperative that the reader understand that I am not suggesting that the loved ones and acquaintances of those who take their own lives or take the lives of others are responsible for those events. I must also acknowledge that messages are much clearer in hindsight than they are in the midst of our busy lives. However, while being sensitive to these facts, I do not think we should ignore the possibility that sometimes we can see what is about to happen if we look for it.

Several years ago, one of my students saved the life of another student. My student was a resident assistant in a dormitory and had participated in a suicide prevention seminar I had conducted for all dormitory personnel. I had trained him to look for signs indicative of suicidal ideation. This young man approached me one day and said he was concerned about one of the men on his floor. He explained the symptoms he had observed and told me why he was concerned. I called the student in question to my office, and as soon as I saw him I realized the resident assistant's concerns were justified. The young man's facial expression was one of hopelessness, he had not showered in several days, and his shirt was haphazardly buttoned. He was clearly in crisis. In the process of my intervention, the student told me he had, indeed, been planning suicide and had intended to take action in the next few days. With help, this young man survived and is now coping fairly well. I credit the resident assistant for saving a life because he was observant.

In Chapter 8, I discussed a list of warning signs. Sometimes we may be unable to see symptoms. At other times we may see the warning signs, but for some reason we are powerless to intervene. However, in many of the homicide cases I have researched, there were points at which intervention was possible, but those who had the power to intervene either ignored the warning signs or did not know what to do about them. Rather than blaming victims and survivors, however, I am suggesting that we learn from our past and apply what we know to our future as we become more aware of warning signs around us.

Mentoring. Mentoring is a buzz word in educational circles these days, but it is nothing new. In fact, mentoring has been around for centuries. The term refers to Odysseus' guide, in Homer's epic poem, *The Odyssey*, whose name was Mentor. To be a mentor is to be a trainer, confidant, guide, educator, and resource for wisdom and knowledge.

A parent fills the role of mentor for a child when the parent looks for opportunities to teach the child both formally and informally. Many parents see this as part of their responsibility, but many do not. When a child is left without this resource, he or she is dependent upon his or her very limited knowledge and resource base to find the answers to questions that are a natural part of development.

One can become a mentor for a child at school, on the athletic field, in the music or dance hall, or in any other environment. The concerned adult becomes a mentor by involving himself with the child beyond the activity that has brought them together. Learning the child's name, interests, hobbies, goals, and desires opens the door to a relationship based on trust and concern. This provides a needed resource for a child who does not otherwise have such access.

Whenever I address schools, I am pleased when the audience includes the entire school community—custodians, cafeteria workers, teachers, secretaries, and administrators. I tell them that any of them can function as mentors. Children may pick the most unlikely person (a maintenance worker or a secretary) as a confidant if the opportunity exists.

When a child has a mentor, he has someone with whom he can share his successes and pains. In turn, this strengthens his social support system. When he sees he is not alone in the world, he is more likely to see the world as a hopeful place of solutions rather than a lonely, hopeless, and powerless place.

Empowerment. Nietzsche argued that we have a "will to power" in that we have a need to discharge the power that lies within us.[1] In other words, we have a need to have control and power over things. When we fill the need to be in control of something, we see ourselves as self-sufficient and capable. When our will to power is unmet, we see ourselves as hopeless and at the mercy of others.

We can gain power over our lives when we find something we can do that provides a sense of control in a world that can often seem out of control. People become empowered when they find some area of interest that they can master. The area of mastery may be in music, dance, writing, sports, mechanics, martial arts, computers, or some other activity.

I help the parents of children who are under my care to empower their children by suggesting that they find one or two things that their children enjoy and focus on them. If it becomes evident that the child does not like an activity or does not seem to have the necessary aptitude for it, move on to another activity. I discourage allowing a child to pursue too many activities. The child's time will be unproductively divided and the lack of focus will make mastery of any single activity less likely.

Summary of the HOME-Safe Project. Critics can find a variety of reasons why programs like this will not work with some populations and in some environments. I do not disagree. No program is universally applicable. However, I am convinced that this program will work with many populations and I resist the idea that we should do nothing until we find the perfect solution. The effectiveness and willingness of the people within a given system (e.g., school, church, athletic team) largely control the success or failure of a project. Dedicated, caring adults can make a tremendous difference in the lives of those who are drowning in despair.

Employee Assistance Program Intervention

We spend more time at work than almost anywhere else. Therefore, intervention at work is a necessary inclusion in any violence prevention plan. The HOME-Safe project is applicable to adult working environments. The first step in providing an effective EAP plan is to ensure that employees are aware of the programs that are available and know how to access them.

The second step is to train EAP staff on the warning signs of potential violence. The company should have a plan for addressing workplace threats that includes securing the site as well as providing individual and family therapeutic intervention for the potentially violent individual. I suggest to companies that EAP personnel also take the lead in training employees on what to do in the event of a violent incident.

It is generally much less expensive to keep and "repair" a problem employee than it is to hire and train a new one. Not only does effective intervention in the workplace make good fiscal sense, but it may also save lives.

EAP intervention is not without problems. The Americans with Disabilities Act (ADA) makes many companies hesitant to intervene. Once the company acknowledges that an employee has a problem (by providing counseling, for example), it can no longer fire the employee for the behavior it has addressed through its interventions. The ADA, while it probably has done more good overall for employees and the workplace than harm, has actually hurt the workplace in this way. Companies that I work with are much more likely to fire an employee who is a potential risk, because if therapeutic intervention fails, they are stuck with a security risk on their work site. I advise companies to consult their attorneys before intervention so that they are fully aware of all the ramifications of any decision they make regarding intervention.

Community Intervention

Churches and other religious organizations may be the most likely community groups for informal intervention. Religion provides hope for the hopeless. Therefore, it should be no surprise that dysfunctional people often gravitate to religious groups. Ministers and lay persons should be nondiscriminatory in their approach to potentially violent people. These people are often irritating and socially dysfunctional. They are, therefore, not always pleasant to be around. Approaching them as a mentor is one way to ensure that they are not ostracized, giving them yet another failure. To be rejected by people in a religious environment is especially frustrating. It gives the rejected person the impression that even God doesn't want him. Religious organizations can provide activities for children and adolescents, providing a safe environment, mentoring, and leadership, thus reducing the likelihood of illegal or violent activities. Churches and church-related organizations are well suited to serve the community by providing after-school, weekend, and summer programs.

The community can also provide service opportunities, community watch programs, and big brother/big sister programs. Like religious organizations, these programs can also provide much needed leadership to at-risk young people.

Therapeutic Intervention

Many therapies have been shown to be effective in preventing violent behavior. Generally speaking, research has shown cognitive-behavioral interventions to be most successful. This method of therapy usually includes training in social skills, coping skills, anger management, and other processes vital to reducing the risk of violence. Therapists are not infallible, and you undoubtedly have heard stories of people who have committed homicides after therapists have said they were not risks. Whatever the theoretical orientation of a therapist, the difficulty for those of us in the field is getting the high-risk client to make and keep appointments. Regular contact with clients, of course, provides opportunity for ongoing evaluation and treatment.

Medical Intervention

Medications for mental illness, called "psychotropic medications," have been shown to be extremely effective in helping people function more effectively and become more satisfied with their lives. Psychotropic medications are not the answer to all mental health issues, but I have seen amazing transitions in my clients' behaviors and thought processes when they are appropriately medicated. I always consider the possibility of pharmaceutical intervention, although I do not always conclude that referral to a psychiatrist is necessary.

People are often reluctant to take medications for mental health problems. They believe that there is something wrong with them if they cannot deal with their problems without the help of drugs. We do not hold ourselves to this same standard in other areas of our lives. Diabetics, for example, do not produce sufficient quantities of insulin. As much as they might dislike taking insulin shots, they do not assume they are weak if they cannot deal with their insulin deficiency without medication. Likewise, in some people's bodies, chemicals are overproduced or underproduced, resulting in cognitive and/or behavioral problems. Psychotropic medications assist patients in balancing these chemicals and allowing them to function normally.

Often when a client has reached a physiological balance I can teach him or her to compensate for the effects of the chemical imbalance. Through cognitive and/or behavioral interventions, dependence on medications is reduced and many patients, with their attending physician's consent, can eventually eliminate the need for medications.

All psychologists and counselors have to deal with the frustration of their clients refusing to take medication. Several of the subjects described in this book had been prescribed medication for mental disorders, but they had stopped taking it. I see this phenomenon regularly in my practice. Patients come in for some specified problem such as depression. I may refer them to a psychiatrist for medication. Many drugs for depression take several weeks to fully engage in the body's system and reach their full effects. Some clients, after taking the medication for several days, are frustrated because they are experiencing side effects but they are not yet seeing the results they had expected. In yet another symptom of their depression, these clients give up on their prescriptions. Others endure the side effects for a few weeks and then begin to feel better. Once they start feeling better, they think they do not need the medication any longer, so they quit. Once they quit, they relapse into depression.

Even where patients are hospitalized, there is not a 100% guarantee that they will take their medications. The nursing staff watches patients as they swallow medications and may even check their mouths to ensure they are not hiding pills under their tongues. Even with these drastic precautions steps, some patients figure out ways to sidestep their medical regimens.

Family members of psychiatric outpatients should do their best to ensure that their loved ones take their medications on schedule. This is difficult and frustrating for family members of resistant patients, but I encourage them to do the best they can.

ORGANIZATIONAL PREVENTIVE STRATEGIES

I know we cannot totally prevent some behaviors, but things can be done at the organizational level to lessen the likelihood of violence. Other things may not lessen the likelihood of violence but can make it more difficult for a person to harm others.

Schools

In spring 1999, I met with our state superintendent of schools to discuss strategies for preventing school shootings. The meeting came just a few weeks after the incident at Columbine High School. The superintendent and I were both concerned that other shootings were imminent. Just four days after our meeting, a student opened fire on the commons area of a local high school.

A first step in the long-term solution to school violence is to personalize the school system. Our schools are becoming so big that it is nearly impossible for teachers and administrators to know the children, their personal needs, and their personal problems. In places where it is possible to personalize, it takes extra effort, and I have found that teachers and administrators are not always willing to expend the energy.

Even when the system is impersonal, one can interact personally by looking the children in the eyes. Eye contact is the starting point for being a good listener. In order to demonstrate the power of eye contact to my first-year counseling students, I have them visit any place of business. When they come to a checkout counter, I instruct them to find one thing about the cashier or clerk that they can comment on. For example, if the cashier looks tired, they might say, "You look tired. I bet this is a tough job." As they say it, they have to make eye contact with the cashier. They always report that the cashier hesitates in the transaction or stops altogether to respond. The cashier is not used to being "heard." This same process works in the hall, in the cafeteria, on the athletic field, and in the classroom. Look the child in the eyes and listen. Once we are listening carefully, we are more likely to recognize potential signs of trouble. Training people to recognize the warning signs of violent behavior is the next step in prevention.

Teachers and administrators should also be trained to identify the intentions of violent individuals when an attack is under way. As hostage negotiators know, in some situations it is imperative that the attacker not be provoked by offensive or defensive moves. In other cases, there is little one can do to appease the perpetrator. At Columbine, for example, the boys were clearly prepared to kill as many people as possible. They left little question of their intentions as they moved from room to room, shooting and detonating explosive devices. Negotiations were nearly impossible. On the other hand, in Conyers, Georgia, a young man fired into a crowded commons area several times with a .22 caliber weapon. He ran from the building and was confronted by the vice principal, Cecil Brinkley, who properly assessed his demeanor and successfully talked the boy down. Mr. Brinkley's decision to intervene would have been different if the young shooter had behaved in an extremely agitated manner. As Mr. Brinkley intervened, he made eye contact with the student, he knew what to say that would not antagonize the student, and yet he presented a commanding position that allowed him to successfully intervene. Mr. Brinkley had nearly forty years of experience in handling conflict to guide him, but others with less experience can be trained to make good decisions like his. An educated guess regarding the intentions of the shooter, a decision to flee, to sit quietly, to hide, or to attempt to disarm the perpetrator can be made more effectively with training.

I have suggested that teachers be trained in weapons recognition. This may seem a radical suggestion, but we live in radical times. Knowing what a gun can do, as well as what it cannot do, may save lives. For example, knowing the number of rounds a given weapon can fire without reloading and the firing power of a given weapon may assist victims in deciding whether to flee, hide, or confront their attacker.

Police should be trained in tactical assaults on schools. It has become clear that violence in the school is a part of our culture and there is no way of predicting which school will be a target. Therefore, police should have a plan for tactical assaults on school buildings and not have to develop a plan on the spot. School administrators should have building floor plans readily available for police.

We should conduct escape drills in schools just as we conduct fire drills. For children, knowing where to go and how to get there may save their lives. In one high school where a shooting occurred, an administrator announced on the intercom as the shooting was in progress that students should go directly to their homerooms. This was a mistake, guaranteeing that no matter what hall the shooter was in, students would be heading directly into his path. As it turned out, the shooter left the building and no further injuries were suffered, but things could have easily turned out tragically.

I favor arming principals or other senior administrators in schools where police officers are not routinely stationed. In Pearl, Mississippi, Luke Woodham fired numerous times in the school courtyard, killing two and injuring seven. As the shooting was in progress, an administrator ran to his automobile, parked some distance away, and returned with his gun. He met Woodham outside the school building as the shooter was leaving and held him at gunpoint until the police arrived. If this administrator had been legally permitted to keep his weapon safely in his office, he might have been able to stop Woodham sooner, perhaps saving some students from injury. Of course, any administrator permitted to keep a weapon at school should be properly trained. These weapons would be secured properly to ensure that unauthorized persons could not access them.

As many schools have now done, I suggest that they develop and implement commitment to nonviolence programs in much the same way that we have developed drug-free programs. Nonviolence programs could include mentoring programs, parent-training programs, anger management, coping skills training, and prosocial skills training, as well as awareness programs addressing the results of violent behavior. These programs should include a zero tolerance policy for violence and threats of violence.

Businesses

In the area of organizational intervention and prevention, businesses have as much opportunity to address the problem of violence as other organizations. Most of us place ourselves under the supervision of our employers nearly every day of the week. Since our employers have a great deal of control over our lives, they are in a position to protect us if they invest in policies and procedures that reduce the likelihood of violence.

When employees perceive themselves as powerless to address their concerns, they become desperate. In their frustration and desperation, they attempt to regain control by filing grievances against their employers, bosses, or coworkers. Charles E. Labig, author of *Preventing Violence in the Workplace*, notes that many "employees who have committed murder at the work site were in the process of being disciplined or terminated by their employers."[2] He suggests that companies should ensure that their grievance procedures are clear and functional so that frustrated individuals have an outlet for their complaints. Having grievance procedures that do not work or processes that are unclear may be worse than having no procedures at all. Labig also encourages businesses to review grievances to ensure that action taken by the company is not punitive but rather aimed at changing or correcting behavior. According to Labig, "punishment is punitive, provocative and evocative of childlike behavior. Taking corrective action offers the possibility of the company's actions being supportive, reality-based, and positive."[3]

For these reasons, grievance procedures are one of the first areas I review in a business. Employees must know what to do if they are unhappy. Grievance procedures should explain the proper chain of command, how to present grievances, and what to expect in terms of a response. Obviously, I do not suggest that companies give employees everything they want. What I do suggest is that employees should know what to expect. They should know how long it will take to receive acknowledgment of the grievance, the process for reviewing the grievance, and how long it will take to receive resolution, whatever that resolution may be.

When a risk has been identified, administrators should make sure that security personnel are fully informed of who the potential risk is, what possible threats to expect, and what to do if the risk is seen on the site. An escape plan should be developed, just like a fire escape plan, in the event of an office incident. Business should provide secure parking, especially for potential victims if a risk has been identified.

Offices should be constructed so visitors must enter a receiving area in order to access employees. A perpetrator intent on eluding the receptionist or passing through a receiving area will do so, but the existence of such an area may provide extra time for a receptionist to call police or security and perhaps to warn others.

A person being stalked can avoid his or her home, car, worship center, and other places but cannot easily avoid the workplace. This is why many domestic shootings happen at work. The perpetrator knows exactly where to find the individual at any given time of the workday. Therefore, in the case of stalking, adjust the employee's schedule, move his/her desk, cubicle, or office to a new location, and change routine meeting times. The stalker will then have a more difficult time finding his victim. Employees should be encouraged to communicate problems to management before they get out of hand.

In businesses where uniformed security guards are employed, all visitors should be screened as they enter the facility. I was delivering some documents to the security director of one of the businesses that I have dealt with, a business whose security is better than most. As I entered the gate in my car, I was instructed to wait by the curb as the guards checked my reasons for being on the site and confirmed that I could enter. The agent that took my information stood beside my car with his back to my door. He called the security office where I was to have my meeting to ensure that I could be given a pass and temporary ID. I could hear his entire conversation, including the response from the security office. If I had been there to harm someone, and if the security office had been notified that I was a risk, I would have overheard instructions to deny me a pass and seen their report of me as a threat. I could easily have made that agent my first victim. Therefore, I encourage businesses to utilize the pull-over protocols used by most law enforcement agencies. If they are unfamiliar with this procedure, I suggest that they contact their local police department. Officers can easily provide basic training in pull-over procedure in an hour or two.

Violence response plans should include a central location for addressing threats and violent behavior. Especially in very large companies, an individual may engage in repeated threats or violent acts, but in different locations. Supervisors in each location may mistakenly believe that the employee is engaging in these acts for the first time. When violent and threatening behaviors are reported to a central location, patterns of aggression can be established.

PREVENTION AT THE INDIVIDUAL LEVEL

Even though many things can be done at the institutional level to prevent homicide, one should not suppose that all responsibility or options end with others. People can also act individually to protect themselves and their children.

Prevention and Your Children

Pay attention to warning signs your children exhibit so that you can be aware if your child is a potential perpetrator. Use of drugs, social isolation, fascination with weapons and death, suicidal words or behaviors, and other warning signs (see Chapter 8) may indicate that intervention is necessary to protect your child and others.

Encourage your children to pay attention to the words and actions of their peers. Teach them to bring to your attention or the attention of school administrators any threat made about violence against others at school or home. When we take these threats seriously, we will reduce the number of incidents. Help your children develop an escape plan for every class they attend if no formal plan has been provided by their schools.

Start prevention training with your children when they are young by teaching them to be responsible, accepting life with its ups and downs. Teach your children effective coping skills. Learning to cope with stress, disappointment, anger, and other emotions is imperative in preventing violent behavior.

It has been my clinical experience that parents are more likely to have trouble with their children if they are uninvolved in their children's lives and activities. I encourage parents to do more than attend ball games and recitals. Walks, discussions about books and movies, and meals eaten together on a regular basis provide a foundation for children. They see that they are not alone. The immaturity of their thinking causes children to believe that what is happening to them is happening for the first time in history and they are the only ones to know what it feels like to suffer their current woes. Families whose members are involved in one another's lives provide each other with a solid base that teaches children they are not alone and no matter what they face, they will face it together.

Involvement with high-risk children will enable one to see troubling symptoms at an embryonic stage. Intervention is more likely to be effective when the troubles are caught early. For the past fifteen years I have worked as a therapist with small children. Almost weekly, I receive telephone calls from parents seeking a therapist for their adolescent children. In many of the adolescent clients (and adults for that matter) that I have accepted over the years, their problems date back to issues in their childhood. If I had been able to work with them earlier in their lives, their problems would not have deepened, they would have been treated, and they would have had no need for a counselor in their teenage or adult years.

Never excuse irresponsible behavior in your child. Even if they have been mistreated, children should understand that the behavior of others never dictates one's own behavior. In many of the recent shootings in schools and businesses, the shooter blamed others for his troubles and that, in his mind, made his actions acceptable.

Pay attention to the concerns your children voice about their peers. In the Columbine shooting, several children had expressed concern about the two boys. At least one parent had contacted law enforcement officers due to his son's concerns. In Michigan in 1999, as in several places around the country, school authorities thwarted an attack on a school based on information they received from a parent, who relayed a child's conversations to school authorities. This very likely saved lives.

Prevention at Work

The place to start at work in preventing homicide is to listen to your fears. As I have demonstrated, in many cases where shootings have occurred people have sensed that something was not quite right. Your apprehension may be trying to tell you something.

Have your own violence response plan. If you are in a position to coordinate or order the development of such a plan, do so. If not, and if your company is not interested in developing one, develop one for yourself. Of course I am not suggesting insubordination, but nothing keeps you from deciding on an escape route in the case of a violent incident and informing your supervisors if you perceive a risk to yourself or others on the job. Even if your company has a violence prevention plan, have your own plan that fills in gaps in the company's plan.

Pay attention to those around you and be aware of potential risks. If you know that a coworker is afraid for her safety because of an aggressive ex-husband, that also puts you at risk. Know your options in situations such as this and do not be afraid to implement a plan for your own protection.

Prevention and Stalking

The first step in dealing with a stalker is to make sure someone else knows the situation. In a work environment, a supervisor should be notified, in a church, the pastor, etc. This gives credibility to your case if law enforcement becomes involved or if the case should ever go to court. The victim should make very clear, direct statements to the stalker that all contact should cease. Although kind people do not want to abandon someone they see as lonely, hope only perpetuates the problem. Do not open mail sent by the perpetrator, do not respond to phone calls, and avoid all contact.

Ensure that your home is secure. Lock windows and doors and park your vehicle in well-lighted areas. Vary driving routes and other routines to make it harder for the stalker to find you at any given day or time. Screen your telephone calls using caller-ID or an answering machine.

Develop a paper trail of the relationship. Keep every note and gift, record every phone call, record the date and time whenever the perpetrator drives by your house. This evidence will be useful to convince a court that stalking is occurring.

Experts recommend that one should not try to negotiate with stalkers. If the stalker persists, apply for a restraining order. Unfortunately, the restraining order can act as a triggering mechanism, spurring violence. I have recommended that victims who live alone should temporarily move to a location where help is available if the perpetrator decides to continue stalking after a restraining order is issued. A piece of paper cannot guarantee one's safety. Restraining orders do not stop bullets. This is a volatile situation that may last for days, months, or even years.

If the perpetrator violates the restraining order, the police must be called and the victim must pursue the case to its legal conclusion. If the stalker is released and still persists in stalking, the victim must contact police who can arrest him/her again. Victims sometimes give up because they do not think the law will help them. It can be frustrating and unfair, but the law may be the only recourse.

I was speaking on violence risk assessment at a conference for mental health workers, when a woman came to me and asked me about stalking. She was being stalked by a former boyfriend. This particular man had a position of power in the community and was professionally acquainted with the judges and law enforcement officers in the area. He had threatened her several times, once with a gun, and he had also threatened her children. She had not pursued a restraining order because she did not think any judge would grant it, given this man's position. I told her she had to try. Worrying was not helping her. Stalkers do their best to incapacitate and control their victims. She was playing into his hands by remaining silent.

If the law did not help her, I suggested she move to another county or state. She told me it was not fair that she should have to move. I agreed, but I told her that her options were to stay where she was, leaving both herself and her children at risk, or do the "unfair" thing and move to a safer environment. Of course, moving would not guarantee the perpetrator would not follow, but she would at least be taking control of her life where she could.

Weapons and Personal Protection

I consider weapons a last resort in self-protection, but one of the most frequent comments I receive in regard to prevention is the suggestion that one should be armed or protected by some sort of weapon. There are many weapons available for self-defense. Chemical sprays, clubs, stun guns, personal siren devices, and firearms are among the popular personal protection devices on the market. Each one has its strengths and weaknesses. If one chooses to acquire any type of weapon, it should be safely stored and inaccessible to children. Any weapon that can be used to harm or kill a perpetrator can be used to harm or kill a loved one. Also, one should be properly trained in the use of any weapon one chooses.

Chemical Sprays. Chemicals sprays are illegal in some areas; however, in most places, pepper gas, mace, and other sprays are legal. They can be purchased in various concentrations and are easy to use. Some are organic and are harmless if ingested, making them less of a risk than firearms in homes where children are present. The effects of chemical sprays are temporary. Many people could not make the decision to kill a perpetrator with a firearm. Chemical sprays are less emotionally threatening for the user because there is no risk of taking a life.

Chemical sprays have varying shelf lives. Dated chemical sprays may be ineffective. If they have been test-fired or used, the nozzles can clog. You will not know the nozzle is clogged until you try to use it. That, of course, is a bad time to realize your weapon is ineffective.

Chemical sprays are ineffective against some perpetrators. A few individuals are unaffected by the spray and others may be unaffected while under the influence of certain drugs. Some chemical sprays work instantly and other need a few seconds to take effect. Those few seconds may be too long. Also, when using chemical sprays, one must consider the wind direction. Spraying into the wind might leave the perpetrator unaffected and incapacitate the user, making escape more difficult or impossible. One final limitation is, of course, that a chemical spray is not effective against a firearm.

Clubs and Batons. Many types of clubs and batons are available on the market. My biggest complaint about clubs is that it is difficult to keep them accessible. Keeping a club in the trunk of your car, for example, will only help if you are attacked when you have access to your car and time to retrieve the club from the trunk. Choosing an extension club that can be carried in a purse, on a belt, or in a jacket pocket makes the weapon more accessible, but the user must carry it all the time. Unless you are a law enforcement or security officer, it is unlikely that you will carry a club or baton on your belt. If the weapon is inaccessible, you will find yourself a victim while your baton is out of reach.

Stun Guns. Stun guns are grossly overrated as personal protective devices. Small stun guns lose effectiveness after one discharge. A stun gun that is not fully charged may simply make the perpetrator mad, rather than stopping his advance. Also, the perpetrator has to be within arm's length for effective use. If the perpetrator is that close, he/she would likely be in physical contact with the user of the stun gun; therefore, the electrical current would also stun the user. Long-handled stun guns put some distance between the user and the perpetrator, but they are bulky and impractical as means of personal protection. Stun guns are also expensive.

Personal Alarm Devices. The purpose of these products is to attract attention. They emit a high-pitched noise when activated. They are small enough to carry in a pocket, in a purse, or on a key ring. They are easy to use, they do no damage to the perpetrator or the victim, and they pose no danger to children. These devices sound good in theory, but the theory is based on a number of assumptions. First, it is assumed that the batteries in the device are fully charged, the device will work properly, the user will have easy access to the device, and he/she will have time to use it. Second, it is assumed that someone will be around to hear the alarm. The third assumption is that one or more persons nearby will, in fact, intervene. These devices may have their place, but self-defense experts that I have consulted do not recommend them.

Firearms. Few topics in our country are as controversial as firearms. Advocates of gun rights argue that the U.S. Constitution provides for the right of the citizenry to keep and bear arms, but opponents believe this makes it easier for criminals to acquire weapons. I will make no attempt to debate the issue here. To acquire a firearm is a personal choice, but if one decides on a firearm many things need to be considered.

First of all, buying a gun for personal security sounds good to many people. They believe they could point and shoot the weapon if they had to protect themselves or their families. However, the practice is not as simple as the theory. I know of policemen, fully trained to use lethal force, who could not pull the trigger when circumstances required them to do so. A gun owner has to be certain he/she is willing to take a life. To say you would shoot to wound is false logic. Even trained law enforcement officers are not accurate enough under pressure to aim that carefully. In firearms training, policemen are trained to "shoot to stop." Their target is the center mass of the chest. Even though it is called shooting to stop, a bullet wound from a .40 caliber weapon in the "stop zone" will probably result in death. Therefore, if you do not think you could take a life and live with the aftermath, potential charges by prosecutors, retribution or lawsuits by the deceased person's family members, and so forth, a firearm is not your best choice for personal protection.

A second consideration is the type of protection you desire, which determines the type of gun you buy. Protection in the home is different from protection on the street or in an automobile. At home, a shotgun is the most effective firearm. It takes little training and one's aim does not have to be very accurate in order to achieve a hit. Shotguns, however, are impractical on the street. A pistol is more likely to be the gun of choice in that situation.

If one is considering a handgun, the size and weight of the gun, the ease of use, caliber, and number of rounds available without reloading are important considerations. Handgun caliber varies. Many police departments carry 9mm weapons as their standard issue. Some use .38 or .357 caliber models, while others use .40 caliber or 10mm. All of these are available to the public. A small caliber weapon, like a .22 caliber pistol, is very easy to carry and to conceal. A shot from a .22 can be fatal, but only if it is well placed. Like pepper sprays, a misplaced shot with a small caliber weapon may only make the perpetrator angry.

Accuracy is more difficult to achieve with small weapons as the distance between the shooter and the target increases. Generally speaking, accuracy improves as the length of the gun barrel increases. Small weapons may allow for only two shots without reloading. Larger handguns may allow for as many as ten, the civilian limit. Law enforcement models may hold as many as fifteen rounds.

Handguns come in either revolver or semiautomatic styles. Because of the external mechanical action of a revolver, a perpetrator can keep the weapon from firing if he grabs the cylinder, hence preventing the cylinder from turning and chambering a round. Semiautomatic weapons have a clip that slides into the handle, eliminating this problem.

Yet another issue with handguns is safe storage. Storing a gun unloaded, in a gun safe, and using a trigger lock are all good ideas. However, they make the weapon practically inaccessible in a crisis. If someone were breaking into your home, you would have to open your gun safe, remembering the combination under pressure, find and use the key to the trigger lock, load the weapon, and fire before the perpetrator got to you or the loved ones you were trying to protect. However, disregarding these safety steps places children at risk. Many states have laws that allow for prosecution of the gun owner if a weapon that was not properly stored is acquired by a child and used in an accident that results in death.

A fifth issue is the license to carry a concealed weapon. Some states do not allow anyone outside law enforcement to own handguns. Other states allow for the ownership of handguns, but they have concealed-weapons laws that govern when and where one can and cannot carry them. Even in states where one can be licensed to carry a concealed weapon, there are many places and situations where one cannot carry it even with a civilian permit (i.e., airports, some public buildings, public functions, churches). For all these reasons, carrying a gun for personal protection may not be practical without risk of violating the law, thus risking prosecution and revocation of the right to carry.

There are many other issues concerning firearms, but I want to address just one more. One of my friends once told me that she felt safer at home because her husband had a gun in the house. I asked her how often he practiced. She said he did not practice at all. I suggested to her that the weapon was probably a greater risk to her home than a help, if someone in the house was not properly trained and regular in practice. I have seen a number of law enforcement training films regarding critical incidents—those incidents where an officer had to fire a weapon. In many of these films, multiple rounds are fired. It is not uncommon for an officer to fire ten or fifteen rounds but make only one hit. These are trained men and women who qualify annually to use their weapons, and yet a 50% hit ratio or less is not uncommon. If this is true for seasoned officers, one should not expect any better of untrained citizens.

In summary, if one chooses to purchase a firearm for protection, there are many serious considerations involving selection, purchase, training, storage, and the law. Forethought, training, practice, and safety must be a part of any decision.

CONCLUDING REMARKS

In this chapter I have presented a number of ways to approach violence prevention. I have addressed intervention, prevention by organizations, and preventive strategies for individuals. In the past few years I have participated in several brainstorming sessions on homicide prevention hosted by educators, law enforcement organizations, psychologists, and other interested groups. In each of these meetings, our groups generated some ideas that were admittedly bad. We also came up with good ideas, but ones that were impossible or impractical to implement. Yet despite our bad ideas and our impractical ones, every brainstorming session also generated good, conceivably workable ideas.

I attended one such focus group at the invitation of a police chief in a large southern city. Several homicide officers were present in the focus group, which was also attended by people from mental health, medicine, religion, and education. During the session I noticed one ranking homicide detective seemingly uninterested in our work. During a break I asked him if our "idealistic talk" drove him crazy. In no uncertain terms, he said he disliked it very much. In one room we had a variety of expensive experts from various fields who had come together on their own time and at their own expense to search for solutions. Yet this man was not interested in any help. Businesses have paid me several hundred dollars for a single hour of my time to work on problems of violence. The time of my medical colleagues in that room was worth even more than that. Even so, we had volunteered our time to a search for solutions and make this detective's job easier. Yet he was content to continue cynically viewing the problem as hopeless.

Similar cynics can find plenty of fodder for argument with the suggestions I have presented in this chapter. I remain undaunted. I believe that individuals can make a difference. Working as a volunteer school counselor in President Jimmy Carter's Atlanta Project several years ago, I participated with hundreds of people from every possible walk of life who committed two years of work to improve the lives of the underprivileged in the city of Atlanta. Even though the Atlanta Project was not perfect, it had a dramatic impact on the lives of both the underprivileged and the volunteers. Participation in that project taught me that no problem is too big to overcome with time, help, and will.

The city of Boston, Massachusetts, has attacked the problem of violence with astounding results. Its multifaceted plan to address violence has produced dramatic effects on various types of violent crime. Most impressive, not a single juvenile "has been killed with a firearm in Boston" since July 10, 1995 (through the publication of "The Boston strategy to prevent youth violence" in spring 1997).[4] Equally impressive, juvenile homicides dropped nearly 80% from 1990 to 1995.[5] Boston's success is due to a well-designed program that included the entire community—law enforcement, safe-neighborhood initiatives, programs addressing domestic violence and child abuse, the business community, the media, and the religious community all working together toward the same goals. Despite the cynical attitudes of some critics of "idealistic thinking," it is clear from the Boston experience that effective programs are possible and dramatic results can be achieved.

NOTES

1. Frederick Copleston, *A history of philosophy: Fichte to Nietzsche, Vol. VII* (Garden City, NY: Image Books, 1985), 411.

2. Charles E. Labig, *Preventing violence in the workplace* (New York: RHR International Co., 1995), 86.

3. Ibid.

4. "The Boston strategy to prevent youth violence," *The Boston Police Department and Partners*, Spring 1997, 3.

5. *Youth violence: a community-based response* (Washington, DC: United States Department of Justice, September 1996), 2.

Seven Mistakes That Can Cost People Their Lives

Discussing prevention as I have done in Chapter 9 is less threatening when I address homicide generically and I do not mention specific names or cases. Yet, one of the most elusive answers I seek in each case refers to the question, "Could this homicide have been foreseen or prevented?" This may be one of the most difficult questions I have to address in this book, not only because the process is inexact but also because the answer can be quite personal. As I have said previously, I realize that it is easy to look backward and lay blame. I have no intention of blaming victims or survivors. Victims of trauma endure enough physical and emotional pain without someone complicating their recovery with allegations and blame. In fact, it is not uncommon for wounded survivors as well as those who were uninjured to blame themselves and to struggle with a sense of guilt that they themselves did not die. They may feel they have betrayed those who died by surviving or by escaping injury altogether. I do not wish to compound the pain of those who survived or who have lost loved ones by suggesting that they are somehow liable for the deaths and injuries that occurred.

However, I privately struggle with each case, looking for places where intervention might have saved lives. I have sifted through the information in hundreds of conversations I have had with clients, police officers, perpetrators, relatives, survivors, and other victims, searching for clues to the causes of the tragedies that touched their lives. Avoiding the appearance of blame in the presentation of my conclusions requires tact and sensitivity. Rather than laying blame, however, I am interested in learning from the choices people made that preceded their deaths, their injuries, or the deaths and injuries of others. These victims did not have the benefit of experience and training that might have saved their lives; therefore, they cannot be held accountable. But even among those who have been trained, responses to crises do not always reflect their training. The intensity of tragic events is such that unless we have been there, we cannot know what decisions we would make ourselves. We have an advantage over these past victims, however, since we can look at the history of their encounters and learn from them. This knowledge does not guarantee that we will make the right choices, but it at least provides us with tools for making choices if we are confronted with similar circumstances. In this chapter I outline seven common mistakes in the homicides that I have studied. I describe how inattention to one or more of these seven issues contributed to the murders that occurred. I also show how attention to one or more of these issues saved lives.

With each homicide case I review, there comes a point when a light comes on in my mind as I see where intervention might have changed the course of events that resulted in someone's death. It pains me to realize that people might not have died if they had made different choices. I am especially discouraged by cases where organizations had the power and the opportunity to intervene, but they ignored warning signs, either by ignorance or by deliberation, and people lay dead in the wake of their decisions. I am even sensitive to the plight of perpetrators who desperately sought resolution to the figurative demons that possessed them, but who found no answers or relief.

There have been only a very few cases where I was forced to concede that little could have been done to prevent the actions of an angry killer. Sometimes the crime is seemingly so random that prediction would have been difficult even if the opportunity for intervention had availed itself. In some cases, especially stalking cases, the perpetrator's dysfunction was so severe that he could not have been appeased. Violence at some level in these cases may have been inevitable. In still other cases, the shooter's resolve to destroy may have resulted from mental illness and/or a rage that built silently over months or years, making proper diagnosis even by trained psychologists difficult or pragmatically impossible. Yet these are exceptions. More often than not, I can see places where different decisions might have saved people from injury or even saved their lives. The mistakes that I have observed can be grouped into seven categories: ignoring or failing to respond adequately to threats, failing to help oneself, failing to develop or implement a plan, attempting to defuse the situation alone, failing to call for help soon enough, panicking, and not taking medications (in the case of perpetrators).

MISTAKE 1: IGNORING OR FAILING TO RESPOND ADEQUATELY TO THREATS

If I could prevent only one mistake in all the homicides I have addressed, this would be the one. It is my firm belief that all our behaviors have a purpose. If we wear a T-shirt that has a message on it, chances are the message means something to us. If we wear suits, ties, or dresses, then chances are we are trying to communicate an appearance of professionalism through our clothing. We select the type, color, and model of vehicle we drive, in part, by what it communicates about us. Nothing about our communications, either verbal or nonverbal, is accidental. In therapy I invest tremendous energy in reading the nonverbal messages my clients present along with their verbal messages. More often than not, when the two types of messages are incongruent, I can place more trust in the nonverbal message. These messages in harmony, however, produce a message in which we can have great confidence. In other words, we can trust that message to be genuine.

When I am assessing risk for violent behavior, one of the things I look for is a message from the subject that tells me his or her intentions. Verbal statements of intent can be evidence of violent potential, but so can nonverbal ones. As I look over numerous homicide cases, I never cease to be amazed by the number of people that have either missed or ignored verbal and nonverbal messages of intent to kill. One clear case where these messages were missed, ignored, or inadequately addressed was the case of Clifton McCree discussed in Chapter 3. As I studied this case, I was stunned to see how many times McCree clearly threatened his coworkers and others and yet, according to statements from those who worked with him, no disciplinary action was taken. His violent temper tantrums, threats, and aggression became more and more frequent over the months that preceded his eventual dismissal after a failed drug test. According to one coworker, McCree became so bold as to behave aggressively even in front of his foreman.

Why was no action taken against him? His supervisors were not totally responsible for their failure to act. In their statements to police, several employees reported that they had complained to supervisors, but others had kept their concerns to themselves. But even those who complained to supervisors admitted that they had refused to sign formal statements for fear they would be identified. Therefore, the supervisors, especially those at high levels in the system, were unable to take any action, even if they had wanted to, because there had been no formal complaint.

However, McCree's foreman, described as a very kind individual, did not want McCree to lose his job; witnesses said they believed he did not take action to fire McCree because he was concerned about McCree's welfare. I have found that even in very large corporations, there are compassionate people who look for ways to deal with a potentially violent employee short of firing him. This compassion, while noble, perpetuates a violent person's control and allows a high-risk employee like McCree to remain in the environment. Eventually, McCree's fellow employees provided supervisors with the information that they needed to act, and the man was dismissed.

Failure to act in this case had its roots in several places. First, employees were either afraid to say anything or they chose to ignore the problem. Second, those who did lodge complaints were afraid for their own safety so they were reluctant to sign formal complaints. Third, according to witness statements, at least one supervisor had the information he needed to fire McCree on several occasions, but he elected not to act because of his personal compassion for the employees in his charge, who included McCree. Finally, upper management could not have acted, even if they wanted to, because the paper trail that they needed did not exist.

As well as making directly threatening statements, McCree also nonverbally told his coworkers he was a potential threat to them. McCree's verbal aggressiveness, his volatile temper, his use of an illegal substance (antisocial behavior), and his contempt for his superiors were all indicators of a potentially violent man. There is no way to know what would have happened if McCree's coworkers had formalized their complaints earlier or if the supervisor had acted earlier to dismiss him. Critics might argue that McCree would simply have killed his colleagues sooner. This may be true, but I would argue that the earlier the intervention takes place, the more likely the situation can be defused. Addressing this situation earlier would at least have been an attempt at intervention rather than inaction.

Of the many homicides that I have reviewed, none compares to the tragedy at Littleton, Colorado, for failure to see and address symptoms of serious distress. Over a period of many months, both Eric Harris and Dylan Klebold showed numerous signs of the trouble that brewed within their minds. Yet professionals, relatives, and friends missed these symptoms. The few people who did recognize troubling symptoms in these boys incorrectly assumed the symptoms were isolated events and dismissed them.

Harris and Klebold planned their revenge on students at the high school for nearly a year, but the symptoms of their troubles began even earlier. A former girlfriend of Harris told reporters that she had broken up with him four years earlier because he had "behaved in a weird fashion."[1] This statement by itself is meaningless, and many normal middle and high school students may be classified as "weird" by their former girlfriends, boyfriends, and classmates, but the kinds of things that Harris did were anything but normal. The former girlfriend described an incident in which a friend had requested that she come to his house. She arrived to find Harris lying in the "back yard with fake blood spattered around him, as if he had committed suicide."[2]

In the months that preceded the tragedy at Columbine High School, Eric Harris maintained a web site that identified people with whom he was enraged. "LIARS!!! OH GAWWWWWWWD I HATE LIARS" proclaimed Harris's web site, in an apparent reference to an athlete from Columbine who had reportedly escaped punishment for aggressive behaviors.[3] The web site included statements of hatred toward blacks and Jews, and also announced that Harris and a friend had constructed pipe bombs.[4] Additionally, it reportedly included both indirect and direct threats. "Well, all you people out there can just die. You all better hide in your houses, because I'm coming for everyone soon, and I will be armed to the teeth, and I will shoot to kill, and I will kill everything," the site warned.[5] A parent of one child was so concerned about the hateful and threatening language, some of which threatened his son by name, that he took pages from Harris's web site to police. Yet the police did not intervene because they said no crime had been committed. (The sheriff's department said that the parents had "refused to swear out a complaint with their names, fearing for their son's life."[6]) The parents also complained to America Online (the site host), but they received no response.[7]

Both Klebold and Harris had produced creative writing with violent themes. Their stories were so troubling to an English teacher that the teacher addressed the stories individually with Harris's father and Klebold's mother. Klebold described killings and Harris described himself as a "shotgun shell."[8] A school counselor became involved in Klebold's case but later concluded that the boy was not a threat. In the case of Harris's writings, the teacher dropped the matter after discussing it with his father. The boys produced a video as a class project and it was reviewed in class during the fall prior to the shooting. In hindsight, it provided a chilling premonition of the events to come. This video showed Klebold and Harris using toy guns to shoot other students in the school hallways.[9] A friend of the boys said he helped the two make several other videos of a "similar genre."[10]

The behavior of the boys communicated hatred and contempt for others. Fellow students say that Klebold was disrespectful to teachers, misbehaved in class, and sometimes lost his temper.[11] The group of students that the two boys associated with dressed in the "gothic" style that included dark clothing and trench coats. Harris was "obsessed" with Nazi and World War II history, he reportedly liked to speak German and mimic Nazi behaviors, and he seemed to glorify Hitler.[12] The attack itself happened on Hitler's birthday. Klebold was known to wear a shirt that said "Serial Killer," a shirt he reportedly wore early on the day of the shooting. Classmates' descriptions of the two boys said they had "sick minds," they were "totally creepy," and "everybody was weirded out by [their behavior]."[13] They were also described as bullies, impossible not to notice, anti-everything, obsessed with death, and despising God.[14] One student claimed Harris had told him specifically that he would kill him.[15] A classmate said that the boys waved a pistol out of the window of their car the summer before their rampage.[16] These behaviors alone would give me cause for concern as a counselor. The boys paraded in distinctive dress and participated in a visibly distinct social group (the Trenchcoat Mafia) that was clearly identified in the school yearbook. Teachers, counselors, and students were openly concerned about them, and the boys publicly presented disturbing writings and class video projects—yet, the principal said he was unaware of any group called the Trenchcoat Mafia or any problem with the boys.[17]

There was evidence of trouble in their homes, as well. They purchased a firearm in January for $500, they constructed numerous explosive devices, and they possessed three other firearms, provided by Klebold's 18-year-old girlfriend, that they used in their rampage. So many explosives were found in the school building that investigators initially believed that the two must have had an accomplice.[18] In their examination of the home of one of the boys, investigators found "clear evidence out, sitting in the room, of what was about to happen," saying "a lot of this stuff was clearly visible, and the parents should have known."[19] Jefferson County Sheriff John Stone said that a sawn-off shotgun barrel and bomb-making material were found in one boy's room.[20] Harris kept a diary that detailed the plan of the assault. This diary showed that Harris had planned the attack for nearly a year, and it included maps, schedules, and other information designed to maximize the impact of the shooting, resulting in the most deaths.[21]

Yet the many hours that went into making bombs, the money spent on buying supplies, weapons, and ammunition, and the detailed planning of the attack somehow unfolded without attracting the attention of the parents. The two boys told others they were angry and wanted to kill. They said it in their behavior, and they clearly said it several times in their words, both in print and face-to-face. Seemingly every area of their lives provided clues to their disturbances. If one of these boys had been my son, I am sure I would want to believe I could not have known the depth of their troubles, but I do not believe the people who said "they were such nice boys." I agree that they may have been capable of presenting themselves in such a way as to look respectable on the surface, but "nice boys" do not engage in the lifestyles and behaviors of these two. The preponderance of the evidence, especially in the year prior to the shooting, without a doubt indicates two very troubled boys. Yet somehow, despite all this evidence, counselors, a principal, teachers, court officers, at least one judge, friends, the parents of classmates, and the parents of the boys themselves did not recognize the extent of the explosive potential in these boys in the days, weeks, and months prior to the attack. In fact, the level at which this tragedy blind-sided some people is poignantly shown by the statement of a spokesman for Klebold's mother, that the attack came "as a bolt out of the blue."[22]

How could two boys produce so many explosives, buy expensive weapons, express such hatred for others through their actions, words, writings, videos, and web pages, and yet leave bright, educated people completely blinded to their potential? I suggest that the blindness came from two sources. First, some were privy only to pieces of these boys' lives—mere snapshots out of context from the broader picture of their lives. Neighbors, teachers, the judge—none of them could have learned the whole story unless they had known to ask the right questions and look in places beyond their own domains. Second, some did not want to see the picture. As I have suggested in previous chapters, we protect ourselves by pretending the dangers in the world around us cannot invade our towns, our schools, or our homes. The disturbing signs that were picked up by some people in the lives of these boys were dismissed because, in part, they did not want to make a big deal out of an attitude, a story, a videotape, or a web site.

It would be easy to become depressed on reviewing these two cases. There have been, however, a number of cases where individuals responded adequately to threats and where attacks were thwarted. In the aftermath of the Columbine High School shootings, many schools instituted a zero tolerance policy toward threats of violence. They educated their students and faculty on the process for dealing with threats and provided information on dangerous warning signs. After the tragedy at Littleton, only a few weeks of school remained before summer break, but with their newfound education on threats to the school environment, many schools found themselves dismissing students weekly or even daily because of threats and false alarms. One high school in the Atlanta metropolitan area suffered so many false alarms that they changed their policy almost as soon as they had initiated it. They decided they would not empty the school building because of threats of violence. They decided to announce the fact that a threat existed and to give the students the opportunity to leave if they wanted. I was holding my breath, waiting for the school year to end, hoping that no other shootings or bombings would take place.

But not every case ended as a false alarm. At Bishop Brady High School in Concord, New Hampshire, administrators learned that a student had a "hit list" and they searched his locker. There they found a .22 caliber revolver and 400 rounds of ammunition. In Palatka, Florida, an attack was averted when 17-year-old William Black and 16-year-old Jeffrey Carter were arrested for conspiracy to commit second-degree murder. An alert history teacher found a drawing depicting a violent theme involving another student. The teacher confronted one of the boys and was told they "planned to do a better job of killing than was done at Columbine High School."[23] Six months before the Columbine shooting, three teenage boys in Burlington, Wisconsin, were charged with conspiring to murder between fifteen and twenty of their classmates. In this case, the plot was not disclosed by an outsider, but by two boys who had originally been a part of the plan and had changed their minds.[24] Copycat crimes and bomb threats occurred in nearly every state in the union in the weeks following the Littleton tragedy, but very few resulted in injuries or deaths. These cases provided evidence that attention to warning signs and threats can, in fact, be helpful in assessing risk and intervening to prevent tragedies. Would any of these children actually have followed through on their plans and threats? Thank God, their plans were interrupted so we have no answer to that question.

MISTAKE 2: FAILURE TO HELP ONESELF

A second common mistake that people have made involves victims taking no action at all to save their own lives. One of the most frustrating interviews I heard on television in the aftermath of the Columbine High School shooting was with a young man who was in the library when Klebold and Harris were killing his classmates. He said that one of the two shooters put the gun about eight inches from his head. The boy then said, "I put my head down, closed my eyes and waited on the gun to go off." According to this student, the shooter did, in fact, pull the trigger, but miraculously, he missed. However, other students present during the attack noted that all the shootings were "at close range."[25] I wonder how many lives might have been saved if one or more of the people present had said to themselves, "I may die, but I'm not going to just lie down and let them shoot me." I understand these were very young people and in the panic of the moment, it would be unrealistic to expect them to have responded differently. However, with minimal training, I suggest that they *could* have acted differently.

Taking action against an armed perpetrator is not always a good idea. In some cases it is better to wait and see what a perpetrator's intentions are. One does not want to antagonize a nervous, armed individual when he may be willing to negotiate. However, this was not the case in the Columbine shooting. The shooters had already demonstrated their intent to kill as many people as possible. In fact, one student recognized the intent of the shooters even in the heat of the moment. This young man said, "Finally, I started figuring out these guys shot to kill, for no reason. . . . They didn't care what race you were. It didn't matter. They wanted to shoot to have fun."[26] Another student echoed this observation when she said, "They didn't care who they shot at. They just kept shooting."[27] In this case, it would have been reasonable to assume the perpetrators would pull the trigger no matter what the young victims did. The gun was "eight inches" away from a victim, well within his reach. He had absolutely nothing to lose by seizing it. Instead, he obediently put his head down and allowed the perpetrator to shoot at him, giving this cowardly bully the passively obedient victim he counted on.

In Poland, during World War II, the Sobibor concentration camp was run by a handful of Nazi guards. The inmates were mostly Jews from Poland, Czechoslovakia, Germany, and Austria. In July 1943, a prisoner named Leon Feldhendler led a movement to escape from the camp. The camp was being reorganized and the changes would certainly have led to the inmates' deaths. They recognized that, even though some of them would die in their attempt to escape, some would be freed and live. They stormed the fences and about 300 escaped, killing a number of SS officers and Ukrainian guards in the process. Even though many were killed in surrounding minefields and others were later captured, fifty survived until the end of the war. The camp was closed following the revolt of 1943. During the seventeen months of its operation, 250,000 inmates, mostly Jews, were killed. At least fifty survived certain extermination because they were willing to take control of their lives and their situation where they could. As a therapist I find that many people have difficulties in their daily lives because they do not take control when they have the possibility. They leave their fates in the hands of others.

Like the inmates of Sobibor, many victims have taken action in the midst of a crisis and lived to tell about it. One young man who was in the library at Columbine acted differently from those I described above. When one of the perpetrators threw an explosive device in the area where this boy and others lay hiding, he did not wait for it to go off. Instead, he picked up the device and threw it away.[28]

In Honolulu, Hawaii, a recently fired employee of a concrete company took several hostages at his former workplace. In the process of taking hostages, he shot his former boss. As control of the situation began to slip from the gunman's hands, he taped the barrel of a shotgun to an employee's head. He then taped the trigger to his own finger, ensuring that if he were shot, the weapon would discharge and kill the employee. After a standoff with police that lasted seven hours, the gunman indicated that he was going to kill the employee on the count of sixty. He attempted to force his hostage to count backwards from sixty, planning to shoot him when he reached zero, but the hostage would not comply. The gunman himself began counting. Knowing he was going to die anyway, the hostage felt the location of the barrel of the gun on his neck, spun around, pulling the barrel away from his neck, and grabbed the gun. The perpetrator fired the weapon, narrowly missing the victim's ear. A second shot discharged into the pavement. The hostage then dropped to one knee, giving the police a clear shot at the gunman. Police on the scene took advantage of this and killed the gunman.

In Memphis, Tennessee, a Federal Express employee carrying his guitar case hitched a ride on one of his company's cargo planes. Inside the case he had concealed four hammers, a spear gun, and a diving knife. During the flight he attempted to hijack the plane. He entered the cockpit and struck the flight crew repeatedly with the hammer. Spear gun in hand, he demanded control of the plane, but one injured member of the flight crew grabbed the weapon. In the scuffle that ensued, the hijacker was detained and the plane landed safely. On the ground, the perpetrator was arrested. All three members of the flight crew survived, although one pilot's injuries were so severe he was unable to continue his career. The perpetrator's plan was to crash the DC-10 into a Fed Ex package-sorting hub, killing himself in the process. He had taken out a $1 million life insurance policy, and he believed his heirs would receive the money upon his death. Even though all three members of the crew were injured, they survived the incident and their actions saved property and countless lives on the ground.

When a gunman fired an automatic assault weapon at the White House in Washington, D.C., bystanders took advantage of an opportunity to disarm him when he stopped shooting because his weapon was either empty or jammed. In several school shootings, bystanders took action that ended the violence. In Pearl, Mississippi, an assistant principal retrieved his personal weapon from his car and held Luke Woodham at gunpoint until police arrived. In West

Paducah, Kentucky, a football player and student charged Michael Carneal as he fired into the crowd of students in the hallways. In Springfield, Oregon, despite being shot already, a wrestler tackled Kip Kinkel and ended his shooting spree.

Perpetrators of violent crimes like the ones I have described in this book are often cowards. They use explosives and weapons to give them a sense of power and control and they use that power to bully other people. Once they have been disarmed, or they recognize they are surrounded by police and cannot escape, it is not uncommon for them to whimper and beg for their lives or take their own lives. If they meet with resistance, they realize their victims are not going to be intimidated. They may then choose to leave the scene or surrender. This is a dangerous situation, though, and fighting back should never be an automatic choice. Many perpetrators are looking for a reason to kill, and any affront to their control may be all it takes. When there are no alternatives, however, it is better to take action to save yourself than simply wait your turn to die.

MISTAKE 3: FAILURE TO DEVELOP OR IMPLEMENT A PLAN

Once people are aware their lives are in jeopardy, they often have weeks, months, or even years to develop plans for saving themselves. Stalkers, obsessed ex-spouses, and angry coworkers almost always demonstrate their potential for violence long before they actually attack. During these days or weeks, potential victims can develop plans for hiding, escaping, or defending themselves. In the case of Robert Helfer, for weeks before the incident, numerous coworkers had harbored concern both publicly and privately that he might be a threat to them. The most vivid example was his coworker, Donna Archuleta, who had requested that her office area remain separated from Helfer's because of her fear for her safety. Her plan for protecting herself included being more alert and aware of her surroundings. She educated herself on Helfer's behaviors by observing him and she learned to identify the seriousness of his confrontations with others based on his demeanor. She became attentive to her surroundings at work, in the parking lot, and away from the office. Even though she did not have a specific plan at the point when a coworker told her that Helfer was approaching with a gun, she quickly developed one. She had the clarity of mind to recognize that she was completely vulnerable in her office where she could easily be found. Instead of hiding in her office, she fled down the hall, although she stumbled and fell. A co-worker helped her into another office where she hid behind a large printer. Helfer, crawling through the halls with a broken ankle, made it to the doorway of her office, but found it empty. Archuleta described herself to me as literally paralyzed with fear, but even so, her good sense enabled her to make a plan that saved her life. Karla Harding told me about the plan of defense she developed even as she sat in Helfer's presence, just minutes before the shooting. She said that even though she did not know what she would do next, she knew she had to charge him. She was not going to be a passive victim. One physician who treated Harding suggested that her plan saved her life because she was a moving target.

In the case of Clifton McCree, in contrast, many employees had heard his threats and known of his violent behavior, in some cases for several years, yet the day he arrived and began killing, all but one of the employees were totally unprepared. The exception was one of McCree's coworkers, who engaged in a routine that made him less accessible in the event that McCree ever lived up to his threats. On the day of the shootings, his plan paid off and he escaped unharmed. Devising a plan should include knowledge of possible exits, places to hide, ways to contact help, recognition of cover (e.g., desks, filing cabinets), and ways to avoid contact with the potential perpetrator altogether. Remaining calm in the midst of a crisis can also help a potential victim modify a current plan or develop a new plan very quickly.

MISTAKE 4: ATTEMPTING TO DEFUSE THE SITUATION ALONE

Sometimes people die when they try to defuse problems on their own rather than referring the matter to the police. In a southern Georgia town, a patron of a bar made a lewd comment to a female bartender one evening. The following night, the man returned and was confronted by the owner of the bar. After a verbal confrontation with the owner, the patron was expelled. Later that evening, another patron who had witnessed the confrontation saw the expelled man on the sidewalk outside the bar. He was concerned to see the man hanging around; he later said he thought it was odd that the man had put on a jacket that hot August evening. The patron informed the bar owner that the man was back. Even though there is no evidence that the man was trying to enter the bar, the owner confronted the expelled man, intending to physically keep him from entering. As he confronted the man on the sidewalk, the two argued briefly. Then the man pulled a weapon from his jacket and shot the owner four times at nearly point-blank range. The owner died from his wounds. The gunman then entered the bar and discharged his weapon numerous times, wounding several people. He eventually surrendered to police. If employees or the bar owner had called police when they first saw the man on the sidewalk, the owner might have survived.

Patrons are expelled from bars every night, and it would be unrealistic to call the police every time. However, the bar owner missed several clues to the man's intentions. The man had already behaved inappropriately both the previous night and again on the evening of the shooting when he was confronted by the owner. After leaving, he donned a jacket that was inappropriate for the weather conditions. Finally, he was making no attempt to force his way into the bar, but neither was he making any attempt to leave. The man was clearly looking for a fight. Unfortunately, he found it and an innocent business owner died as a result.

MISTAKE 5: FAILURE TO CALL FOR HELP SOON ENOUGH

Attempting to handle threatening situations alone is closely related to the next mistake—failing to call for help soon enough. Sometimes witnesses are aware something is happening, but they take no action until it is too late. At an Ohio trucking company, an angry employee engaged in a loud argument with a former coworker and then struck him. In the course of the argument, coworkers overheard the victim say he would call the police and file assault charges against the employee. A problem situation was clearly developing. At least two people heard the argument and one of them saw the employee strike his colleague, but no one called the police until the perpetrator pulled a gun and shot his victim several times. Calling the police early might not have saved the life of this worker, but it might have saved the life of two others whom the perpetrator hunted down and killed. These events unfold very quickly. It is unfair to expect that either of the witnesses should have known enough to call police or that they should have correctly assessed what was occurring. However, if they had been trained to recognize the volatility of such situations, they would have known they should call police as the argument escalated. The police could have been on their way even before the first man was shot.

A policy by which fired employees are prohibited from returning to the work site can provide the reason to call police. In Boston, a stockbroker returned to the office the day after he was fired. The supervisor had graciously agreed to continue discussions in regard to outplacement counseling. The angry ex-employee entered the office, withdrew a .22 caliber pistol from his brief case, and shot the supervisor. Even though he was wounded, the supervisor managed to exit the office and enter the adjoining hallway where the perpetrator beat him with the weapon and then fired at him several more times. Workers eventually overpowered the perpetrator and held him until police arrived. The supervisor died at the hospital about an hour later. Employees stated that they assumed the perpetrator was returning to continue a discussion from the previous day.[29] Again, if employees had been informed of his dismissal and if the business had engaged in a policy that forbade dismissed employees from returning to the site, the employees would have known something was amiss. They would at least have had the opportunity to consider calling security or the police. As a side note, I recommend outplacement counseling be handled at the time of dismissal. This boss's gracious offer compromised his own safety and potentially that of the other workers. If outplacement counseling cannot be completed at the time of dismissal, it should be conducted over the telephone to avoid situations such as this.

Whether it is at work, at home, or in some public place, people are often reluctant to call the police because they do not want it to appear that they are overreacting or are incapable of handling stressful or difficult circumstances. This same mentality leads to the deaths of heart attack victims every year. They begin to suffer symptoms of a heart attack, but they do not want to overreact. They sometimes live in denial for hours or even days, assuming their pain is caused by something they have eaten or some other less threatening health problem. They do not want to admit that they could be dying from a heart attack. By the time they finally accept that they are, indeed, suffering a heart attack, it is sometimes too late for them to be treated successfully. Similarly, when an argument or assault is under way, people do not want to believe that anything tragic could happen to them or in their presence. They perpetuate their denial by assuming that shootings and murders happen to other people in other places—not in their own offices and living rooms. The reality of what is happening grips them only when they see a weapon or hear a gunshot. By then it is too late to call for help. Believing that the worst is possible moves people to call for help.

It would be naive to suppose that calling the police immediately will always prevent a homicide or assault. Sometimes, even when witnesses call the police at the first hint of trouble, it is not soon enough. In the case of Samuel Quick (discussed in Chapter 4), employees called the police almost immediately. By sheer coincidence, several senior police officers were just minutes away when they heard the call over their radio. They arrived on the scene almost immediately, but it was too late to prevent Quick from shooting his victim in their presence. However, most cases present an opportunity for help to be summoned. As these incidents unfold, we lose nothing by calling the police. If the perpetrator negotiates and surrenders or even if he leaves the scene before the police arrive, there is no cost to the police, the caller, or the bystanders. Failing to call, however, can be costly in terms of both dollars and lives.

MISTAKE 6: PANIC

I am sure I could make a fortune if I could develop some pill or process for preventing panic. Even trained soldiers sometimes panic when they face the possibility of their own deaths in battle. It should be no surprise, then, that civilians, when surprised by gunfire or explosions, panic and do not know what to do. "I was terrified and I didn't know what to do at first" was the comment of one student at Columbine High School.[30] Certainly, such initial panic is not exclusive to this student, nor is it exclusive to Columbine. Many of Richard Farley's victims were killed because they were in the wrong place at the wrong time. They heard shooting and stepped into hallways to see what was happening. Others were killed as they panicked and tried to leave the building. In his statements to law enforcement officers, Farley said he shot several people because they scared him. They came running in his direction in their panic, not realizing what they were doing, so he shot them. In another shooting, on a military base, the shooter fired at a senior officer. The commanding officer stepped into the room to see what was happening. When he did so, the gunman shot and killed him. Ironically, the gunman's original target survived.

The commanding officer should have recognized gunfire and known better than to enter the room. Yet his actions were much the same as those of the untrained civilians in the office building where Farley conducted his shooting spree. His poor decision cost him his life.

One employee in the Farley shooting, however, did not panic. She quietly hid underneath a desk. As Farley moved throughout the large room with many desks, by chance he stopped beside the desk where she was hiding. He discovered this woman and talked with her briefly. If she had panicked and charged him, or if he had believed that she was trying to attack him as she ran, she would likely have been killed. But instead this woman remained calm and asked Farley if he wanted her to stay. In her statements to police, she said she was afraid he would shoot her if she tried to leave, but even in her fear, she remained calm. Farley allowed her to walk out of the building unharmed.

MISTAKE 7: PATIENTS NOT TAKING MEDICATION

We have seen how confused the thinking processes of patients can become when they have either refused altogether to take their prescribed medications or ceased taking them or were never properly diagnosed and given a prescription. The case of Russell Weston is representative of this sort of individual. It is reasonable to assume that if Weston had been properly diagnosed and appropriate prescriptions were made available to him, his delusional thoughts would have been controlled. Of course, it is impossible to know "what if" in Weston's case and there is, likewise, no guarantee that any patient, either hospitalized or outpatient, will take his or her medications. What we can learn from this is the importance of maintaining a mental health patient's regimen. Supervising physicians, attending therapists, and family members should be educated on the importance of consistency in the patient's prescribed medical interventions.

I cannot know how many patients have *not* engaged in violent acts because of the effectiveness of their psychotropic interventions. Therefore, I cannot cite cases where medication has prevented an act of violence. I can, however, deduce that many cases exist where the patient has been properly medicated and that medication has pre-empted violent actions. My deduction is based on the sheer number of patients on medication and the relatively small number of these patients who actually commit violent acts.

Many of my clients over the years have not been fully informed by their prescribing physicians about the side effects and expected results of their medications. For example, some antidepressants have side effects such as appetite loss, sexual dysfunction, and sleep disturbances. These side effects may only last for the first few weeks the patient is taking the medication. Yet, some of these medications do not begin to produce their full effect for several weeks. The patient thinks he is taking medicine that is producing unpleasant side effects and yet is not providing the expected relief from his symptoms. When my clients are considering discontinuing their pharmaceutical regimens or have done so already, education concerning what they should expect from the drug is sometimes all it takes to encourage them to continue their treatments. Patients must also be counseled in another problem of medical intervention. Once their symptoms begin to abate, they think they are cured and cease taking their medications. Teaching patients, and family members where possible, to recognize the urge to discontinue the medical regimen, and the dangers of following such an urge, is the responsibility primarily of the prescribing physician and secondarily of attending therapists.

CONCLUDING REMARKS

I have outlined seven mistakes that people have made, but where do we go from here? In summary I would suggest that we give careful attention to threatening behaviors, both verbal and nonverbal. These behaviors are warnings to us, and we make ourselves vulnerable when we fail to adequately respond. I suggest that we take action to help ourselves where we can. In our culture, we often lay blame on others and rely on our friends, our parents, the government, or the police to protect us. While each of these entities may intend and desire to help, sometimes the best help lies within ourselves. Our determination to survive and our resourcefulness may be our best tools for survival. Helping ourselves includes planning. As a child I remember sitting around the dinner table with my family discussing how each of us would get out of our house in case of a fire. We each developed our own plan and explained it to the others, while we also contributed ideas to our siblings regarding their respective plans. If our house had caught fire I could have implemented my plan and escaped my home. I knew what I was supposed to do and I could have done it. Many children die in fires because they have no idea what to do. Instead of putting a plan into action they cower under beds or in closets, only to die of smoke inhalation as they await rescue. When there is a clear risk to you from someone in your environment, do not wait for tragedy to strike before you make a plan. If you wait, you will be forced to develop a plan while under the intense pressure of panic and fear.

Do not try to defuse or handle an escalating crisis by yourself. A businessman came to me for counseling after a shooting occurred at his office. No one was injured. The perpetrator escaped and was never apprehended. My client told me that immediately after the event he called the police, but he felt responsible for checking the building to make sure the perpetrator was no longer present. There was no reason for him to do that. No one else was at risk in the building, and his good intentions only placed his life in jeopardy. Likewise, do not be afraid to call for help. There is no cowardice in doing so. I sometimes hear people snicker at video images of SWAT teams storming a house in which a perpetrator has barricaded himself. Ten or more armed officers may be dispatched to deal with a single perpetrator. To the ill-informed observer, it may seem as though these police officers are overdoing it, but the police know that there is power and security in their numbers and in their training. Their caution protects them. Let the police and security forces do what they are trained to do.

If you find yourself in the middle of an incident, do not panic. Your panic is nearly as dangerous to you as the perpetrator is, because panic clouds your judgment and inhibits your ability to act. Having a plan that is practiced and clearly thought out is the first step in remaining calm. The calm, fearless characters we see in war movies are more fiction than fact. You can expect to be afraid, but fear does not necessarily mean panic.

Finally, if you or someone you are responsible for is being treated for a mental health problem, encourage the patient as best you can to take his medication consistently and on schedule. My clients often have problems in more than one area of their lives. They may be diagnosed with depression, but they may also have difficulty in decision-making. Their presenting symptoms are only a part of the bigger picture of their mental state and their level of functioning. Because they have trouble making good decisions, they need supportive family and friends to assist them in dealing with their finances, their health, and their responsibilities. These include the responsibility of taking medications. As a concerned family member, call the prescribing physician for information if necessary. Do not suppose that

those of us in the mental health field have any control over patients
when they leave our offices.

On Monday mornings I enjoy talking about Sunday's football
games with my colleagues. We analyze the games from the previous
day and confidently explain to each other what we think went wrong
in each game and how it would have ended differently if quarterbacks,
coaches, and referees had behaved differently or made different decisions. Part of our confidence is based on the fact that since the game
is history, we cannot be proven wrong. In the homicide cases I have
cited in this chapter, I concede that I could be wrong in my analyses
and I acknowledge that the dynamics of each of these cases are so
complex that I may not fully or accurately understand what occurred.
I can, however, assure the reader that I have not made these analyses
casually or flippantly. The conclusions that I have drawn are my best
effort; I have tested them as new cases develop, and the results have
been the same. It has often been said that those who fail to learn
from history are condemned to repeat it. I hope the reader will see
that the information presented in this chapter can alter the course of
our destinies.

NOTES

1. Mike Williams, "Terror resounds in frantic 911 calls: gunshots boom
in background of phone conversations recorded during Littleton attack,"
Atlanta Journal/Constitution, April 24, 1999, 12.

2. Ibid.

3. Lorraine Adams and Dale Russakoff, "Dissecting Columbine's cult
of the athlete: in search for answers, community examines one source of
killer's rage," *Washington Post* (Internet Edition), June 12, 1999.

4. "Portrait of school killers," *CNN On-Line, www.cnn.com/US9904/
29/BC-CRIME-SHOOTING-PORTRA.reut/index.html*. April 29, 1999.

5. Ibid.

6. T. Trent Gegax and Matt Bai, "Searching for answers," *Newsweek,*
May 10, 1999, 34.

7. Eric Pooley, "Portrait of a deadly bond," *Time*, May 10, 1999, 26.

8. James Brooke, "Teacher of Colorado gunmen alerted parents," *New
York Times* (Late New York Edition), May 11, 1999, A14.

9. Williams, "Terror resounds in frantic 911 calls," 12.

10. "Gunmen made video that foretold rampage," *CNN On-Line,
www.cnn.com/US/9904/22/school.shootings.video.ap/index.html*, April 22,
1999.

11. Jim Hughes, "Descriptions vary of suspects," *Denver Post Online*, *www.denverpost.com/news/shot0420d.htm*, April 21, 1999.

12. Ibid.

13. Angie Cannon, Betsy Streisand, and Dan McGraw, "Why? There were plenty of warnings, but no one stopped two twisted teens," *U.S. News and World Report*, May 3, 1999, 16.

14. Ibid., 19.

15. "Portrait of school killers."

16. Matt Bai, Daniel Glick, Sherry Keene-Osborn, T. Trent Gegax, Lynette Clemetson, Devin Gordon, and Daniel Klaidman, "Anatomy of a massacre," *Newsweek*, May 3, 1999, 27.

17. Cannon, Streisand, and McGraw, "Why? There were plenty of warnings," 17.

18. "Columbine student rescued from window making 'incredible' recovery," *CNN On-Line*, *www.cnn.com/US/9905/07/school.shooting.02/index.html*, May 7, 1999.

19. "Columbine investigation turns to parents' role: police: 'trenchcoat mafia' members advised by lawyers," *CNN On-Line*, *www.cnn.com/US/9904/25/school.shooting.04/index.html*, April 25, 1999.

20. Mike Williams, "Diary: year's plotting went into school shooting: maps of school, schedules, date of 'rock-and-roll time' were noted in deadly detail," *Atlanta Journal/Constitution*, April 25, 1999, A6.

21. Ibid., A1.

22. "Columbine investigation turns to parents' role."

23. "Two students arrested for allegedly plotting school attack," *CNN On-Line*, *www.cnn.com/US/9908/25/SchoolPlot-Arrest.ap/index.html*, August, 26, 1999.

24. "Wisconsin boys charged with conspiracy to murder classmates," *CNN On-Line*, *www.cnn.com/US/9811/school.plot/index.html*, November 18, 1998.

25. "Bodies remain inside school as police check for bombs: 15 people, including gunmen, dead in Colorado massacre," *CNN On-Line*, *www.cnn.com/US/9904/21/school.shooting.03/index.html*, April 21, 1999.

26. "Quotes from Columbine High School shootings," *CNN On-Line*, *www.cnn.com/US/9904/20/AM-SchoolShooting-Quotes.ap/index.html*, April 21, 1999.

27. "Two suspects among possible 18 dead in Colorado school rampage," *CNN On-Line*, *www.cnn.com/US/9904/21/school.shooting.01/index.html*, April 21, 1999.

28. "Wounded student: shooter 'an all-right guy,' " *CNN On-Line*, *www.cnn.com/US/9904/23/victim.released/index.html*, April 23, 1999.

29. "Fired broker had troubled past: charged in shooting death of boss," *Patriot Ledger*, April 8, 1988, 13.

30. "Quotes from Columbine High School shooting."

Conclusions

Homicide among the historically nonviolent is nothing new. We are beginning a new millenium in a violent culture but murder has been a part of human experience since the beginning of time. The first homicide in recorded history is reported in the Bible. When Cain murdered Abel out of jealousy, the children of the very first people on earth became murderer and victim.

The early part of the twentieth century saw a mass homicide strike the Taliesin home of the famous architect, Frank Lloyd Wright. Wright had been sharing his home with his mistress, Mamah Borthwick Cheney, for a number of years. The relationship between Wright and Cheney was regarded as unconventional and even scandalous in 1914. It would later be suggested, although never confirmed, that the reason for the massacre was to punish Wright for his immorality.[1] Ms. Cheney had two children, Martha and John, from a marriage that preceded her relationship with Wright. The two children occasionally traveled to Wright's home in Arizona to visit their mother.

While Wright was working on his Midway Gardens project in Chicago, he took the recommendation of an associate there and hired Julian Carlton, a native of Barbados, and his wife, Gertrude, to work at the Taliesin estate. Carlton served as waiter, butler, and general handyman in the Wright home and his wife served as the cook.

On August 15, 1914, Mamah Cheney and her children had gathered together on a screened-in porch for lunch while several others met around the table in the main dining room about twenty-five feet away. Present around the main table were Billy Weston, a 35-year-old master carpenter who had helped build Taliesin, his 13-year-old son Ernest, 56-year-old foreman Thomas Brunker, 30-year-old Emil Brodelle and 19-year-old Herbert Fritz, both draftsmen, and a landscape gardener, David Lindblom.[2]

After serving lunch, Carlton asked Weston for permission to get gasoline to clean stained carpeting. Then, he barred all of the windows and doors with the exception of one door. Warning his wife to flee the house, he poured gasoline around the doors and windows and set fire to the house.

He then ran to the screened-in porch where he killed John and Mamah Cheney with a hatchet. They were killed while still seated at the table, apparently unaware of the fire. Martha, however, attempted to flee, but was caught and repeatedly attacked with the hatchet.

Meanwhile, in the main dining room, the men noticed gasoline flowing under a door just before it caught fire. Fritz escaped through a window, although his clothes were ablaze and he broke his arm when he fell. He would be the only one to avoid assault from Carlton's hatchet. As he tried to extinguish the flames he could see Carlton running around the house with a hatchet in his hand.[3] Both Billy Weston and Emil Brodelle were attacked as they attempted to leave the burning house through the window. Weston helped Lindblom, who had been burned and beaten, to escape the house. The two of them then ran a half-mile to call for help.[4] Weston, however, returned to Taliesin in a vain attempt to put the fire out.

A friend of Martha's was on her way to Taliesin when she saw the flames. Reaching the burning home, she saw several burned bodies. One badly burned individual, still alive, attempted to mouth her name. It was Martha Cheney, who would die a few hours later.

In all, seven people, including Mamah Cheney, her children, Brodelle, and Brunker died at the scene. Ernest Weston and Lindblom died later. Only Billy Weston and Herbert Fritz survived.[5] Fortunately for Wright, he had left Taliesin in the middle of the previous week for Chicago and was not home when the slayings occurred, or he might also have been a victim of the servant's rage.

Carlton was found the next day hiding in rubble in the basement furnace room and was arrested.[6] Carlton's own story was that he was seeking revenge against a fellow employee who had insulted him (most likely Brodelle). In an apparent suicide attempt, Carlton had consumed muratic acid while hiding in the basement, but although he was severely burned, the acid did not kill him. Instead, he would die in prison several weeks later from self-starvation.[7]

A neighbor described Carlton as "a mild-mannered man,"[8] while others said he was well-educated, intelligent, not known to drink, and "not generally disliked or distrusted."[9] As in most of the cases described in this book, however, numerous signs revealed he was a troubled man. Billy Weston, who would survive hatchet blows and burns, described him as as "the most desperate, hot-headed fellow he had ever met."[10] Lindblom also stated he had witnessed Carlton's anger.

There was some indication that people were concerned about Carlton before his lethal behavior on August 15. Although he had only worked in the Wright home for a few weeks, Mamah Cheney did not like him. The Carltons reportedly had given their two week notice, saying they were leaving Taliesin because Gertrude was homesick for Chicago, but there is evidence that Ms. Cheney had asked them to leave by the day of the killings.[11] The very morning of the murders, she sent a telegram to Wright in Chicago saying, "Come as quickly as you can. Something terrible has happened."[12] Wright would receive the telegram around the same time Carlton was attacking the Wright home. According to biographer Meryl Secrest, Carlton's own wife had noted that he had been acting strangely, talking about killing people and sleeping with a hatchet in a bag beside his bed.[13]

What drove Carlton to his actions will never be known for certain. While it has been suggested that he acted to punish Wright and Cheney for their lifestyle, other factors may have been at work instead of or in addition to this. For example, Brodelle had called Carlton a "black son of a bitch" because Carlton refused to use a saddle on his horse.[14] It was in defense of his honor over this insult that Carlton would say he committed his crime.[15]

Murder is not new and it will undoubtedly be with us as long as people inhabit this planet. This book has described many different homicides. The purpose of these descriptions is not to entertain. In every case I read about or investigate, I look for things that can help prevent future tragedies. In summary, here is what I have learned.

First of all, not all homicides are the same. As police and other investigators attempt to make sense of a killing, they must first determine what type of killing it was. The forces that motivate a robbery suspect to kill a business proprietor or a customer are distinctly different from the forces that drive a jealous husband to kill his wife and her lover. Just as these homicides differ in their causes, they differ in the way they are committed. Workplace killers may plan their rampages, and they use firearms far more often than not. Killers on the highway, who kill because of road rage, may use a firearm, a crossbow, or their vehicle as a weapon, and they have almost no time to plan. Domestic partners may use almost any imaginable weapon in the commission of their crimes. Sometimes domestic homicides are crudely planned yet often they happen with the impulsivity of a road rage crime.

Finally, as we have seen, the aftermath of these crimes differs. Where children are the perpetrators, they are often caught. Investigations of their crimes may take only days. Children's sentences are mitigated by their ages and the type of prosecution. If they are prosecuted as juveniles, their records are secret and they will likely be released by age 21. If they are prosecuted as adults, they may even be sentenced to death.

Workplace killers, as we have seen, often make no plans to leave their crime scene. They either take their own lives at the scene, or they lay down their weapons and wait for the police to arrive. The very first homicide case I reviewed involved a former employee of a trucking company. This man entered his former workplace after being fired. A secretary saw him enter his former boss's office. Minutes later she heard shouting and then gunshots. The gunman traveled the building encountering other employees and he calmly informed them that he would not harm them. He apparently was searching for the dispatcher, a woman with whom he had a grievance. When he found her he shot her. She crawled out of the building and died on the front lawn. As police arrived on the scene, the gunman nonchalantly strolled around the outside of the building and said, "I'm the man you're looking for. I killed them all." He laid his weapon on the hood of a vehicle and was arrested without further incident. Other workplace homicides, as seen in Chapter 3, end in the death of the perpetrator by his own hand. Investigation, while time consuming, is relatively easy.

Mental illness, while often a factor contributing to homicide, is rarely the root cause. Of the thousands of homicides committed every year, only a small fraction can be attributed directly to mental illness. While many murderers are diagnosably mentally ill, the same thing can be said of most of us. The mitigating differences are our coping skills and our levels of functioning.

In the introduction to this book I stated that the purpose of good research is to describe, explain, predict, and control. I have described many homicide cases in the chapters of this book. I have explained what happened in those cases and how I believe they could have been predicted. The most important part of the process is control. What can we do to prevent homicides from happening? In Chapters 8, 9, and 10, I addressed the assessment of risk, prevention, and people's common mistakes. If one reads the chapters of this book but neglects to implement the prediction and control issues, this work is of little value.

IS THERE EVIL AMONG US?

I have addressed homicide from a psychological perspective and I have also discussed social issues contributing to homicides. One final question haunts me. Our world is most palatable when we can find meaning and purpose in its events. When the inexplicable happens, we search in the darkest corners for answers to our questions. Neither our minds nor our hearts are satisfied when we cannot establish a cause-effect relationship in events. Yet, on occasion, there is a homicide so cold and so cruel that I am at a loss to explain it.

Some perpetrators have committed such horrific crimes that I wonder if perhaps they were simply evil. For example, Ronald L. Shanabarger suffocated his 7-month-old son in a crib. Tragic as infanticide is, it is unfortunately not uncommon. What sets Shanabarger's crime apart is his method and motive. Shanabarger was angry with his wife, Amy, because of an incident that happened before he and Amy were married and more than two years before the death of the baby.

In 1996, while he was dating his future wife, Amy, Shanabarger's father passed away. Amy was on a cruise at the time with her family. When she refused to come home early from the cruise to comfort Shanabarger, he reportedly began planning his revenge. He believed she did not understand his grief so he concocted a cruel plan to teach her a lesson. According to his confession, he married her, had a child with her, and waited until she bonded with the child.[16] Then, in cold-blooded cruelty, he wrapped the baby's head in plastic wrap and placed the baby facedown in the crib. He then left the room to get something to eat and to brush his teeth.[17] He came back about twenty minutes later and found the baby dead. Initially, the death was thought to be SIDS (sudden infant death syndrome), but guilt and the look on the face of his dead son haunted Shanabarger. Just a few hours after he and his wife buried their son, he confessed to his wife and he would later confess several times to investigators. He would later plead not guilty in court.

There was some speculation that Shanabarger committed the homicide in order to collect a $100,000 life insurance policy on the child, but his own confession refers to the motive already described. It seems unlikely that one would admit such a cold-blooded motive if a less dastardly motive were available. Shanabarger is currently awaiting trial on murder charges.

In Griffin, Georgia, a small town just a few miles from my home, lived Wendell White, a 23-year-old man with only two misdemeanors in his criminal history. White and Ayiesha Middlebrooks, a teenager, met when she was an employee at a local restaurant. The couple began dating and eventually conceived a child, Wendell "Bubba" Middlebrooks. However, in October 1997, just five months after the birth of their son, Ayiesha ended her relationship with White when she discovered he had previously fathered a child by another woman. Living in her grandparents' home along with a number of other relatives, she began dating other men.

White was unwilling to let go of the relationship. He phoned Ayiesha repeatedly and showed up outside her grandparents' home when she was on a date. In November, one month after the breakup, White met Ayiesha, then 19 years old, outside her grandparents' house. She refused to talk with White and refused to let him see his son. Around 1:00 A.M., he broke into her home, wrested his son from the arms of the baby's aunt, and kidnapped him before anyone could react. The Middlebrooks called police, who searched for White for nearly two hours before he was seen walking down the street near the Middlebrooks' home.

Four police officers and about a half-dozen relatives surrounded White in an elementary school parking lot, but the police were unable to take him into custody because he used the baby as a shield, threatening to kill him. As police tried to negotiate with White, he said he wanted to talk to Ayiesha. Several relatives were present and heard his demand. One returned to the Middlebrooks' home and informed the mother.

As she arrived she saw White holding their son and immediately begged him to give the baby to her. As she and relatives looked on, he suddenly raised the baby over his head and without warning slammed the baby to the pavement. Then, as the stunned police and relatives watched, he grabbed the boy by the ankles and slammed him to the pavement a second time. Tossing the baby aside, he attempted to flee but was tackled by family members and law enforcement officers. Family members cursed and kicked him until police placed White in a police car, while Ayiesha cried out for her son "not to leave mommy."[18]

There was some speculation that the baby was dead prior to White's actions because he was very still and quiet through the entire ordeal. However, an autopsy indicated that the child was in fact alive at the time White slammed him to the pavement and it was those two blows that killed the child.[19]

White claimed to be jealous after he had attempted reconciliation with Ayiesha but she was uninterested and was seeing other men. He was also upset at the attention the Middlebrooks paid to the baby at White's expense. According to prosecutors, he showed no remorse and claimed to have killed the boy to "get back at" Ayiesha.[20] White was tried and found guilty of murder, burglary, and kidnapping, but jurors spared him the electric chair. Instead, he was sentenced to life in prison without the possibility of parole. Jurors said they chose life without parole because it would make him suffer more and they did not want a potential jury deadlock on the death penalty to leave open the possibility of a sentence (life with the possibility of parole) that might one day allow him to go free.[21]

White's troubled background as one of ten children, a foster child after his mother was imprisoned, and a student at a school for emotionally disturbed children cannot fully explain this amazing cruelty. White's brother tried to explain that White did not intend to kill the child. He said that White accidentally dropped the child, but that does not even begin to explain why he would pick him up and "drop" him a second time.[22]

What could drive men and women to such desperate acts of cruelty? This book is not a theological work, but some behaviors are so unconscionable that they defy explanation. In the years I have invested seeking answers for homicides, in some cases, I have no answers. That leaves me with the possibility that perhaps there is something beyond quantification at work in this world and in the hearts of men. If this is true, programs, checklists, psychologists, and social workers will continue to be at a loss in preventing these perpetrators from committing their vile acts.

CONCLUDING REMARKS

This book has covered a variety of homicides, and the lives of many people have been discussed. One final subject must be addressed. There are more victims of these crimes than it may seem from reading these pages. The spouses, parents, and children of perpetrators are often as grief-stricken and anguished as the families of the victims. They wonder how the one they loved so dearly could do something so dreadful. They wrestle with guilt, wondering if they could have prevented the tragedies that occurred. Sometimes the grief of the perpetrator's survivors is complicated when they are sued by victims, leaving them not only dealing with the actions of their loved ones but also suffering financially.

Police officers sometimes find it difficult to cope with the crimes they investigate. When they see children lying in hallways and schoolyards, they think of their own children and how they themselves could easily be the ones planning funerals and grieving. Images of dead children haunt the thoughts and dreams of these men and women as they try to cope with the savagery of our world. The perpetrators of murder continue doing damage through agonizing memories, lawsuits, and personal grief, long after they are gone. While their actions may fade in the memories of some, they remain vivid in the minds of others. To all these "forgotten" victims, I extend this honorable mention.

Where do we go from here? Most of you who are reading this book will never be victims of homicide. Once finished reading, you may put the book away and move on with life, never considering that what has been described in these pages might befall you. The prudent reader, however, will carry some of this book in mind. Before I began working in this area, I almost never thought about becoming a victim of any crime. I live in a very small rural town, I have never been robbed, I have never had my car stolen, and I have never been seriously assaulted. After studying nearly 300 murders, I see the world differently. When I drive into a gas station, I look carefully around me before I even stop my vehicle. At the college where I work, a very unlikely setting for a homicide, I never fail to consider the possibility of homicide by former coworkers or students. When people ask my opinion about a situation, I never dismiss the possibility that it could result in murder. I assess every client that comes through my office door for the possibility of violent behavior.

Some may argue that I am overreacting and blowing circumstances out of proportion. I do not agree. I concede that in almost all the circumstances I described in the preceding paragraph, the statistical likelihood of violence to me or to others is minimal. However, I still accept its possibility. I do not live my life in fear, but I live my life controlling those circumstances that I can. My hope is that in reading this book you have become more aware of threats to your own life and the lives of those that you love. That awareness is like an insurance policy. Hopefully, you will never need it, but if you do, it may save your life and the lives of others. Gavin de Becker, in his book, *The Gift of Fear*, suggests that "belief is a key element in recognizing when you are in the presence of danger. That belief balances denial, the powerful and cunning enemy of successful prediction."[23]

NOTES

1. Robert C. Twolmby, *Frank Lloyd Wright: an interpretive biography* (New York: Harper & Row, 1979).

2. Meryl Secrest, *Frank Lloyd Wright* (New York: Alfred A. Knopf, 1992), 216.

3. Ibid., 219.

4. Ibid.

5. Ibid.

6. Twolmby, *Frank Lloyd Wright: an interpretive biography*, 136.

7. Secrest, *Frank Lloyd Wright*, 220.

8. Ibid.

9. Ibid., 217.

10. Ibid.

11. Ibid.

12. Ibid.

13. Ibid.

14. Ibid.

15. Ibid.

16. "Police: suspect fathered child to kill the infant," *CNN On-Line, http://www.cnn.com/US/9906/28/revenge.killing.02.ap/index.html*, June 29, 1999.

17. Paul Bird, "Killed son to get even with wife, man says: plot reportedly began in 1996," *Indianapolis News*, June 25, 1999, C1.

18. Ralph Ellis, "Griffin man goes on trial in son's death," *Atlanta Journal/Constitution*, October 13, 1998, B04.

19. "Baby's horrifying, violent end spurs second-guessing. Police criticized: some say officers should have shot and killed the infant's father instead of trying to negotiate," *Atlanta Journal/Constitution*, November 22, 1997, G02.

20. Ralph Ellis, "Griffin man avoids death penalty: convicted of killing his son, Wendell White given life without parole," *Atlanta Journal/Constitution*, October 17, 1998, F1.

21. Ibid.

22. Ralph Ellis, "Griffin man on trial in his baby's slaying. Graphic testimony expected: suspect accused of killing his son by smashing him into the pavement," *Atlanta Journal/Constitution*, October 5, 1998, C01.

23. Gavin de Becker, *The gift of fear: survival signals that protect us from violence* (New York: Little, Brown & Company, 1997), 10.

Bibliography

"Accused slayer of seven tells of obsession." *Los Angeles Times*, August 21, 1991, A20.

Adams, Lorraine, and Russakoff, Dale. "Dissecting Columbine's cult of the athlete: in search for answers, community examines one source of killers' rage." *Washington Post* (Internet Edition), June 12, 1999.

Adler, Jerry, Carroll, Ginny, Smith, Vern, and Rogers, Patrick. "Innocent lost." *Newsweek*, November 14, 1994, 26–30.

American Psychiatric Association. *Diagnostic and statistical manual for mental disorders, 4th edition*. Washington, DC: American Psychiatric Press, 1994.

Anderson, S. C. "Anti-stalking laws: will they curb the erotomanic's obsessive pursuit?" *Law and Psychology Review, 17* (1993), 171–191.

Bai, Matt, Glick, Daniel, Keene-Osborn, Sherry, Gegax, T. Trent, Clemetson, Lynette, Gordon, Devin, and Klaidman, Daniel. "Anatomy of a massacre." *Newsweek*, May 3, 1999, 24–31.

Beck, Melinda, Rosenberg, Debra, Chideya, Farai, Miller, Susan, Foote, Donna, Manly, Howard, and Katel, Peter. "Murderous obsession: can new laws deter spurned lovers and fans from 'stalking'—or worse?" *Newsweek*, July 13, 1992, 60–62.

Blank, Jonah. "The kid no one noticed." *U.S. News and World Report* (Internet Edition), October 12, 1998.

Blank, Jonah, and Cohen, Warren. "Prayer circle murders." *U.S. News and World Report* (Internet Edition), December 15, 1997.

Blank, Jonah, Vest, Jason, and Parker, Suzie. "The children of Jonesboro." *U.S. News and World Report* (Internet Edition), April 6, 1998.

"The Boston strategy to prevent youth violence." *The Boston Police Department and Partners.* Spring 1997.

Buckley, William F., Jr. "The Susan Smith case." *National Review* (Internet Edition), August 28, 1995.

Bureau of Justice Statistics Special Report. In *Workplace Violence* [Online]. Available at FTP: *http://www.ojp.usdoj.gov/bjs/pub/ascii/wv96.txt,* 1998.

Cannon, Angie, Streisand, Betsy, and McGraw, Dan. "Why? There were plenty of warnings, but no one stopped two twisted teens." *U.S. News and World Report,* May 3, 1999, 16–19.

Chisholm, Patricia. "Teens under siege." *Maclean's* (Internet Edition), May 3, 1999.

Chua-Eoan, Howard. "Mississippi gothic: in a dramatic turn, an alleged one-man rampage may have become a seven-pointed conspiracy." *Time,* October 20, 1997, 54.

Cloud, John. "Of arms and the boy." *Time* (Internet Edition), July 6, 1998.

Coon, Dennis. *Introduction to psychology: exploration and application, 8th edition.* New York: Brooks/Cole Publishing Company, 1998.

Copleston, F. *A history of philosophy: Fichte to Nietzsche, Vol. VII.* Garden City, NY: Image Books, 1985.

D'Antonio, Michael. "The strangest stalking case ever." *Redbook,* June 1996, 108–111+.

de Becker, Gavin. *The gift of fear: survival signals that protect us from violence.* New York: Little, Brown & Company, 1997.

Dickinson, Amy. "Where were the parents?" *Time,* May 3, 1999, 40.

Ehrenreich, Barbara. "Susan Smith: corrupted by love?" *Time* (Internet Edition), August 7, 1995.

"Family Violence: breaking the cycle for children who witness." International Association of Chiefs of Police, Alexandria, VA, 1997.

Fein, R. A., and Vossekuil, B. "Preventing attacks on public officials and public figures: a Secret Service perspective." In J. Reid Meloy, ed., *The psychology of stalking: clinical and forensic perspectives,* pp. 176–191. San Diego, CA: Academic Press, 1998.

Foster, Buddy, and Wagener, Leon. "The real story behind Jodie Foster's haunting ordeal." *McCall's,* June 1997, 48.

Gegax, T. Trent, and Bai, Matt. "Searching for answers." *Newsweek,* May 10, 1999, 30–34.

Gibbs, Nancy. "The Littleton massacre." *Time,* May 3, 1999, 20–32.

———. "Noon in the garden of good and evil: the tragedy at Columbine began as a crime story but is becoming a parable." *Time,* May 17, 1999, 54.

Gibbs, Nancy, and Roche, Timothy. "The Columbine tapes." *Time*, December 20, 1999, 40–57.

Gleick, Elizabeth. "No casting of stones." *Time* (Internet Edition), August 7, 1995.

Hall, Doris M. "The victims of stalking." In J. Reid Meloy, ed., *The psychology of stalking: clinical and forensic perspectives*, pp. 113–137. San Diego, CA: Academic Press, 1998.

Harris, G. T., and Rice, M. E. "Risk appraisal and management of violent behavior." *Psychiatric Services, 48*, 9 (1997), 1168–1176.

Hewitt, Bill, Bane, Vickie, Arias, Ron, Bates, Karen, et al. "Sorry and outrage." *People Weekly* (Internet Edition), May 3, 1999.

Hewitt, Bill, Harmes, Joseph, and Stewart, Bob. "The avenger." *People Weekly* (Internet Edition), November 3, 1997.

"Intimate partner violence fact sheet." Centers for Disease Control and Prevention. Available at FTP: *www.cdc.gov/ncipc/dvp/ipvfacts.htm*, 1998.

Keeney, B. T., and Heide, K. M. "Gender differences in serial murderers: A preliminary analysis." *Journal of Interpersonal Violence, 9* (1994) 383–398.

Kelleher, Michael D. "An obsession with Laura," *Sartore Township*. Available at FTP: *www.svn.net/mikekell/farley.html*.

———. *Profiling the lethal employee: case studies of violence in the workplace*. Westport, CT: Greenwood Publishing Group, 1997.

———. *When good kids kill*. Westport, CT: Greenwood Publishing Group, 1998.

King, Patricia, and Murr, Andrew. "A son who spun out of control: an Oregon teen is charged with killing his parents and his classmates. The road to the cafeteria." *Newsweek*, June 1, 1998, 32–33.

Labash, Matt. "The power of Cassie Bernall: to evil, she made the perfect answer." *Reader's Digest*, August 1999, 53–60.

Labi, Nadya. "Mother of the accused." *Time* (Internet Edition), April 13, 1998.

Labig, Charles E. *Preventing violence in the workplace*. New York: RHR International Co. (a division of the American Management Association), 1995.

Lardner, George. "No place to hide." *Good Housekeeping*, October, 1997, 104–106.

Magid, K., and McKelvey, C. A. *High risk: children without a conscience*. New York: Bantam, 1989.

Mantell, M., and Albrechte, S. *Ticking bombs: defusing violence in the workplace*. New York: Irwin Professional Publishing, 1994.

McFadden, Robert D. "Brief romance, growing fears, then 2 deaths." *New York Times* (Late New York Edition), April 9, 1994.

Meloy, J. Reid. "The psychology of stalking." In J. Reid Meloy, ed., *The psychology of stalking: clinical and forensic perspectives*, pp. 1–23. San Diego, CA: Academic Press, 1998.

Moffatt, Gregory K. "A checklist for assessing risk of violent behavior in historically nonviolent persons." *Psychological Reports, 74* (1994), 683–688.

———. "Subjective fear: preventing homicide in the workplace." *HR Focus*, August 1998, 11–12.

———. "Violence risk assessment and clinical treatment of the client at high risk for violent behavior." *Georgia Journal of Professional Counseling, 8* (Spring 2000).

Monahan, J. "Causes of violence." *Law Enforcement Bulletin, 63* (1994), 11–15.

———. *Predicting violent behavior: an assessment of clinical techniques.* Beverly Hills, CA: Sage Publications, 1981.

Monroe, Sylvester. "A boy and his lawyer." *Time* (Internet Edition), April 27, 1998.

"Murder in America: recommendations from the IACP murder summit." International Association of Chiefs of Police, Alexandria, VA, 1995.

Oster, Gerald D., and Caro, Janice E. *Understanding and treating depressed adolescents and their families.* New York: John Wiley & Sons, 1990.

Phillips, Andrew. "When children kill." *Maclean's* (Internet Edition), April 6, 1998.

Pooley, Eric. "Portrait of a deadly bond." *Time*, May 10, 1999, 26–32.

Public enquiry into the shootings at Dunblane Primary School on March 18 1996. The Stationery Office, *www.official-documents.co.uk/ document/scottish/dunblane/dunblane.htm*, 1996.

Rogers, Patrick, Haederle, Michael, Leonard, Elizabeth, and Dodd, Johnny. "Mortal lessons." *People Weekly* (Internet Edition), June 8, 1998.

"Safer schools: strategies for educators and law enforcement seeking to prevent violence within schools." International Association of Chiefs of Police, Alexandria, VA, 1998.

Safran, Claire. "Justice for Debra." *Good Housekeeping*, March 1994, 136–137+.

———. "Was justice done?" *Good Housekeeping*, March 1995, 95+.

Secrest, Meryl. *Frank Lloyd Wright.* New York: Alfred A. Knopf, 1992.

Simon, Robert I. *Bad men do what good men dream.* Washington, DC: American Psychiatric Press, 1996.

Snow, Robert L. *Stopping a stalker: a cop's guide to making the system work for you.* New York: Plenum Trade, 1998.

Stroff, D. M., Breiling, J. and Maser, J. D., eds. *Handbook of antisocial behavior.* New York: John Wiley & Sons, 1997.

Sullivan, Randall. "A boy's life." *Rolling Stone* (Internet Edition), September 17, 1998.

Tharp, Mike. "In the mind of a stalker." *U.S. News and World Report*, February 17, 1992, 28–30.

"Theodore Robert Bundy or Ted Bundy." *www.crimelibrary.com/bundy/attack.htm*.

Thomas, Irene Middleman. "Are you afraid to come to work?" *Postal Life* (Internet Edition), *www.usps.gov/history/plife/p1090198/afraid.htm*, September/October, 1998.

Thompson, Charles L., and Rudolph, Linda B. *Counseling children, 4th edition*. New York: Brooks/Cole Publishing Company, 1992.

Tjaden, Patricia, and Thoennes, Nancy. "Stalking in America: findings from the national violence against women survey research in brief." U.S. Department of Justice. Available at FTP: *www.ncjrs.org/txtfiles/169592.txt*, April 1998.

Trebilcock, Bob. "I love you to death." *Redbook*, March, 1992, 100–114.

Twolmby, Robert C. *Frank Lloyd Wright: an interpretive biography*. New York: Harper & Row, 1979.

Van Biema, David. "A surge of teen spirit." *Time*, May 31, 1999, 58–59.

Verner, Chris. "Newsmaker: slaying of actress haunts accused fan." *Atlanta Journal/Constitution*, July 19, 1990.

Wescott, Gail Cameron. "The reckoning." *People Weekly* (Internet Edition), August 7, 1995.

Wulf, Steve. "Elegy for lost boys." *Time* (Internet Edition), July 31, 1995.

Youth violence: a community-based response. Washington, DC: United States Department of Justice, September 1996.

"Youth violence in America: recommendations from the IACP summit." International Association of Chiefs of Police Alexandria, VA, 1996.

Index

Abuse, 4, 8, 41, 73, 106, 108–109, 169; child, 4, 13, 55, 62, 68, 108–109, 123, 207; neglect, 106, 173; physical, 13; sexual, 13, 62, 68, 123, 139; spousal, 4, 8, 13, 57, 178; substance, 33, 40; verbal, 44

Aggression/aggressive behavior, 3, 4, 14, 15, 17, 32, 41–42, 46, 56, 89, 106–107, 128, 131, 142, 165, 167–168, 173, 175, 177–178, 185, 211, 213; against inanimate objects, 168; and boys, 181; childhood, 105–106; drivers, 167; ex-husband, 201; externalized, 13, 175; fantasy, 176; history of, 139, 167–168; internalized, 13; language, 168; models, 178; passion, 177; patterns of, 199

Air traffic controllers, 40

Alcohol, 13, 156, 173

All-Tech, 71–72

America Online, 141–142, 158–159, 214

Americans with Disabilities Act (ADA), 191

Anderson, Robyn, 144–145

Antidepressants, 142, 226

Archuleta, Donna, 1, 46, 48, 220–221

Assessment, xi, 3–5, 15, 18, 23, 35, 49, 101, 106, 163–184, 195, 202, 211, 217, 222, 235, 239; absent or weak support system, 171–172; age, 181; antisocial behavior, 171; available weapon, 180–181; clear feelings of being wronged, 174; false positives, 164; fantasies of violence, 176–177; frequent divorce, 179; history of aggressive behavior, 3, 167–168; job instability, 177; lack of or weak social skills, 172–173; loss of a job, 179; male gender, 181; poor self-image, 174–175; potential for violence, 164; poverty, 179–180; problems with, 163–167; self-fulfilling prophecies, 165; severe situational stress, 177–178; social isolation, 170; specific victim, 178–179; subjective fear by others, 168–169; substance abuse, 173; suicide attempts/ideation, 175–

176; threats of intent to do harm, 169–170
Atlanta Christian College, 2
The Atlanta Project, 207
Auerbach, Sarah, 80

Barbarin, Sergei, 31–33
Bardo, Robert John, 94–96
Barton, Debra, 67–69, 73
Barton, Leigh Ann, 68–69, 72
Barton, Mark Orrin, 66–74
Beck, Matthew, 49–52
Behavioral Science Unit, xi. *See also* Federal Bureau of Investigation
Bellanger, Jerry, 100
Bernall, Cassie, 145, 151–152, 155
Bishop Brady High School, 216
Black, Laura, 88–94
Blame, 17–18, 40, 43, 46, 53, 65, 69, 73, 110, 120, 157, 174, 189, 200, 209–210, 226
Boone, Gayle, 98
Bowman, Margaret, 9
Brady, James, 96
Bragging, 128, 140
Brinkley, Cecil, 195
Brown, Brooks, 141–142, 145
Bundy, Theodore, 8–9, 11–12, 43

Caliber, of gun, 205; .22 caliber, 32, 44–45, 117–118, 127, 130, 195, 205, 216, 223; .25 caliber, 115; .30 caliber, 125; .32 caliber, 129; .38 caliber, 10, 27–28, 60, 156, 205; .40 caliber, 204–205; .44 caliber, 36; .45 caliber, 70, 72, 121; .357 caliber, 44, 205; 9mm, 30, 44, 47, 50, 70, 80, 127, 130, 158, 205; 10mm, 205
Carjacking, 61, 63
Carlton, Julian, 231–233
Carneal, Michael, 115–119, 220
Carrey, Jim, 85

Carter, Jeffrey, 216
Carter, Jimmy, 207
Cartier, Michael, 79–80
The Catcher in the Rye, 95
Catharsis, 181
Centers for Disease Control and Prevention (CDC), 80, 82
Central Intelligence Agency (CIA), 29
Cheney, Mamah Borthwick, 231–233
Cheney, Martha, 231–232
Chestnut, Jacob J., 28–29
Chi Omega sorority, 9
Clark, Bruce William, 37–39
Clifton, Madlyn (Maddie) Rae, 111–113
Cocaine, 173
Colorado Department of Transportation (DOT), 46–49
Columbine High School, 16, 43, 132, 137–159, 194–195, 200, 213–218, 224; aftermath, 154–156; choir room, 149–150; day of the shooting, 144–154; growing rage, 139–140; Harris and Klebold, 138; indications of problems, 141–143; the library, 150–152; preparations, 143–144; the siege draws to a close, 152–154; trouble brewing, 140–141; the web site, 141–143
Communicate, viii, 1, 24, 92, 159, 198, 211, 214
Conflict, 14, 195
Connecticut Lottery Corporation, 49–52
Conscience, 106
Context, 15–18
Control, 2, 15–16, 32, 46, 56–58, 69, 81, 89, 99, 127, 138, 157, 179, 190–191, 197, 202, 212, 218–220, 225, 228, 235, 239; controlling anger (temper), 3, 14; controlling behavior, 67, 202; gun control, 11, 180; lack

of, 80; loss of, 74, 121; uncontrolled, 56

Coping, 12–15, 18, 52, 84, 122, 157, 177–178, 187, 188, 189, 199, 238; skills, 13–15, 17, 52, 58, 66, 107, 165, 167, 172–173, 175, 178–179, 192, 196, 199, 235; strategies, 14–15, 18, 25, 52, 107, 173, 178

Crazy, 12, 21, 39, 89, 207

Dahmer, Jeffery, 21
de Becker, Gavin, 101, 164, 168, 239
Dearborn, Michigan, 37
Death penalty, 12, 113, 125, 237
Death sentence, 65, 93
Defense, 51, 87, 99, 221, 233; in court, 11, 60, 63, 90, 92–93, 95, 100, 112–113, 122; defenseless, 155; defensive, 110, 117, 195; self-defense, 202, 204
Delta Airlines, xi, 5, 35
Denial, 58, 223, 239
DeShazor, George, xi, 6
Diagnostic and Statistical Manual, 4th Edition (DSM IV), 21–23, 84
Dietz, Park E., 101
Discrimination, 174
Dobson, James, 9
Domestic violence, 7–8, 11, 35, 55–77, 168, 198, 207, 234; prevalence of, 56; psychology of, 56–58
Doom, 107, 142, 143, 144
Drug test, 41–42, 212
Dumb and Dumber, 85
Dunblane, Scotland, 43–46
Dunblane Primary School, 43–46
Dungeons and Dragons, 107
Duy, De-Kieu, 30–31
Dysfunctional, 3, 8, 13, 37, 40, 72, 106–107, 172, 178, 192, 210; behavior, 49; sexual dysfunction, 226; thinking, 58, 60, 67, 86

Edmond, Oklahoma, 37
Electromagnetic Systems Lab (ESL), 87–94
Ellul, Guy, 99–100
Employee assistance, 3, 191
Erotomania, 83–84
E. T. Booth Middle School, 110
Evil, 13, 93, 120, 159, 235

Fantasy, 95, 107, 119, 176
Farley, Richard, 87–94, 224–225
Fatal Attraction, 100
Fear, vii, 1, 16, 23, 32, 43, 45–49, 82, 83, 92, 98, 99, 112, 148, 165, 168, 170, 172, 200, 212, 214, 220–221, 225, 227, 239; fearless, 227; God-fearing, 61; subjective, 168–169
Federal Bureau of Investigation (FBI), 6, 28, 180; Behavioral Science Unit, xi; FBI National Academy, vii, xi, 4, 6, 35
Federal Express, 219
Fight or flight, 14, 195
Florida Institute of Technology, 49
Florida State University, 9
Forms and causes of homicide, 7–12
Fort Lauderdale, Florida, 41–43
Foster, Jodie, 94–96
French Revolution, 180
Frye, John, 9–11

Gangs, viii, 16, 140; gang behavior, 16, 35, 123, 158, 172
Gender, 26, 171, 181
Georgia State University, 15
Gibson, Debbie, 94
Gibson, John M., 28–29
Golden, Andrew, 122–126
GoldenEye, 157
Gothic behavior, 140, 214

Grievance, 46, 49, 174, 197, 234; procedures, 40
Grijalva, Ruben, 92

Hadley, Nicole, 116–118
Hallucinations, 84
Hamilton, Thomas, 43–46
Harding, Karla, 1, 47, 49, 221
Harassment, 24, 47, 81, 89, 97, 139, 171, 174
Harris, Eric, 138–159, 213–217
Hawaii Pacific University, 126
Heath High School, 115–118
Helfer, Scott, 1, 4, 46–49, 167–168, 221
Henderson, William J., 40
Heritage High School, 132, 158
High-risk, 5, 177, 185, 192, 200, 212
Hilburn, Mark Richard, 37–38
Hinckley, John, 94–96
Historically nonviolent, viii, 2–4, 231
Hitler, Adolf, 140, 144, 156, 214
Hollensteiner, Patrick, 98–99
Holmes Social Readjustment Rating Scale (SRRS), 177
Homer, 189
HOME-Safe Project, 186–191; empowerment, 190; hope, 187–188; mentoring, 189–190; observation, 188–189; summary of, 190–191
Hoshizaki America, 59–60
Hostage, 115, 219; negotiator, 92, 195
Huberty, James, 17–18
Hugo, Victor, 179

Impulsive behavior, 7, 14, 107
Infanticide, 235
Internal Revenue Service (IRS), 49
International Association of Chiefs of Police (IACP), 7
Internet, 68–69, 116, 118–119, 127, 141, 158–159

Intervention, 5, 23, 46, 84, 164, 170, 182, 185–210, 212–213, 225–226; Americans with Disabilities Act (ADA), 191; community, 192; employee assistance, 191; hope, 185–188; medical, 193–194; therapeutic, 192. *See also* HOME-Safe Project
Intimidation, 110, 167, 168, 220
Ireland, Patrick, 145, 152, 154–155
Isolation, 16, 174; social, 170, 179, 199

Jackson, Arthur, 94, 96–97
Jasion, Larry, 37–38
John D. Long Lake, 62, 63–65
Johnson, Mitchell, 122–126

King, Stephen, 57, 107
Kinkel, Kipland, 16, 126–132, 220
Klebold, Dylan, 138–159, 213–217
Kroth, 119, 121–122
KSL Television, 30–31

Labig, Charles E., 197
Lang, Leigh Ann. *See* Barton, Leigh Ann
Lardner, Kristin, 79–80
Lavallie, Tracy, 59–60
Law suits, 205
Layoff, 179
Leach, Kimberly, 9
Leawood Elementary School, 147, 152, 154
Les Miserables, 179
Letter writing, 24–25
Level of functioning, 23–26, 227
Levy, Lisa, 9
Listening skills, 179, 194–195
Luvox, 142

Marijuana, 108, 116, 173
McCarthy, Timothy, 96
McClendon, Jason, 107–109

McCree, Clifton, 41–43, 46, 211–212, 221

McDonald's, 17, 87

Menefee, Christina, 119–122

Mental health continuum, 22–23

Mental illness, 21–23, 27, 33, 45, 58, 66, 83–84, 95, 115, 131–132, 181, 185, 193, 210, 234; attachment disorder, 106–107; delusion, 24–25, 29, 72–73, 84, 86, 89, 93, 157, 225; depression, 13, 25, 33, 49, 63, 69, 128, 142, 193–194, 216, 226–227; failure to bond, 106–107; insane, 22; normal (normalcy), 4, 26; paranoia, 24–25, 27, 31–33, 44–45, 67, 74; sanity, 21–22; schizophrenia, 23, 26–27, 31–33, 83; sociopathic thinking, 84. *See also* Suicide

Mentally ill, homicide by, 25–33

Mentoring, 186, 189–190, 192, 196

Middlebrooks, Ayiesha, 236–237

Miller, Johnathan, 109–111

Mistakes that cost lives, 209–228; attempting to defuse situation alone, 221–222; failure to call for help soon enough, 222–224; failure to develop or implement a plan, 220–221; failure to help oneself, 217–220; failure to respond/ignoring threats, 211–217; panic, 224–225; patients not taking medication 225–226

Momentum Securities, 70–73

Mormon Church Family History Library, 32

Motivation, 99, 112, 116, 233

Motive, 29, 44–46, 63, 116, 119, 132, 145, 158, 235–236

My Sister Sam, 94–95

Myers, Gary, 46, 48–49

Nail, Sharlene, 47–48

Natural Born Killers, 142

Nazi, 140, 214, 218; neo-Nazi, 140, 144

Nielson, Patricia, 150, 153

Nietzsche, F., 190

Obsession, 57, 83, 87–89, 91, 93–96, 127, 143, 177, 180, 214, 220; obsessive personality, 84; obsessive stalker, 81, 94

The Odyssey, 189

Otto, John, xi, 5

Pacific Southwest Airlines, 36

Pearl High School, 121–122

Peers, 25–26, 107, 115, 117, 199–200

Penn State University, 12

Personality, profile, 182; traits, 84

Phillips, Joshua, 111–113

Phobia, 23

Porter, Candace, 123–124

Post office, 37–40

Potential, 1–2, 4–5, 10, 16, 18, 22, 46, 51–52, 74, 106–107, 137, 171, 178, 191–192, 197, 201, 211–212, 215–216, 220, 223, 237; charges, 204; deadlock, 237; defendant, 155; embarrassment, 172; perpetrator, 159, 185, 199, 221; problems, 137, 176; signs, 195; stalker, 84–85; victims, 179, 185, 198, 220–221; witnesses, 111

Poverty, 179–180

Power, 57–58, 69, 107, 187, 189–190, 194, 196, 202, 210, 220, 227; powerlessness, 189, 190, 197

Predict, 2, 5, 18, 26, 49, 84, 106, 163–164, 167, 177, 196, 210, 235, 239

Prediction of violence. *See* Assessment

Premeditation, 7–8, 112, 157

Prevention, 18, 35–36, 52, 185–210, 235

Prevention, individual strategies, 199–
   206; with children, 199–200; per-
   sonal protection, 202–206; stalking,
   201–202; at work, 200–201. *See also*
   Weapons and personal protection
Prevention, organizational strategies,
   194–199; business, 197–199;
   schools, 194–196
Principle of least interest, 57–58
Probability, 15, 18, 163–164, 181
Prosecute, 13, 68, 81, 97, 234
Prosecution, 60, 63, 65, 99, 112, 205–
   206, 234
Protection, 98, 101, 201, 204, 206
Protection, personal. *See* Weapons and
   personal protection
Prozac, 128
Psychometric instruments, 5, 175,
   182
Punishment, 8, 41, 65, 96, 130, 197,
   213, 231, 233

Quake, 142
Quick, Samuel, 59–60, 224

Race, 42, 83, 218
Rage, 7, 8, 17, 43, 64, 73, 107, 109,
   120, 139–142, 144, 176, 210, 232;
   road rage, 35, 234
Rage, 107
Reagan, Ronald, 94–96
Restraining order, 79, 80, 90, 93, 100,
   201–202. *See also* Triggering mecha-
   nisms
Revenge, 42, 89–90, 120–122, 141,
   150, 176–177, 213, 232, 235
Ritalin, 128
Robbery, 5, 7, 11, 16, 37, 68, 172,
   233
Robbins, Jullian, 12
Rose Madder, 57
Rosenthal, Richard, 11
Roses, Brandon, 105
Ryker, Jacob, 130–132

Safety, 36, 40, 46, 48–49, 62, 73, 98,
   106, 113, 147, 164, 168, 201, 205–
   206, 212, 220, 223
Saldana, Theresa, 96–97
Sanders, Dave, 147–148, 153, 155
Sanity, definition of, 21–22
Santa Rosa Community College, 87
Satanism, 120
Schaeffer, Rebecca, 31, 94–96
School shootings, 113–159
Scott, Rachel, 146, 154–155
Scream, 107
Secrest, Meryl, 233
Secret Service, 25, 27, 29, 94, 96
Self-esteem, 84
Self-fulfilling prophecy, 165
Self-image, 174–175
Serial killers, 7–8, 11, 13
Shanabarger, Amy, 235–236
Shanabarger, Ronald L., 235–236
Sherrill, Patrick Henry, 37–38
Side effects, of psychotropic medica-
   tions, 193–194, 226
Simon, Robert, 82–83
Simpson, O. J., 57
Smith, Susan, viii, 61–66, 74
Snap, 120, 128, 178
Snow, Robert, 83–84
Sociopath, 84
Sorbibor, 218
Special Weapons and Tactics (SWAT),
   32, 147–148, 152–154, 227
Spivey, Debra. *See* Barton, Debra
Stalking, 31, 79–103, 198, 201–202,
   210, 220; celebrity stalkers, 94–97;
   complications with, 97–100; defini-
   tionof, 82; prevalence of, 82; profile
   of perpetrators, 82-83; psychology
   of, 84–86; types of, 83–84; victims
   of, 82–83
Stress, 10, 15, 18, 40, 49, 171, 175,
   177–178, 179, 181, 187, 188, 199,
   223; stressors, 66, 177

Sudden Infant Death Syndrome
(SIDS), 236
Suicide, 11, 17, 26, 49, 51, 61–62, 65–
66, 69, 130, 151, 169, 175–176,
187–189, 213, 233; ideation, 169,
175–176, 189; note, 10, 80, 159
SWAT. *See* Special Weapons and Tactics

Taliesin, 231–233
Terrorists, 56; behavior, 137; threats,
97
Testosterone, 181
Theft, 129, 131; pilfering, 174
Threat(s), 1, 5, 25, 32–33, 42–43, 51,
101, 110, 119, 141, 159, 169, 179,
191, 196–199, 221, 239; threatening
behavior/comments, 1, 27, 42–43,
46, 49, 57–58, 71, 79, 81, 83, 89,
90, 92, 96–97, 99, 109, 117, 124,
128, 139, 142, 145, 159, 168–169,
185, 199, 202–203, 209, 211–214,
221–222, 226, 236; threatening letters, 25, 94
Thurston High School, 126, 128–131
Trenchcoat Mafia, 140, 214, 215
Triggering mechanisms, 16–18, 167,
178–179, 201; loss of job, 179; poverty, 179–180; restraining order, 79–
80, 90, 93, 100, 201–202; severe
situational stress, 177–178
Tsang, Sabine, 100

U2, 95
Union, South Carolina, 61, 63–64

US Airways, 35–36
U.S. Capitol, 27–30
U.S. Constitution, 204
U.S. Post Office, 2, 37–40
U.S. Postmaster General, 40

Varela, Rick, 80

Warning signs, 5, 52–53, 191, 195,
189, 199, 210, 216–217
Weapons and personal protection, 202–
206; chemical sprays, 202–203; clubs
and batons, 203; firearms, 204–206;
personal alarm devices, 204; stun
guns, 203
West Side Middle School, 122, 124–
125
Westinghouse Corporation, 35
Weston, Russell, 27–30, 225
White, Wendell, 236–237
Whooper, James, III, 37–39
Woodham, Luke, 116, 119–122, 196,
219
Workman's compensation, 174
Workplace, homicide in, 5, 17, 26, 35–
54, 67, 172, 180, 186, 191, 198,
218, 234; killers, 51–52, 234; shootings, 39, 67; threats, 191; violence,
35–36, 40, 52
Wright, Frank Lloyd, 231–233

Yale University, 96

Zero tolerance, 169, 196

About the Author

GREGORY K. MOFFATT has been a college professor for 15 years. Since 1987, he has also been in private practice as a therapist, specializing in children. He has addressed hundreds of audiences, including law enforcement, parenting groups, and schools on the subject of homicide risk assessment, and has lectured many times at the FBI Academy at Quantico, Virginia. He is also a Diplomat in the American College of Forensic Examiners. He authors a local newspaper column that addresses family and children's issues, and consults with business in regard to violence risk assessment and prevention.